FILM
&
VIDEO
MARKETING

by

Michael Wiese

Published by Michael Wiese Productions, 11288 Ventura Blvd, Suite 821, Studio City, CA 91604, (818) 379-8799 in conjunction with Focal Press, A division of Butterworth Publishers, 80 Montvale Avenue, Stoneham, MA 02180, (617) 438-8464.

Cover design by Scott Mednick & Associates, Los Angeles
Back cover photograph by Geraldine Overton

Printed by Braun-Brumfield, Inc., Ann Arbor, Michigan.
Manufactured in the United States of America.

ISBN 0-941188-05-1

Books by Michael Wiese

Film & Video Marketing
The Independent Film & Videomakers Guide
Film & Video Budgets
Home Video: Producing for the Home Market

Books from MICHAEL WIESE PRODUCTIONS

Fade In: The Screenwriting Process by Robert A. Berman
Hollywood Gift Catalog by Ernie Fosselius
Film Directing Shot by Shot by Steven D. Katz
Film Directing Cinematic Motion by Steven D. Katz
The Writer's Journey by Christopher Vogler

FOR MORGAN SMITH

CONTENTS

CONTENTS

Acknowledgments

Authors always thank their spouses and that's as it should be because writing is a very disruptive process. Book writing takes a lot of time away from any primary relationship. Even when I'm not writing I am sometimes thinking about it and distracted—in another world. Spouses and close friends are the first to feel this withdrawl. During the writing my wife Morgan Smith, and now best friend, was generous and nurturing, knowing that writing is my process for getting at and sharing hard-learned knowledge— something vital to my own growth. As usual she's been absolutely terrific and stood behind every key stroke on this, my fourth book.

These books seem to take two years. No matter how quickly I think they'll come together, two years is what it takes.

The experiences gathered for this book come through a great many people and organizations. First, of course, is my experience at Vestron where I was able to exercise my programming and marketing wings and try a great many things that nowaways you just can't do. The market was very forgiving then. Vestron Video president Jon Peisinger was my boss and continues to be a good friend. We wrestled and struggled with many programming and marketing ideas. Few got away. It was my interaction with Jon, my staff and the other departments at Vestron that gave me many of the opportunities that I write about in this book.

The Vestron Pictures folks, Mitchell Cannold, Steve Reuther, Jimmy Ienner, M. J. Peckos, Al Reuben, Pat Caufield, Susan Senk, Sharon

Streger and especially its president, Bill Quigley, and Vestron Video president Jon Peisinger provided me, and hence you, an inside look at how DIRTY DANCING came to be. They were very open and willing to share their good and their not-so-good ideas so that others could learn from them. For this I am very thankful.

Shirley MacLaine and Bella Abzug had the confidence in me as producer and director to hire me for Shirley's new video. This allowed me to bring all my programming and marketing skills to the forefront. Our creative exchanges created a program we can all be proud of. I thank both Shirley and Bella for the opportunity and Vestron for signing up for the adventure.

These books cannot be written in a void. Rather, the experiences shared here have come out of my interaction with many people and organizations. Without them these ideas would never have been developed or tested. I would like to thank the following people for giving me the opportunity to participate in some terrific projects: Tim Kelly & Dennis Kane, National Geographic Television; Sheldon Rochlin, Mystic Fire Video; Emily Laskin and James Hindman, The American Film Institute; Michael Nesmith, George Steele and Al Cattabiani, Pacific Arts Video, Adrian Malone, Paul Johnson, Karen Loveland and Elizabeth Brownstein, The Smithsonian Institution.

The most unconventional testing of many of these marketing ideas came in the development, manufacturing and marketing of Goin' Hollywood, our new board game. My partner Greg Johnson was absolutely terrific to work with—totally supportive, and he contributed fully in making the game real. Although it was a board game and not a film or video, we employed everything we knew about marketing other media to make it a hit. Thanks go out also to Betsy Zeidman, who got in the marketing trenches selling sponsorship and retail accounts. She also was my associate producer on Shirley MacLaine's INNER WORKOUT and covered for me when I didn't have enough hands or brainpower left.

Scott Mednick was the art director for the cover design which Mari Migliore executed. Scott also did the art direction for the board game Goin' Hollywood and Dan Simon executed it. (I thank them here because there is no acknowledgment page on a board game!)

Karen Speerstra, senior editor at Focal Press, is an unseen but frequent voice on the phone. Although we've never met face to face she has signed up for nearly every book I've brought her. (We joke that if we ever meet, it'll jinx the deal!) She prods, cajoles, and injects just enough good will and humor to keep this author very happy.

Behind the scenes but very much a part of things since the very first book is Mary Murrel, my account representative at Braun-Brumfield, the printing company. She steadfastly oversees the manufacturing, delivery and fulfillment of the books. Her counterpart, Dick Bunnell at New England Book Components oversees the printing of the color covers. We're talking great people.

We've yet to do a book together, but nevertheless senior editor Ellen Lazer at Knowledge Industries has twice asked me to contribute a chapter for her home video books. This encouragement (someone really wanting to read what I write) and the fact that one chapter isn't too hard to write got me going on this and the last book. It's kind of a way I trick myself into getting started. Ellen, thank you for that.

Suzanne Steve scampered around getting last minute permissions on artwork, correcting and editing typos and generally getting me to get it done. Shelley Mahr did the proofing and copyediting. She too has a Macintosh. I told her editing my work would be easy and fun. Hah, I lied! She did a terrific job.

CBS photographer Geraldine Overton found time in her busy schedule between her photo sessions with television stars to make the photograph for the back cover. Her charm and great eye brought me out. No easy feat. The author looks friendly—like someone I'd like to meet.

PERMISSIONS AND CREDITS

I would like to thank the following companies for so generously allowing me to reproduce their outstanding marketing materials (posters, sell-sheets, ad mats, cassette packaging, photos, advertisements, P.O.P displays, etc.)

Artwork from the film and/or video courtesy of:

ALIVE FILMS; *Betty Blue*, ATLANTIC ENTERTAINMENT GROUP; *Wish You Were Here*, CALLAN PRODUCTIONS CORP.; *Callanetics*, CINEPLEX ODEON CORP.; *Sign O' The Times*, *Madame Sousatzka*, GOIN' HOLLYWOOD INC., Greg Johnson/Michael Wiese; *Goin' Hollywood: The Movie-Making Game*, HBO VIDEO; *Raquel: Lose 10 Lbs. in 3 Weeks*, *Dear America*, HOME VISION; *Paul Gauguin*, *The Architecture of Frank Lloyd Wright*, *Toni Morrison: Profile of A Writer*, ISLAND PICTURES INC.; *River's Edge*, *She's Gotta Have It*, *Dark Eyes*, J2 COMMUNICATIONS; *Dorf and the First Games of Mt. Olympus*, MEDIA HOME ENTERTAINMENT, INC.; *Pee Wee's Playhouse : Rainy Day, Vol. 3*, *Kathy Smith's Fat-Burning Workout*, MYSTIC FIRE VIDEO; *Joseph Campbell: Power of Myth* , NATHAN/ TYLER; *In Search of Excellence*, NEW LINE CINEMA CORPORA-TION; *Hairspray*, *Nightmare on Elm Street 4*, NEW WORLD PIC-TURES; *Elvira: Mistress of the Dark*, *Man Facing Southeast*, POLARIS MEDIA GROUP INC.; *Esquire Dance Away: Get Fit With The Hits* series, PYRAMID FILMS; Ernie Fosselius/Michael Wiese, *Hardware Wars*, SKOURAS PICTURES; Cheryl Pellegrino, *My Life as A Dog*, *Living on Tokyo Time*, VESTRON INC.; *Dirty Dancing*, *Platoon*, *Gothic*, *NOVA Video*, (*The Shape of Things*), *The Beach Boys: An Ameri-can Band*, *Let's Go Mets*, *The Dead*, *Audubon Video* series, *The Unholy*, *Shirley MacLaine's Inner Workout*, *Arnold Palmer: Play Great Golf*, *Stars & Bars Media Blitz* promotion, *Videogift* promotion, *National Geographic Video* (*Rhino War*, *Secret Leopard*, *Secrets of the Titanic*). *Paul Reiser: Out on A Whim*, *Dolphin Adventure*, VIDMAR COMMU-NICATIONS INC; Hollywood, CA., *Pre-Recorded Home Video* Chart, WOOD KNAPP VIDEO; *Highlights of the 1988 Summer Olympics*.

INTRODUCTION

INTRODUCTION

"My first film was for the birds."

Journey Through Marketing

I never really thought much about marketing. That's probably why my first dozen or so films still sit on a shelf.

I learned filmmaking from the ground up. My first film job was as a production assistant to a documentary film unit. I got all the lousy jobs: carrying heavy gear, cleaning up the film bins after a long day of editing. Finally I got my first break. I got to shoot a film. Well, an animated film. Of concentric circles. It had to be done perfectly though, because it was a research project for some scientists who were studying pigeon navigation. They would hook wires up to the pigeons, show them my film and study their brain waves. I guess my first film was for the birds.

Many of us come into filmmaking through a creative door. We've been camera operators, editors or writers. Few of us have worked on the marketing side or even know what that entails. Film students learn how to run film (or videotape) through the camera, how to make an image and edit. Nowhere in our formal film education did I or any of my filmmaker friends learn anything about marketing.

During our experimental filmmaking days in the sixties we were most concerned about creating our art, about "finding our voice," about making statements. For years I believed that if a film was well crafted, well lit, had engaging characters and was well edited, it would find an audience. Not so. What usually happened was that the film got made, was shown a few times in museums or film festivals, won an award and that was that. Rarely would the film find distribution. What were we doing wrong?

Novice and experienced producers all face the same problem: *How do we get our films and videos made?* A bigger and perhaps concurrent issue is: *How do we get them seen?* Getting them seen by paying audiences often means a trickle of revenue returning to the filmmakers. This trickle, if large enough and from enough different sources, can not only repay costs incurred during the original production but, perhaps, yield a profit and a sense of accomplishment. *People actually paid to see my work! Amazing.*

The goal we all share as communicators is to get our work seen. And the more people who see it, the greater the revenue streams. The successful film or video will go through normal distribution channels and maybe even find some new niches. This does not happen haphazardly. Unknown to most, successful films and videos are actually designed to be successfully distributed by producers who not only have their craft under control but know how to get an audience for their work when completed. That's marketing.

I stumbled into the process of marketing. I really knew nothing about it nor did I care to. In fact, the sixties milieu was such that "going commercial" or getting your work on television was antithetical to the movement. We wanted change, but we did not want to use any of the proven and established means for achieving it. Not only were we trying to create a new language of film and express new ideas, but we also wanted to create a new distribution system to deliver the message. Ambitious? Absolutely. Most projects failed to get off the ground. Even so-called anti-establishment films like EASY RIDER were distributed through the traditional studio system. Many filmmakers forget these things.

So for years I stumbled along, raising money from private investors to make my short and documentary films. Most were seen briefly. As long as I pushed them I could get them seen. But little happened on its own.

Then there was HARDWARE WARS—the short film parody of STAR WARS I produced. It was written and directed by my friend Ernie Fosselius. We didn't set out to have a hit independent short, we just wanted to make a film that would get George Lucas's attention. We naively thought that maybe he would give us a job if he liked the movie.

We chose STAR WARS to parody at the time because it was a good example of a big-budget movie with lots of special effects. We didn't know that it would be the hit it was.

Within a few years our thirteen-minute short film—shot on a budget of $8,000—had grossed $500,000 in a variety of markets. It was being distributed theatrically, nontheatrically (to schools and libraries), on home video, and it was shown on PBS, HBO and on many cable systems. It was the first time I didn't have to keep breathing life into a movie to get it seen. It was selling itself. The press was positive and the word of mouth was tremendous. It was

5

an underground hit, then a cult hit and is now a short film classic. Every time another STAR WARS movie came out (either theatrically, on pay cable or video), the sales and rentals of our little movie picked up. None of this was planned—but it could have been. It was a well-made movie that found its audience because timing, word of mouth and all the other factors that one usually has to orchestrate came together spontaneously. I learned about marketing in a very backward manner, because luck, not planning, made HARDWARE WARS a success. (I had made dozens of award-winning short films before this one. About half never found distribution.)

After HARDWARE WARS, I paid more attention to marketing. I thought about every new project and asked the big questions: *Who will want to see it? Why? How can they learn about the film?*

A few years later I made DOLPHIN, a film about human and dolphin interspecies communication. This time I constructed a plan to reach the audience. The idea was to release the film in San Francisco where I lived. I figured I could get the most publicity there. I hired a publicist who wrote the press release, contacted the press, got the film reviewed. We had a one-week local premiere in a theater we rented. We placed ads in the San Francisco Bay area newspapers and cross-promoted our other showings, thus maximizing the advertising and publicity that appeared. We spent $20,000 on the campaign and the movie in all its local showings brought in $20,000. It was a wash. But now we had reviews and articles in hand. We tried the same approach in Los Angeles, Seattle and Denver. Not a whole lot of people turn out for documentaries.

We quickly learned that it was a break-even proposition at best. We then moved on to exploit the other markets in a conscious manner.

First came the nontheatrical market. There was the original one-hour version and then I cut a shorter version of THE WONDER OF THE DOLPHIN for children. Then came television (PBS) and thirty foreign networks. Later, as cable grew, there were sales to the Disney Channel and the Discovery Channel. Finally came home video. In hindsight we were very naive about what kind of film we had, who would really go see it and what to do with it. Nevertheless, I was learning how to design a marketing plan.

I decided it was time to get a "real job." I became a segment producer for a live variety/entertainment show in San Francisco which aired five nights a week. My job was to produce segments. I was thrilled that I would have a chance to try out lots of ideas. But I learned that what they wanted were "promotable" segments—those that looked appealing in *TV Guide*. The producers' main concern was getting more people to watch the show. By improving their ratings the station could increase their advertising rates, so my segments had to be promotable. Every morning I would rush in to see what the overnights (ratings) were. They showed—to the quarter hour—how many people were watching. Different shows had different numbers and a pattern began emerging. Every time we did anything that featured "sex, food or baby animals," we got good ratings. I always figured if I could only think of an idea that combined all these subjects into one segment, I'd have a hit. But that's another story.

The station was very serious about the fledgling show. So serious that they hired a market research firm who asked focus groups about the show and how to improve it. The researchers' results caused the station to redesign the set, book more Hollywood stars, shoot a new opening and replace some of the staff. I was replaced by two comedy writers. None of this worked, however, and the show was off the air soon thereafter. Nevertheless, they did their best to redesign the program and find an audience through market research.

My next job as a producer of television and radio spots for political candidates had an even steeper mandate: Get votes. The TV ads attempted to change public opinion in a positive manner toward our candidates, but the viewers then had to take action and vote. The research was very sophisticated. Polls were done almost every week to identify the issues the candidate should or should not address. The polls told us all kinds of things about how the constituents perceived our candidate. The resulting television spots had little to do with who our guy really was, but tried to move the public's perception of him regarding the issues to get him the most votes. It was the ultimate in media manipulation. We shot a candidate in a ghetto with his sleeves rolled up. He'd never been in the ghetto before. Minutes later he stepped back into his limo. As we sped off I told him, *"You know, when you get the job, you're going to have to come down here."* He looked shocked. The public's perception of him was quite different; they saw as a hard-working man who rolled up his sleeves in order to get things done. Disillusioned, I quit. Another lesson in marketing. There were elements of presentation and positioning that I felt I could use later, however.

Next I became director of on-air programming and production for The Movie Channel (and later Showtime when the two cable networks merged). My job was to oversee the production of all interstitial material (original program segments between feature films which included profiles, promos, IDs, contests, teases and bumpers), to create an on-air look that differentiated our network from HBO, our ferocious competitor. It was important that cable subscribers know when they were watching The Movie Channel. Especially after market researchers came to us with stories like, "We asked viewers if they had seen The Movie Channel and they said, *'Yeah, you mean HBO.'*" We had a lot of work to do.

We created programming to promote The Movie Channel which made us look different (even though, at that time, everyone was broadcasting the same movies). Since we were The Movie Channel, we could justify doing interviews with stars, writers and directors and run soft profile pieces on the same stars who would appear in our upcoming movies. We also created clever network IDs and reminders that viewers were "watching The Movie Channel. Movies 24 hours a day." The short interstitial programs were anywhere from ten seconds to twenty minutes and ran between the feature films. They were designed to make the consumer feel good about subscribing to The Movie Channel. (Subscriber "churn" was running rampant. Although it was kept secret, a very large number of people—5 percent of our subscribers every month, 36–60 percent a year!—were disconnecting once they learned they didn't need to subscribe to two pay services to see the same movies.) Our job was to keep them happy with our service and to disconnect the other guy's. We also ran monthly sweepstakes with big prizes to keep people involved with the network.

My next job had different marketing parameters and limitations. It was clearly the most exciting and gratifying. I was vice president of original programming at Vestron Video. When I joined, they only had about fifty employees. Now there are over 500 in twelve international offices. The mandate: "Come up with non-feature programming. You can do whatever you want." Oh boy! "As long as it sells." Oh.

At Vestron I wasn't going after ratings or votes or trying to keep millions of viewers happy. It was much more one-to-one than that. A program was not successful unless someone, somewhere (a video retailer) bought one copy of the tape. And then this single transaction had to be replicated thousands of times (5,000 or more), depending on what it cost either to acquire it or to produce it. As the video market expanded in mass outlets with tapes for sale (rather than rental), the programs had to be perceived as valuable enough that tens of thousands of customers would buy one and take it home. In the "go-go" years of home video (1984–86) thousands of new video stores were opening and they needed product to fill their shelves. They were not knowledgeable about the video business. They were not very discriminating about video programs. They bought and bought. Life was good. But once the shelves filled up, it became much tougher to sell programs. There were a lot more suppliers of programs. We had to find more and more elements to promote to make a show marketable to the wholesaler, the retailer, and the consumer. We were in the packaged goods business. The video business, as we shall explore in greater detail, became an even greater marketing teacher.

As of this writing I have returned to the independent arena. I've dusted off all those projects I've always wanted to do and created some new ones. But with it comes a new perspective—creative marketing. Ways to get the program to different audiences.

At Vestron I worked on nearly 200 projects. Since leaving I've consulted for National Geographic, the Smithsonian Institution, the American Film Institute and numerous video distributors and program producers. The task for all of us is to redefine ways to deliver programming to the viewing public.

Making a good show isn't enough. Don't get me wrong. A good product is necessary. But quality alone won't ensure success. I've trained myself to make programming and marketing decisions at the same time. When I read a script, I am thinking about marketing. When a producer pitches an idea, I try to see the poster. I listen to the title. I imagine the audiences that will want to see the work. I think of how to get it to them.

Ten years ago I put my head in the sand. I was afraid to think about marketing because I thought it might compromise the creative process. I was afraid if I thought about how to make something successful, somehow the "soul" or the artistic integrity of the work would be lost. I now believe that it is the responsibility of the artist, the producer or the writer—during the creative process—to have part of his or her attention on marketing, on the task of making it easier to deliver his or her communication to audiences. Communicating implies communing with someone; it doesn't happen in a vacuum. Who then do we want to see our work? How will we deliver it to them? Answering these questions is our job during the making of the film or video and in delivering the work. It's not finished when it's finished. It's finished when an audience has seen it. Marketing is the process bridging these two events.

It is my sincere wish that this book helps producers in pre-visualizing their projects and creating inner images of marketing strategies which may bring them outward success.

Michael Wiese
Studio City, California
March 1, 1989

MARKETING

"There are many forms through which we can communicate."

Marketing

Marketing is a much-touted, popular concept of the eighties, but few producers understand its significance. We hear the word all the time, but what does it mean? Looking it up in the dictionary is always fun. *Marketing* comes from the word *market*. The dictionary also lists *bazaar, carnival, circus* and *fair*. Knowing what I do of the film and video markets, I guess that's a pretty accurate description. There's lots of confusion, lots of noise, lots of competition, and lots of product. The word *marketing* also implies *selling, merchandising, distributing, peddling, retailing, wholesaling,* and *vending*. My interpretation combines the two. Could you say that marketing is a colorful, noisy, memorable way of selling your product? I guess so.

A more formal definition might be: Marketing is the strategy employed to find the most effective way to get to your audience or buyer. This book is therefore about how to market your films and videos to your audience in the most effective manner. And in our business, throwing in some noise and color won't hurt.

Who Do You Want To Be?

The best place to start is at the beginning. Hopefully you will be willing to ask yourself some very difficult questions long before writing and producing your films or videos. And hopefully you will have some answers before embarking on production, because the answers to the questions that are about to be posed will help you tremendously down the line when it comes time to market your films and videos. Why? Because marketing really begins with identifying who you are and what you want to be in this business and how you stack up against the competition.

This process is not much fun because you have to be honest with yourself and really get at some important personal issues. I guess that's why most filmmakers and videographers avoid marketing as long as they can, because marketing is—in the final analysis—tied in with some very personal issues. It's tough to ask these questions and sometimes even tougher to answer them. But it is the only place to start.

First off: *Who are you?* (I don't mean in the spiritual sense, though for many of us that's probably not a bad question either.) Who are you in the marketing sense? What level player are you? Are you an indie with your first feature or documentary to distribute? Are you a mid-level film producer with relationships among various distributors? Are you a videographer of special-interest videos? Realistically, who are you? Make a list of descriptive elements that describe you. Be honest. <u>Try to see yourself as others might.</u>

Now you have stated who you are. *Who do you want to be? What career move do you want to make?* Once you know that you are a documentary filmmaker and you want to be a director of narrative features, for example, you can more clearly see what skills and contacts you have and use this to understand what you need to do to reach your goal.

Are you competitive? If you've looked at yourself, at who you are and who you want to be, really honestly, you'll find that you are not competitive in many, many ways. There are hundreds, maybe thousands of people who—if logic had anything to do with it— would be picked for the next project before you because of their qualifications. But as you delve into answering these questions in detail, you will also find areas where you are unique, where you bring something to the party that few people do. This is where you find some leverage and your power, where you have something different to offer than the competition.

This advantage may be some personal experience that gives you special insight. Or some special relationships within a group of people that no one else has. Or some special writing or drawing or communication skill that makes you stand out. Maybe you have a visual style that others acknowledge is really different. Or a different musical sense. It could be any number of things. These aspects make you more competitive. If you focus on the things that others also do well, you become less competitive because there are so many people who can do the same job.

As creative people we need to find our own special skills to make the greatest contribution and then place ourselves in an environment where we can maximize those skills. If you can identify your special gifts, you can begin to use them to create films and videos that will be competitive in a world of too much product. You have to find the right job for yourself.

My dear friend and teacher Bucky Fuller said that it was a waste of humanity's resources to keep people in their jobs. He said that if we sent everybody home and just let them discover <u>what they naturally want to do</u>—what they really, really want to do—one or two people would come up with something (like discovering electricity) that would make such a tremendous contribution to the rest of humanity that it would more than make up for everyone else not working. The notion was that everyone would benefit if we were given time to do our own thinking. Maybe the guy at the post office should be fishing; while he's fishing he could have a brainstorm about how to grow giant tomatoes to feed the world. *What do you really, really want to do?* Once you know that you can begin to determine how to bring that ability to the marketplace.

Dream It or Do It?

During my mid- and late twenties I wanted only to make feature films. It was not uncommon for me to work on a single project for years only to run out of steam, potential investors or whatever before wearily setting it back in the file cabinet. It was tough. I'm sure many of you have experienced this. At the end of the process you are frustrated and angry. Frustrated because you know that your idea is sound and that you would make a terrific film. And angry because somehow the forces that be rejected your project.

This whole cycle is very dangerous for filmmakers or any sensitive creators. We start out with so much enthusiasm and positive intent, only to end up rejected, frustrated and angry. As the years pass, we become more broke and embittered.

It doesn't have to be like this. There is a way out. And it is much simpler than I imagined.

This became very clear to me recently when I was invited to Sundance Institute in Utah to speak to a group of seventy or eighty minority women in a three-day conference organized by PBS and the Corporation for Public Broadcasting. I was one of the few men there and I felt very privileged to be among such a powerful group of highly intentioned women. There were Hispanics, Blacks, Native Americans, Asian-Americans and many others. They weren't first-timers but women whose collected works had won numerous awards, favorable reviews and acclaim within their own communities. Usually, however, their work—if it was ever completed—was shown once or twice on PBS and that was that.

My job was to give these women some ideas about how to distribute and market their work. Award-winning novelist Alice Walker, author of THE COLOR PURPLE, was the speaker the first night and gave one of the most moving and eloquent talks and readings from her journals that I've ever heard. Most of the material revolved around her struggles with Steven Spielberg during the production of THE COLOR PURPLE. Everyone was very high on their own hopes and dreams: "If Alice's work can find it's way into mainstream America, maybe mine can too."

The next morning I was on a panel with several executives from the major studios. I looked around at the faces in the audience before it was my turn to speak. Everyone was still high after Alice's presentation. The women in the audience were thinking about how their socially relevant idea would be the next COLOR PURPLE. The presence of the studio people only encouraged the feeling that there really was a receptive audience for this kind of filmmaking in Hollywood.

I don't begrudge anyone their dreams. Nor would I ever thwart anyone's desire to see their socially relevant idea brought into being in the form of a feature film. But I am also a realist. I could not go along with the collective fantasy in the room. I just didn't believe that Hollywood was waiting to turn the best ideas of these women into the next COLOR PURPLE. And I said so. The room was dead still. I popped the bubble. These women were not happy.

I hated to see their expectations get so high and for them to put all their energy into getting their movies made in Hollywood. For Alice Walker to hook up with Spielberg was an anomaly. It's the exception. It just doesn't happen everyday. Not that I felt that these women should not hold on to that dream. They should. But if, years later, it doesn't materialize, they will have sacrificed valuable time, money and energy. The outcome will leave them even more bitter, angry and resentful than they are now. I've been there. And not just once or twice.

We find ourselves in that situation when <u>we think there is only one form through which we can communicate</u>. For some people, it's the feature film. For others, it's a television special. What I encouraged this group to think about was not dropping their dream to work with Steven Spielberg on the next COLOR PURPLE, but to use their communication skills to express themselves in a variety of ways and not to fixate on just one. I suggested that they put on one-act plays, write books or poetry, do posters or murals or radio shows. Find other, viable means of expression. Means that are accessible. Forms that are open to them. Otherwise, with no creative outlet for expression, their frustration and hopelessness will undoubtedly mount.

Well, I didn't get a standing ovation. But over the next few days women came up to me one by one and thanked me. They said they had thought about what else they could do and felt empowered. They had wonderful ideas—wonderful <u>non-feature</u> ideas—that they wanted to talk about. They became excited about these smaller projects because they knew they could return to their own communities and actually get them done.

When we stop thinking of ourselves as filmmakers, or writers, or videographers and start thinking of ourselves as communicators, many more forms of expression instantly open up. We can take power into our own hands. We have a voice. We can be heard.

Of course there are features I'd like to make. Lots of them. But realistically I know that I'll really be lucky to do any of them. That's just the way it is. It doesn't even have that much to do with my abilities; it's more a function of power and timing and luck.

Different Relationships to Different Projects

In the meantime, I want to keep going, to get things accomplished. So I consult with people on their projects and help them along. I oversee the process as executive producer on those projects I want to nudge along. And things I want most to get made, I will produce or direct. Like the concentric circles within a tree, the stronger I feel about a project, the more involved I get. Consulting is the outermost circle, then comes executive producing, then producing, then directing. By the time you get to directing you have little time for anything else because directing is so intensely focused. You have to be myopic to do it. Executive producing, on the other hand, allows you to do many things simultaneously. I have different relationships to different projects, depending on my level of passion.

There is also nothing wrong with consulting and working on other people's projects. In fact, it feels good to see the work get done. But for directing, the passion must be there because you have to sustain energy over the course of production, which could be many years. And the project you are directing must have enough depth to it so that you will stay interested and keep finding value within the material. And that's not every project. For me, each project is different and must be assessed individually.

It was a valuable insight for me to understand that it is appropriate to respond differently to different projects, that my level of participation and outlay of energy can be different. I find that I can get a lot more done. I am happier when <u>I have a creative outlet for my expression, regardless of the form it takes</u>. And when the feature comes along, I'll be ready for that too. But in the meantime, I haven't put myself into a situation that begets frustration, bitterness or disappointment.

Pitching the Vision

With any project or media endeavor it is very useful to think not only about the project but how that project fits within the context of the industry as a whole. It is not enough to dream up a great film or video. You must also see where it fits in the bigger picture. Beyond your passion for the project is the marketplace with its own set of needs. At some level it will have to be accepting of your film. Are there already many pictures of the same type in the market-place? Are there many similar pictures about to be released? How has the market responded before? If you are doing something entirely new, will this present opportunities or obstacles in market-ing? Will people easily understand it and want to see it? How will you position it in the marketplace?

This kind of thinking returns us to the *Who do you want to be?* question. What kind of supplier of programming do you wish to be? How will you present yourself? How do you want to be perceived in the marketplace? If you know what you are going after you can better prepare yourself for those inevitable series of pitch meetings that reverberate off any project. I've found the preparation on and around the big question of *Who do you want to be?* to be very valuable. With the answer comes understanding, a sense of pur-pose and a greater clarity about your own work and how it fits into the marketplace.

Once I was preparing a presentation for some investors who wanted to put up money for some feature films. They didn't really know much about the movie business nor did they have any specific ideas about what they wanted to make. Instead, they wanted to know what I wanted to make. They didn't want to finance just one picture but two or three low-budget pictures. I thought about the resources available and what I wanted to do and how that fit into the overall scheme of things. Here are some of the pitch notes that I used for that investors meeting to help define what we wanted to be. You may wish to do a similar exercise to clarify your career path.

MW ENTERTAINMENT GROUP

THE MW ENTERTAINMENT GROUP is a development, production and marketing company specializing in high-concept/low-budget, quality films.

FILM PRODUCT: Upscale, "intelligent" comedies, relationship movies, dramas, and genre "movies with a twist" with "crossover" potential.

TARGET AUDIENCE: Sophisticated, urban audiences (20–40 age group) reached through exclusive runs in specialized theaters. Limited print release, controlled targeted marketing through regional roll-outs.

GOALS

- Develop a slate of low-budget features with marketable elements.

- Identify 1 or 2 films for 1989 production/1990 release and 1 or 2 films for 1990 production/1991 release.

- Maximize on-screen production value within limited budgets.

- Leverage the most favorable distribution agreement through print and advertising financing.

- Maximize return on investor capital.

DEVELOPMENT OBJECTIVES

Acquisition/Development Strategy:

- Writing Original Scripts.
- Optioning Scripts, Plays, Books and Dramatic Properties.

Concept Requirements:

- Genre Movies with a Twist. (comedy, romance, music, adventure)
- Fresh, Original Concepts and Titles.
- Design for "Crossover Potential."
- Intriguing Stories.
- Fascinating and Memorable Characters.
- Realistic Dialogue.
- Unusual Settings and Locations.
- Sophisticated Production Techniques/Effects.
- High Production Value.
- At Least One Promotable Cast Name.

Marketing Development:

- Pre-Design Key Art, Hooks and Copy.
- Test Marketing Concepts.
- Control Marketing Campaign.
- Publicity and Promotion Budget.

<u>Improved Distribution Agreements Through:</u>

- "Rent-A-Distributor" Concept (reduced fees)
- Print and Advertising (P & A) Commitment
- Splintering of Television and All Foreign Rights

After you've tried this, you will perhaps begin to see yourself in a different way. I go through this process again and again and have done so for many years. We change, and what value we then bring to the party changes. Until we step away from ourselves and try to make an honest appraisal, it isn't always clear to us what ace we have to play.

Once you learn what you do best, you can identify the primary product you want to produce. As discussed before, it may be a feature, a documentary, a television show or a video. It could also be a postcard, a poem or a song.

When you've identified the product, you can start to look for the appropriate markets and distribution channels to deliver the product to its audience.

<u>Potential buyers may exist but there may not be a distribution channel to reach them</u>. Say the market of potential buyers is everyone who wants to re-tile their bathroom floor. Terrific. Maybe they could use a home video that tells them how to do it. But how do you reach them? No sense producing the product unless you have a way of getting it to them. The video store isn't going to carry

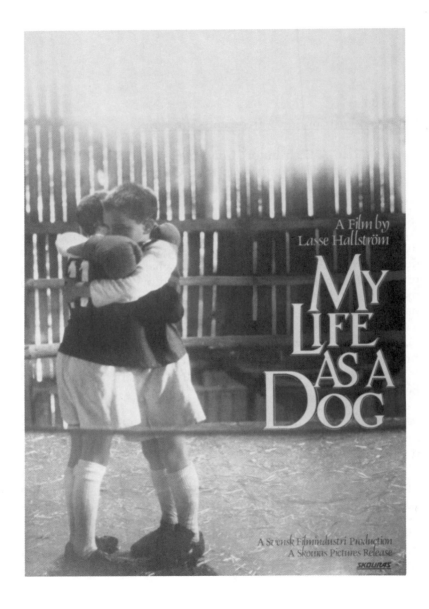

this tape. Maybe it has to be sold through hardware and tile stores. But to do that you'll have to create a whole new channel of distribution, because tile stores don't sell videotapes.

Or maybe you want to make a movie about a group of freedom fighters in Central America. Fine. But is a movie the best way to communicate their plight? Will it really be shown in theaters beyond film festivals and PBS? Who is the audience for the film and where will they be able to see it? How can you effectively communicate to an audience so that they'll see it? All the pieces have to fit, from the product to the distribution system to the market itself. Without very strong existing distribution streams between the communication piece and its intended audience, you will be terribly disappointed. All that work will be for naught. It won't get seen.

At the moment you conceive your idea for a film or video, you must know then and there what market you are going after. It's not enough to have a good idea; you must know how to deliver it to an audience. Many filmmakers and videographers put their heads in the sand, thinking only about how to make their film or video and not about how it's going to get out into the world. I know about thousands of films and videos that never found an audience! What a waste. Worse still, you've got a lot of talented, creative people around whose work—even after the agony of making it—was never seen. How is it going to be distributed?

Potential distribution resources were addressed and included in my investors pitch notes. Even though, in the final analysis, there were probably only a handful of distributors for the pictures we

wanted to make, the number of potential distributors offered assurance to the investment group.

POTENTIAL DISTRIBUTORS

We have identified many potential distributors and co-venturers for our films. We have ongoing contact (*) at the executive level among the independent film, television and video distributors. Here is a "hit list" of potential partners.

*ACT III
ALIVE
*AMERICAN PLAYHOUSE

ANGELICA
APOLLO
*ATLANTIC ENTERTAINMENT
*CINECOM
CINEMA GROUP
CINEPLEX ODEON
*COLUMBIA
CONCORD
*DISNEY
*EMPIRE
*FILM DALLAS
FIRST RUN FEATURES
*FOX/LORBER
*FRIES ENTERTAINMENT
*HBO
HEMDALE
*INTERSCOPE
*IRS WORLD MEDIA
*ITC PRODUCTIONS
*ISLAND PICTURES
J&M
*LBS
*LIGHTNING PICTURES
*LIGHTYEAR ENTERTAINMENT
*LORIMAR
MANAGEMENT ENTERTAINMENT COM-
PANY
MEDIACOM FILMWORKS
MIRAMAX

*MULTI-MEDIA
*NELSON ENTERTAINMENT
NEW CENTURY/VISTA
NEW HORIZONS
*NEW LINE CINEMA
*NEW WORLD ENTERTAINMENT
NEW YORKER FILMS
ODYSSEY FILMS
*ORION
*PARAMOUNT HOME VIDEO
*PRISM ENTERTAINMENT
RANK
*SAMUEL GOLDWYN CO.
SKOURAS PICTURES
*SHOWTIME
*SONY
SPECTRACORE
*TELEGENICS
*TBS
*TRI-STAR
TWE
*UNITED ARTISTS
*VESTRON
*VISION PICTURES

Financial Model Assumptions

The financial model and accompanying rationale for low-budget features that was pitched to the potential investors made the following assumptions:

1. Box-office gross is a function of <u>the quality of the film</u> and not the budget level. Public awareness is enhanced by smart print and advertising expenditures. Income is not necessarily a result of this exposure. Good word of mouth is vitally important. A good low-budget film that can be well marketed can make money.

2. A $2.5 million <u>budget</u> assumes one name cast member at a fee of $200,000–400,000 for a six-week shoot.

31

3. The theatrical model assumes that fifty prints are worked for a minimum of twelve weeks, during which time the on-screen average is $5,000, resulting in a box-office gross of $3 million. The distributor receives 50 percent of this gross or $1.5 million. Assuming our investors put up the P&A (print and ad) money, the distribution fee will be 15 percent. (Perhaps this fee increases to 17–20 percent once we've recouped our investment.) Deduct the $500,000 P&A costs and the production company nets our $775,000 from theatrical exhibition.

4. Once upon a time the rule of thumb for home video was that a manufacturer/supplier would pay an advance equal to the P&A budget. Whatever was spent on the theatrical release (in terms of prints and advertising) would have the same value (as an advance against royalties) in the home video market. While this is no longer the case, we believe we can create a picture with even greater value through astute scripting, casting, production and marketing.

We believe that a film distributor with an output deal with a home video supplier should be able to get back 40 percent of the budget, hence improving the home video deal from the previously mentioned rule of thumb. For these efforts a distributor will want a 25 percent override (fee).

In the final analysis, however, advances are really based on how well home video suppliers think a film will perform. An independent producer might be able to sell the video rights separately, but that leaves him or her with the enormous problem of finding theatrical distribution without also granting the home video rights. Nowadays, film distributors also want home video rights as down-

LOW BUDGET FEATURE   "Rent A Distributor" Scenario

BUDGET	*2,500,000*
Prints & Ads	*500,000*

THEATRICAL (Domestic)

Wkly Average	5,000		
# of Prints	50		
No of Wks	1 2		
Total Box Office Receipts			3,000,000
Exhibitor % of Box Office		.50	-1,500,000
Distribs % Share		.50	1,500,000
Distrib % Fee		.15	-225,000
P&A Costs Recouped			-500,000
		NET	775,000

775,000

HOME VIDEO

Units Sold	*50,000*		
Wholesale Ea	*56*		
Net Wholesal	*2,800,000*		
25% Royalty	*700,000*		
Advance as % of Budget		.40	1,000,000
Distribution Fee %		.25	-250,000
		NET	750,000

750,000

PAY TELEVISION

License Fee as % of Budget	.20	500,000
Distribution Fee %	.175	-87,500
	NET	412,500

412,500

SYNDICATION

License Fee		600,000
Distrib. Fee %	.20	-120,000
	NET	480,000

480,000

FOREIGN

All Rights as % of Budget	.40	1,000,000
Sales Rep Fee %	.15	-150,000
	NET	850,000

850,000

TOTAL NET RECEIPTS		3,267,500
Investment Interest %	.20	-500,000
Budget Recouped		-2,500,000
NET PROFIT		267,500

Profit Split: 50% Investors/50% Prod. Co.	133,750
Total Money to Investors	3,133,750
% Return on Investment	.25

33

side protection. The theatrical and home video rights can no longer be "splintered." Film distributors know that theatrical release builds home video value and they want to share in that income as well.

Therefore in our model we assume an advance of $1 million (or 40 percent of the budget) with 25 percent going to the theatrical distributor as an override fee.

We also assume that the home video supplier will sell 50,000 units, netting $56 each at wholesale, for a total of $2.8 million. A 25 percent royalty would yield $700,000, so an advance of $1 million would not be that much of a stretch if the film was good and one or more suppliers wanted it. (If, of course, the film is poor, the whole model breaks down.)

5. A film distributor will take a 17.5 percent fee to agent a <u>pay television sale</u>. (Or the production might might hold onto these rights, thereby avoiding the fee. This is unlikely, however, as the film distributor will want as many rights as possible.) On a $2.5 million dollar budget and a $3 million box office the pay TV sale could yield $500,000.

6. <u>Syndication rights</u> may be held onto by the producer, nevertheless a TV sales agent is still necessary. Figure a 20 percent fee of $120,000.

7. <u>Foreign rights</u> (theatrical, home video and TV) are sold outright via a sales rep who will try to collect high advances (and not realistically look to future royalties). There is a 15 percent sales com-

mission. Foreign sales are heating up and can account for 40–45 percent of the budget in monies returned. On a $2.5 million film, 40 percent can yield $1 million less 15 percent fees. (This assumes the film is of a genre that "travels" well internationally.)

8. After paying back the $2.5 million negative cost and interest of 20 percent paid to the investors on their money ($500,000), the profits of $267,500 are split fifty-fifty. The investors make an additional 25 percent on their money. This scenario should be viewed as a break-even situation. All the film's costs including P&A are recouped, the investors make a little bit on their investment. The upside potential is why investors would invest.

The assumptions here are exactly that—assumptions. Many factors in the market could change the amounts returned from each market. Distribution fees are negotiable and, depending on the other product in the market, you might strike a more or less favorable deal. This chart represents only a superficial level of cash flow from these markets. Subtle, creative accounting practiced by distributors could significantly lessen the return to the production company. These assumptions should not be taken as real or meaningful in any other context than as an example of how revenues from various markets could come together. Obviously the picture, its quality, the timing, marketing and performance in the marketplace are all factors that bear on potential profits. This is purely a conceptual model for discussion purposes during a pitch to potential investors.

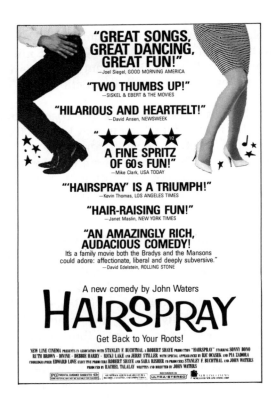

Model Yourself

The best way to get started is to model yourself after a producer, distributor or movie that has been successful. Spike Lee (SHE'S GOTTA HAVE IT) and Robert Townsend (HOLLYWOOD SHUFFLE) exemplify filmmakers whose work with black actors has crossed over to white audiences. They busted their chops until they made their films. Both were comedies that appealed to black and white audiences alike. Both were very successful. Their debut films opened Hollywood doors to their next works. Don't read their press releases; they won't tell you what you need to know. The business about Robert Townsend using his credit cards to finance his film is great press copy but it's only a half truth. (Everybody uses credit cards!) If you really want to know how these films were made, talk to the producers and the directors. Get the inside skinny. If you are a filmmaker with comedic material for black actors, model yourself after these filmmakers and similar successes. This will get you down the road a lot faster. However, just because their films worked at a certain point in time doesn't mean yours will, but it is a place to start.

In positioning some films I wanted to make, I made a list of similar films, their performance and their distributor. This list of similar film product gave my potential investors a general idea of how the films we wanted to make fit with the competition.

SIMILAR FILM PRODUCT

MW Entertainment Films expects the performance of their films, target audiences, marketing and distribution methods to be similar to the following film product.

	Distributor	Rental ($ millions)
Raising Arizona	20th Cent.-Fox	10.0
A Room with a View	Cinecom	10.4
My Life As A Dog	Skouras	10.0
Friday the 13th Part V 1985	Paramount	10.0
Ernest Goes to Camp 1987	Buena Vista	9.9
Sixteen Candles 1984	Universal	9.7
Nightmare/Elm Street 1984	New Line	9.3
The Sure Thing 1985	Orion	7.9
Mosquito Coast 1986	Warner Bros.	7.7
Diner 1982	MGM	5.6
Krush Groove 1985	Warners	5.1
The Gate 1987	New Cent./Vista	5.1
Creepshow 2	New World	4.9
Critters 1986		4.7
Less than Zero 1987		4.5
Blue Velvet	DEG	4.0
Wish You Were Here	Atlantic	3.2
House II	New World	3.3
Maurice	Cinecom	2.5
Tampopo	New Yorker	2.0
Hollywood Shuffle	Goldwyn	2.3
Jean De Florette	Orion Classics	2.1
House of Games	Orion	2.1
River's Edge	Island	1.7

Personal Services	Vestron	1.7
Withnail and I	Cineplex Odeon	1.7
Dark Eyes	Island	1.7
Matewan	Cinecom	1.6
The Whistle Blower	Hemdale	1.5
Meduses	European Classics	1.4
I've Heard the Mermaids	Miramax	1.3
Manon of the Spring	Orion Classics	1.0
Sammy and Rosie	Cinecom	.6

(Note: This is a working draft and incomplete. Grosses are still being confirmed. Some pictures are still in theatrical distribution and therefore film grosses are still in flux.)

Be careful not to mis-model. Don't expect your abilities or the performance abilities of your projects to go beyond what is reasonable or possible. I've read many scripts that claimed to be the next STAR WARS but had nothing at all to do with space or science fiction or action/adventure. In home video, producers are constantly touting their projects as the next "Jane Fonda." Most producers just don't want to know that their projects *aren't* the next "Jane Fonda." They don't want to know how their ideas stack up to the competition. They'd rather make their movies and leave it up to the fates. It's a luxury to work in a vacuum. But when the day of reckoning comes—which is the release day—wouldn't it be more reassuring to know where you are heading and what you'll be up against in the marketplace? Modeling your business, your project, and its marketing can be very useful.

Summary

Ask yourself the tough questions. Identify the issues. This may make you uncomfortable because you may not have quick answers to these questions. That's all right. The answers will show you how to be your own best resource and how to create product that can be successfully marketed. You'll find yourself thinking about and addressing marketing issues as you proceed creatively on the development of your projects. Later in the book we'll examine the independent feature film hit DIRTY DANCING and see how marketing issues were treated during development, production and distribution. We'll see that they thought long and hard about who they wanted to be which in turn pointed the way to successful marketing.

INDEPENDENT
FEATURE
FILMS

THE PRODUCT

"Take advantage of all the collective knowledge and experience that have gone into other films within the same genre."

The Genres

Any treatment of marketing has to start with the product. Films aren't just films; there are certain kinds of films with different purposes which address different audiences. By studying the various theatrical releases you can begin to identify film product. For your own project you must ask yourself, *What is it?* And you must clearly answer that question before proceeding.

If you can't answer it you won't find the right distributor, the right marketing campaign or the right audience unless you stumble on it. Save time and energy by knowing what you are making—in terms of how films are classified—before you start.

For example, there are various film genres: horror, comedy, action, adventure, documentary, drama and so on. When you are describing your film it will fit into some category. That in itself will give the marketer or distributor or publicist a handle on how to present your film. They will model the release after successful campaigns that have come before. These approaches have been defined and redefined many times. Take advantage of the collective knowledge and experience that have gone into other films in the same genre. From that point you can expand creatively on marketing principles that have worked in the past.

I was recently invited to a screening by a good friend who was director of photography on an action/adventure exploitation film. Actually, I'm not sure what genre the film was; in fact, it looked like the director would be hard pressed to say. It was the kind of film that set out in one direction and then kept changing course. First it was a prison film. Okay, that's a clear genre with clear conventions. But then a virus was introduced into the prison population. Okay, now we're talking science fiction. Then this virus turned the inmates into zombies. Horror film? A sexy scientist comes into the prison. Exploitation film? Every few minutes another convention from another genre was brought in. It was as if the director would shoot some sequences, have screenings, and then take the advice of whoever commented and go out and shoot new material. The movie simply didn't work. Why? Because, by drawing from all these genres (which have very strict conventions) the director came up with a film that will please none of its intended audiences. The people who come to see an action picture will be put off by the sci-fi element. The horror, sexploitation and action audiences will be turned off by any of the elements from another genre. The director, by combining elements rather than consciously making a film for one audience, will alienate all the audiences. In the screening I saw, people laughed at the wrong times and about half of them left early. (It was truly dreadful.) The first-time director made a hybrid that failed miserably because he didn't know which audience he was making the film for. So far, no distributor has taken on the film, and if one does, there's a rough road ahead. You can't be all things to everybody. It doesn't work.

The Audience

When you ask yourself *What is it?* you are also asking yourself *What kind of audience will go to see this kind of movie?* Is the audience made up of teenagers, young adults, women or men? Will it capture an older audience? Is there a core audience, such as in the horror genre, that loves to be scared and will go to just about anything? Is there an upscale, urban audience that prefers art or foreign films? Just who is the audience for your film, where do they live, and why will they want to see your movie? Why will it appeal to them, get them to come out of the house and plunk down their dollars?

The First Buyers: The Financiers

Before you make your movie you will have to address the question: *Who will finance this kind of movie?* What do they want in a movie? There's no sense taking an art film to a producer of gory horror films or exploitation movies. No sense taking a horror movie to an art film distributor, exhibitor or financier. It's a total waste of time. You need to identify potential buyers and the specific kinds of films they buy, finance, co-produce or distribute.

Take an hour to study the latest issue of *Variety*'s box-office chart or the *Hollywood Reporter*'s "Films in Production." It will give you an excellent overview of who is producing/distributing various genres of movies. Compile a "hit list" culling only those who truly are appropriate for your genre.

To proceed blindly and make assumptions about what independent producers or studios or distributors are buying is a waste of everyone's time. Once you finally get an appointment and pitch your title, it will be the fastest meeting you ever attended. There is nothing worse than being in a pitch meeting with the wrong buyer. And you won't be welcomed the next time you call.

You need to know what kind of movie the distributor, financier or co-production company makes. Besides studying the trades, do other research. Call other producers. Find out who the players are in your specific genre. Model your business plan and financial approach after other films in the same genre. When you go to a meeting you will know the parameters of the financing deals, the creative limitations of the genre and how the pictures are marketed.

You should also have some sense of the kinds of deals that are being made. Do they do development deals? Do they do step deals where your project is financed in a step-by-step fashion upon certain approvals? Do they do negative pick-up deals where the film is financed (by investors or a bank) and the distributor will "pick it up" and pay a specified amount once the film is finished? Is your meeting to discuss co-production possibilities among different financial partners who get different rights in exchange for a portion of the financing? What kinds of deals have been made before? What kinds of structures have been used for movies similar to your own? Ask your lawyer to talk to other lawyers to research the deals currently in vogue. You may be able to find out recent deals with other producers. This will give you a place to start if there is interest in your property.

Film Issues

These are the various issues that relate to marketing that need to be addressed when one sets out to sell a film to a financier, a studio or distributor. For example:

Who does the selling?

In the beginning, the most important issue is <u>marketing yourself and your film</u> to distributors. This is accomplished either directly or through agents. Scripts and treatments, budgets and proposals may be sent to distributors and financiers. A formal introduction via a third party known to both yourself and the distributor brings greater credibility. Without it, the uphill battle just to get a meeting can be enormous. Sending a script by mail is an almost certain strikeout. If returned at all, it will be unopened. Very few people will read unsolicited material; the possibility of lawsuits hangs like a cloud over the head of anyone with deep pockets.

Agents can make contacts on your behalf and be there to negotiate should interest be shown. Along the way all kinds of things can and will happen. Someone may like your script and want to buy it— without you attached. You must anticipate these things. If you are going out for the first time, is this really something you want to do? It's very hard to get a film made. Is it better to sell or option your material or should you hang on to it and demand that you have a production role? The answer depends entirely on your own constitution, your personal objectives and whether you have enough leverage in the deal to also be director or producer or co-producer.

Who should be attached?

The script is clearly the most important element. It is the center from which all other things come. If it is good it creates its own kind of leverage for the person who wrote it. Many writers have worked their way into producing and directing by holding on to their scripts and refusing to let them go. But there are an even greater number of properties that remain unproduced because their creators refused to let them go. There are no rules here. Everyone you talk to will offer different advice.

By increasing the credibility of the project, you at least get more people willing to listen to you. If you've written a script and then find a producer and a director, you are on your way. Once you have a star attached you have a package, and your financier and/or distributor will be much more interested. Of course, you've done 80 percent of the work. You've made their life easier because they can visualize the film. Now all you have to do is make it. Many projects go through many different combinations of elements (stars, producers, directors, rewriters), which can be a result of the talent's availability or the studio, producer or financier's desire to bring their own vision to the film. "We'd be interested if you can get _____ to play the lead," is frequently heard. Thus begins the chase to land the star to fill in the blank. And by the time the project is repackaged, the studio or financier is onto another project, or no longer works at the studio, or another similar picture is in production, etc.

51

Agents will be anxious to help with the packaging of a script because it will bring greater fees to their agency. It also means that they can bring their other clients to the project. This is both a plus and a minus. It's a plus because this will help immeasurably with increasing leverage and getting your package together. On the other hand you will be limited to their talent pool because this is where they may start (and end) the search. And all of this goes on <u>before</u> anyone has been pitched the project. The studio or producer or director may also have very different ideas about who should work on the project. The larger the budget and the bigger the name actors or directors, the more complex this dance will become because more people will want to vote. However, it may very well be the inclusion of these names that makes a project go.

Genre pictures (e.g., horror films) do not require stars but only suggestive titles and marketing hooks. They are made for less money and the producer does not have to play musical chairs. While artistry may be lacking in these pictures, the first-time director and producer have much more control because there is much less at stake.

Are there budget limitations?

Each genre has its own budget range. The reason for this has to do with sales. If you only have a limited number of theaters and a limited audience for an art film, then it had better cost a lot less than what it can make. Most comedies do not travel well overseas, so their potential is limited. Action and horror films, however, with

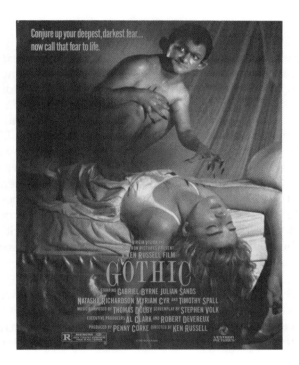

their relative lack of dialogue, are easily understood worldwide. Therefore, more can be spent on the budget for special effects, etc. *Variety* publishes the negative cost of many films. It is a good exercise to study the budget range spent on the various genres. Do not overspend on your genre. You must have realistic expectations about what a film can really earn to make money in this business.

Can I splinter rights?

For a time, the independent producer could divide theatrical and home video rights. The producer could go to two different distributors and receive (as advances) more than the actual cost of the film. He'd make a profit before the film was shot. Nowadays distributors will not assume the risk and expense of releasing a theatrical film unless they also own (or control) the home video rights. Theatrical exhibition builds public awareness for a film and thereby increases the value of home video. People know the film exists and, even though they didn't see it at their local theater, they may rent it when it arrives on their video store's shelf. A distributor can cushion the downside of a theatrical release by also exploiting the home video rights. Therefore, while a producer may sell the home video rights to a film, he or she will be very hard pressed to make a theatrical deal without having the home video rights to sell as well.

Producers are still able to hold on to the domestic and worldwide television rights in their films without coupling them to theatrical or home video distributors. The exploitability of a film in television is a function of the film's genre and the market demand at the time of the sale.

How *Not* to Get Francis Ford Coppola's Attention

Shortly after film school I was trying to figure out how to get a presentation to powerful people in the film business. It wasn't long after Francis Coppola directed THE GODFATHER. He was at the San Francisco Film Festival where they held a retrospective for him and during an interview he said, "If you really want to get my attention do something different. I mean, show me slides or something. You've got to wave your hand a little bit higher than everyone else. That would impress me." I set out to get his attention.

At that time I was working with Steven Arnold and Kaisik Wong. We wanted to make a feature titled MONKEY based on a thirteenth-century Chinese classic. The title character was very magical; Monkey could fly, do amazing transformations and wreak havoc in heaven.

With Francis's words still fresh in my mind, we designed a near-life-size cardboard photographic cutout of Monkey that would pop up when unfolded. In one of his hands was a proposal with some eight-by-ten photographs and a film treatment. In the other hand was a card with our phone number in it. Some friends of ours were carpenters working on Francis's house—they would get it in.

Taking a cue from the horse's head scene in THE GODFATHER, we had the carpenters plant the folded Monkey pop-up under the covers in Francis's bed. (OK, Francis, now you know.) We waited by the phone all night. No call. Weeks went by. Nothing. Could he have missed it?

A year later I had long forgotten our stunt. I went to over to a friend's house for dinner. Ironically, she happened to work as an assistant to Francis. When I walked in I was shocked—there on her wall were the eight-by-ten photos of Monkey from the proposal. I asked her how she got them and she said that one day Francis handed her a bunch of stuff and said, "Throw this out." She told me she liked it so much she kept it.

Obviously we went overboard. If someone put something in my bed, I'd be terrified. What an invasion of privacy; no wonder he never called.

The lesson here is to be appropriate. We weren't. Innovative, yes. Appropriate, definitely not. We should have shown some slides.

Classes of Co-Production Partners

There are many, many groups and potential partners for any project. The trick is recognizing that the world is loaded with potential partners—large and small. And finding ways to work together. The first place to start is with a list of the *class of co-production partners*—the group that might participate. Not every class of partner on the list will be appropriate, but it will get you thinking. Once you've identified the appropriate class, you can break each line down into specific names of companies to pursue. Prioritize those companies into a master "hit list," starting with those you think will be most interested based on what they've done in the past. The list that follows is an example of classes of potential co-partners which was prepared for the previously mentioned investors pitch.

CO-PRODUCTION PARTNERS

Private Investors/Consortiums
Foreign Governments (blocked funds)
Financiers
Corporations
Theatrical Distributors
International Theatrical Distributors
International Sales Agents
Home Video
International Home Video
Pay TV
Syndicators
Record Companies
Music Publishers
Book Publishers
Toy Companies
Licensing and Merchandising Firms
Sponsors (products/services)
Public Relations Firms
Marketing Companies/Consultants
Film Bookers

Budget line items may be bartered, deferred, or invested, thereby reducing the amount of cash investment required.

Budget Items
Actors
Director

Producer
Facilities
  Labs
  Production Houses
  Video Post Houses
  Equipment Rental Houses
  Animation/Title Houses
Law Firms/Lawyers
Brokers
Accountants

Yes, this is marketing. You are marketing your film idea to financiers and co-production partners. This is the first step of many as your film finds its way to an audience.

The primary question is *Who are the buyers and what do they want?* Without the answer you cannot really even begin.

When I find a project I like I spend a long time thinking about and writing down all the possible financiers, backers and distributors for the project. Anyone who really doesn't belong on the list is scratched off. Then I prioritize the list based on what I know or learn about these companies before a pitch is even made. I try to identify the most logical buyers first. I don't want to waste time getting no's. I'd rather be making the project. If you do your homework you can avoid an awful lot of running around.

Feature Distributors

The first step for anyone pitching a project or looking to sell completed films is to identify film distributors and the kind of product they distribute. You must know who distributes what.

Note: When I was at Vestron we screened and evaluated more than 3,000 ideas in a few years. Most of these never should have been sent to us in the first place. Only two or three projects were financed from this group; the others were shots in the dark by producers who did not do their homework to find out what kind of original product Vestron was distributing. (Sending away for our catalog would have been an easy first step.) It seemed unbelievable. We had the unsettling feeling that producers were desperately sending out their proposals—praying that they would stick somewhere.

What a waste of time and money. Buyers have no respect for this shotgun approach, which instantly devalues any project. It cheapens it to shop haphazardly. It shows that the producer doesn't know what he or she is doing. It wastes everybody's time. And since most acquisition and development people have no time, they will quickly turn off to a producer who wastes it.

Who Distributes What?

Who distributes what kind of product? Although individual distributors may change their strategy of acquisition and production from time to time, it is still worthwhile to try to sort out distributors and their product.

What follows is a list of distributors and the kind of product they have carried in recent years. This will help you quickly sort potential distributors. When in doubt, study the distributor to find out what kind of product they currently carry before making a proposal.

THE MAJORS

The major studio distributors handle just about every traditional genre of product except X-rated films.

BUENA VISTA
Comedy, family, adventure.

COLUMBIA
Music, drama, comedy, thriller.

MGM/UA
Comedy, drama, thriller.

PARAMOUNT
Comedy, thriller, action/adventure, concert.

20TH CENTURY-FOX
Thriller, comedy, art, action/adventure, family.

UNIVERSAL
Action/adventure, comedy, drama.

WARNER BROS.
Comedy, sci-fi, horror, action/adventure, thriller, drama.

MINI-MAJORS

CANNON
War action, drama, comedy, sword and sorcery, sexploitation.

DE LAURENTIIS ENTERTAINMENT GROUP
Thriller, mystery, art, action.

ORION PICTURES
Thriller, drama, comedy.

ORION CLASSICS
Foreign, art films, comedy.

TRI-STAR PICTURES
Thriller, sexploitation, drama, action/adventure, music, comedy.

INDEPENDENT DISTRIBUTORS

Distributors with four or more films per year released. There are countless smaller distributors who release one or two films per year.

ALIVE
Drama, art.

ATLANTIC RELEASING
Art, kids, teen comedy.

CINECOM
Art, foreign, comedy, performance piece, drama.

CINEMA GROUP
Thriller, occult, sci-fi, horror.

CINEPLEX ODEON
Kids, drama, art, concert.

CONCORDE
Action, exploitation.

CROWN INTERNATIONAL
Exploitation, action, thriller.

EMPIRE PICTURES
Horror, sci-fi, sexploitation.

EXPANDED ENTERTAINMENT
Animation compilations.

FILMDALLAS PICTURES
Art, drama, foreign.

FILMWORLD
Drama.

FIRST RUN FEATURES
Drama, art.

SAMUEL GOLDWYN COMPANY
Art, kids, horror, comedy, foreign.

HEMDALE
Art, drama, action.

INTERNATIONAL FILM
Art, foreign, drama.

ISLAND PICTURES
Art, drama.

LIGHTNING PICTURES
Horror, exploitation.

LORIMAR MOTION PICTURES
Thriller, comedy, drama.

MIRAMAX
Art, drama, foreign.

NEW CENTURY/VISTA
Horror, thriller, comedy.

NEW LINE CINEMA
Horror, thriller.

NEW WORLD PICTURES
Horror, thriller, sci-fi, kids, drama, action.

NEW YORKER FILMS
Foreign, art, drama.

PLATINUM PICTURES
Sexploitation.

SHAPIRO ENTERTAINMENT
Thriller, action, exploitation.

SKOURAS PICTURES
Art, foreign, drama, comedy.

SPECTRAFILM
Thriller, action.

TRANS WORLD ENTERTAINMENT
Sci-fi, action/adventure.

TROMA
Exploitation, horror, comedy.

VESTRON PICTURES
Art, drama, horror, foreign.

This should be taken as a rough guide to distributors. Occasionally an exploitation distributor will pick up an art movie for distribution. There are also dozens of other smaller distributors not listed here who handle single pictures.

Budget Range

Besides genre, the second distinction you can make between distributors is the budget ranges they handle. The average budget for a studio picture is nearly $20 million. Mini-majors compete with films around $10 million or less. Independent distributors make pictures for $6–7 million or less. Smaller independents' pictures cost around $3 million or less. And finally, the tiny exploitation distributors may make pictures under $1 million. This categorization identifies potential buyers. A studio will not do a super-low-budget film, nor will a small independent take on a big-budget film. Even though you might be able to find exceptions, time will be saved and the resultant "pass" letter avoided by making some distinctions in your approach up front.

Scale of Print and Ad Campaign

By studying the budget range and genres of pictures that distributors handle you can get a pretty good sense of how many prints they distribute on their pictures. This in turn gives you an idea of the print and ad commitment (P&A) they will put up when they release their films.

Some distributors roll out their small art films, dramas or "difficult" films slowly on a regional basis and allow them to find an audience.

They hit the major art houses, collect good reviews and hopefully get strong box-office results. These films will then be advertised with their box-office grosses in *Variety* to interest other exhibitors in showing them. Thus begins the rollout to similar audiences and theaters nationwide. (This strategy is changing because it is also important to get films into home video as quickly as possible. If a film takes a long time playing on a regional basis then the publicity value may be lost on home video when it is released much later.)

The exploitation genres, like horror or action/adventure, do not rely on reviews—people will go to see them regardless. Hundreds and hundreds of prints may be released in a saturated campaign. The distribution capitalizes on widespread awareness from national TV ad campaigns.

An excellent exercise is to study the weekly box-office grosses in *Variety*, which also shows the number of prints in release. You will come to see a correlation between the type of film and its release pattern as described above. You can also find examples in *Variety* of the key art for these films. The key art and layout will illustrate how films are positioned for their audience.

It is very difficult to find out the budgets for the films you will see in *Variety*. When budgets are reported they are often inflated. Why? Producers want distributors to think they spent more money than they actually did. They figure, "Why not say my film cost $3 million when it really cost $1.5 million? This way I may get a higher advance, which may even cover the cost of production and yield a profit immediately." It is also difficult to ascertain what the above-the-line payments (to cast, producers, director) may be unless you have a good idea of what specific fees these people take. On the other hand, any financier will want audited statements of expenditures during or after filming.

When you are preparing a business plan for a specific film, track down a film that was similar in genre, budget range and scope; then find the producer and ask him about the various specifics of production cost and how the film was released by the distributor (number of prints, advertising expenditures, release strategy, etc.).

I firmly believe in modeling what has come before. Why reinvent the wheel? Instead, go to school on someone who's already been down the same path. Capitalize on their successes and avoid their failures. Ask the right questions when you are preparing your project. Otherwise it's like starting from scratch and requires substantially more work.

Deep Pockets

Besides knowing which buyers, it is important to know whether your buyer has any money. Reading the trades will keep you posted on their quarterly earnings. No sense pitching a company that's about to go belly up. A company that has had healthy earnings will no doubt be doing more projects than one that is floundering. What follows is a list of company earnings for 1987. It identifies the most successful companies. By the time you read this, however, the playing field will have shifted again. It's a very volatile business. But this will give you a sense of the players' scale in relation to one another.

Film Distributor Earnings

Over $400 million: Paramount
Over $300 million: Buena Vista (Disney)
Over $200 million: Fox, Orion, Warner Bros.
Over $100 million: Columbia,Tri-Star, Universal
Over $50 million: New Line Cinema, United Artists
Over $25 million: Cannon, De Laurentiis, MGM, New World, Vestron
Over $10 million: Atlantic, Lorimar, Goldwyn

Under $10 million: Alive, Cinecom, Cinema Group, Cineplex Odeon, Cinetel, Crown International, Expanded Cinema, FilmDallas, Hemdale, International Film, Island, Orion Classics, Skouras, Trans World, and TMS Pictures.

About Buyers

Buyers want to buy. Yes, it's true—that's why they are there. They want nothing more than to say yes to a project. They find something. They look good. You get what you want. So you must make the buyers' job easy. You must research what they want and then give it to them. That is why research and pitching are so important. Buyers are very busy people. You can imagine. Everyone with an idea wants to get their attention. Buyers have very short attention spans. Your pitch must work in literally a few seconds. If they like the idea, if it engages, then you can elaborate. Think about how to embody your idea into a few powerful sentences. Then prepare yourself. You will only get one shot.

The Second Buyers: The Exhibitors

Just because a distributor takes on a film for distribution doesn't necessarily mean they can market it to exhibitors. Distributors, of course, don't buy a film unless they think they can book it into enough theaters to make a profit. Nevertheless, because of the abundance of films looking for screens there is another tier of buyer which must "approve" the picture before it hits the screens. That is the exhibitor. The exhibitor may be a buyer for an entire theater chain or the operator of a single independent theater. The exhibitor will want to look at the finished film before making a decision about showing it. For years the studios were able to rent their films to exhibitors through an auction process called blind bidding. This meant that, based on a title and the names of a few stars, theater exhibitors were expected to outbid their competitors for a film that no one had seen. Great business, ain't it? In recent years most states have outlawed blind bidding and it is now routine for distributors to hold screenings for the exhibitors.

It's not enough to make a film that you think an audience will like and that a distributor will distribute—the exhibitor too must be enrolled. But selling your film to the theater is the job of the distributor and falls outside the control of the producer. Part of the distributor's strategy, particularly if he or she is an independent distributor with independent product, is to sell the film to an exhibitor when there are windows of opportunity. The distributor may consciously stay away from holidays and summer when the studios bring out their big pictures and fiercely compete for theaters; a small distributor with a small picture stands very little chance of getting screens. It's better to get out of the way and pick those times when the picture would have a better shot. This is why the release date of the film is so important.

The Third Buyer: The Audience

The goal is to market, advertise and promote your film to <u>the specific audience which will be most interested in seeing it</u>. This is accomplished through advertising in newspapers, on television and on radio, as well as publicizing the film through newspapers, magazines and newsworthy publicity stunts. Different audiences are communicated to in different ways using different media. This is the job of the distributor and publicist (and sometimes the exhibitor, who will contribute to the advertising of the film or to creating publicity stunts)—to get the picture in front of an audience who might like to see it. These issues and the mechanics involved will be addressed in this book in greater detail.

DEVELOPMENT AS IT RELATES
TO MARKETING

"Both programming and marketing issues must be simultaneously addressed. Creative decisions in one area will affect the other area."

Development as It Relates to Marketing

Developing a film is a quest. You will struggle with the content of the film, you will ask yourself why you are making it and what your purpose is. Those are <u>programming</u> questions. You will also ask yourself who the film is for and how that audience gets to see it. Those are <u>marketing</u> questions.

<u>Both programming and marketing issues must be simultaneously addressed in the initial stages of creation</u>. One cannot exist without the other. Creative decisions in one area will affect the other area. Because a film is sold, in part, on its content and the expectation of the audience, these two creative twins must be given their due early on in the development process to best assure the film's delivery to its intended audience. When marketing is done in a vacuum, you don't have the opportunity to refine the program if necessary to reach broader audiences. When programming (the development of content) is done in a marketing void, an opportunity to sculpt the material in a different fashion is missed. It may be much more difficult to market. A hook may have to be developed, found or contrived that is not necessarily part of the film itself. No wonder filmmakers frequently balk at the copy and campaigns designed for their movies. This process should be started early in any film's (or video's) development.

We've all heard that the studios are run by distribution and marketing executives and not filmmakers. Much of that is true. A project is usually evaluated from a marketing point of view because this is a business. Studio and independent distributors want to know whether a film can be sold. They'll ask: *Is there an audience for this film? How do we reach them? How much will it cost to distribute and market this film? Are we best equipped to do that? How much profit can be made?* If the filmmaker has already addressed these issues within the context of the kind of film he or she is making, the difficulty in getting a producer, a studio or a distributor to underwrite the project is greatly reduced. The marketing hooks will be clearly seen within the content of the program.

The title will no doubt be the subject of great debate. Those few words are extremely important because they must convey an entire sense and expectation of the picture. I've worked on numerous projects where title discussions have gone on forever. *Is this really the best title for the movie? What does it mean? What does it evoke? Combined with the newspaper and ad graphics, what does the title communicate?* The title is a direct link to the target audience. *Does our intended audience want to see a movie with this title?* Market research may help answer this. More on that later.

One of the most frustrating issues arises again and again—the problem of predicting public taste eighteen months from now. *What will audiences be interested in a year and a half from now?* Only a crystal ball will tell you that. It takes a minimum of eighteen months to get a film through production and into distribution. By then, other producers may have preempted the market by bringing out simi-

lar product. What about PLATOON? It was one of the first Vietnam movies of its kind to come out in a year when many others (HAMBURGER HILL, HANOI HILTON, etc.) followed and failed. What if PLATOON had come out later? Or what about those three or four movies about an older man in a young man's body that came out in the same year? BIG hit it big *after* the other movies failed, which is a miracle in itself. But BIG wasn't sold on its concept like the others, it was sold on its star, Tom Hanks. The marketers knew they couldn't get an audience to turn out for a theme that had bombed so many times before. So they promoted the acting of the star. The marketing strategy worked. The movie worked.

The Story

Buyers of films, be they financiers, studios, distributors or exhibitors, will study a script to determine the quality of the story and the concept's elements. The basic question is simple: *Is it a good story? Does it work within the framework of the genre? Is it appropriate to the genre?* Action is more important than words: *Is it cinematic? Do the images, not the words, tell the story?*

When does the story take place? How long is it? Does it hold our attention throughout? Is there a clear hook or promotable angle within the script? What is it?

During the evaluation process a script will make its way to one or more readers, professionals (usually writers themselves) who read a script and analyze it. They write up a one- or two-page evaluation, or "coverage" as they say in the trade, which includes a synopsis and comments. These evaluations go to the executive in charge of buying or producing new films. While each buyer has his or her own criteria for evaluating properties, the main script elements that will be highlighted are the uniqueness of the story, its setting and characters. There will be additional comments on the quality of the dialogue, the story structure and plot points. The coverage will also include a review of the visual treatment, the script's pacing and the writer's skills.

This is all very subjective; different readers will have different opinions. If the coverage is good, the executive may read the script. If the coverage is poor but the idea is intriguing, the executive may still read the script and disregard the reader's evaluation. Usually, if one or more readers like it very much, it begins to journey upstream to the executive offices where it will get further review at a weekly development meeting.

If a script is rejected by one buyer, it continues making the rounds of other studios, distributors, producers and financiers. Scripts may float around for years. Producers sometimes think that if they change the title they can submit the same script again to the same buyer. With today's computers, buyers very quickly find similar synopses, directors, etc., to determine if they've seen the script before regardless of title. Any writer or producer who changes a title for resubmission gets a black mark.

It is truly staggering how many scripts are written and submitted to potential buyers. Vestron is a new motion picture producer. In the first year after announcing that they were going into feature projects, they received truckloads of scripts. To give you an idea of the volume, imagine forty large three-ring binders. Each binder contains one- or two-page coverage (evaluations) of scripts. Each book holds about 400 pages. That's 200 scripts per book or 8,000 total!

When I returned to the independent producer ranks I spent a good deal of time going through these scripts to see if there was anything I wanted to produce. The quality of the material was horrendous. We are talking worse than worst. If you ever want to feel good about your own worst ideas, you should read what some people think will make a good movie. There is no way I can impress on you how absolutely horrible most of these ideas sounded. No way.

The dreadful thing is that dozens of poor readers out there had to read this stuff—all the way through! Their minds have probably turned to mush by now from the ordeal. Vestron employed a large staff of freelance readers, most studios and independent producers do. This is what you are competing with. After a few weekends reading as many evaluations as I could stomach, I really began to get a sense of what the industry is reading. You cannot imagine how really sincere script buyers are when they say there are very few good scripts submitted. It's true.

When a good script does finally turn up, the potential buyer will want to know more about the writer's credits and what other elements, if any, are attached to the script: *Is there a director who is attached or interested in directing the script? Who is the producer? What have they done? Can they deliver on budget and on time?*

Many buyers will not pay for development. Why? Because they don't have to. There are an abundance of completed scripts in the marketplace already. Besides, it's expensive and too much work. If a good script never comes of it, they are out a lot of money. A buyer would rather find a script with some elements attached so that the job of packaging is less arduous. They want projects that are very close to production so that they will have to expend less time and money on the project.

The other promotable elements, if any, will be examined: *Who is doing the music? Is there an album possibility? What other promotional opportunities exist within the property? Was it based on a best-selling book? What about doing a novelization of the script and coming out with it at the same time as the movie? Is the idea for the movie newsworthy, current? Will it still be interesting eighteen months from now? Are there stars attached to the project? What is the budget? Is there any key art for the poster or marketing campaign?*

Although I've developed, produced and/or acquired hundreds of videos, with the exception of "made-for-video movies" my work on theatrical features has been limited. Nevertheless, the development and marketing criteria discussed above still apply. What follows is some of the thinking that went behind the decision to fund these films.

The Beach Boys

I executive produced THE BEACH BOYS: AN AMERICAN BAND for Vestron. The budget was $2.1 million. It was essentially a "rock-umentary" with forty Beach Boys songs. (Documentaries don't sell, so it was called a rock-umentary.) The decision to make the film was more a function of creating value for ancillary markets than to create a successful box-office movie. It was clear from the beginning that the theatrical potential of the movie was extremely limited. Everyone knew that very few people would leave their homes to see a Beach Boys movie. Most of their fans are over thirty-five years old, and we knew this wouldn't be one of the few movies they go to see each year.

We booked the film ourselves (through a sales agent—Vestron did not have a feature distribution division then) in about a dozen theaters around the country for a maximum run of two weeks. Did anybody show up? With the exception of Los Angeles, no. We didn't expect them to. What we wanted were reviews, ads and news coverage because this would build value for the home video release (which at the time was Vestron's real business). Once the film finished its theatrical run it could be sold to video retailers as a "movie." After all, it had a movie poster, movie reviews and it played in movie theaters. Hey, it's a movie! As a movie Vestron could charge $69.95 (retail) for it. <u>Had it not been positioned as a movie the video trade would have identified it as a music video</u>. The top price at the time for music videos was $29.95 and it would have been a long journey to recouping the production costs. It sold 20–30,000 units in the U.S.

So, it was launched as a movie. (The ticket sales were a little bit more than the cost of the few prints and ads. Consider it a wash.) It was sold into home video at movie prices. Then it went to Cinemax, which paid a $350,000 licensing fee. Then it was rereleased to home video at $29.95 and positioned as a music video. (This is having your cake and eating it, too.) Then Vestron Television sold it into syndication. (Another few hundred thousand dollars in revenue.) A year later a shortened "greatest hits" home video version was released at $19.95. It wouldn't surprise me if Vestron releases it again someday at $9.95. This same strategy was employed in a variety of foreign territories. With revenue coming in from all these different streams and having initially sold the documentary as a movie, it made a good profit for Vestron beyond the $2.1 million budget and additional marketing costs.

Much of the marketing strategy was conceived before the film was made. This became a "go" project because the Beach Boys have been around for twenty-five years and are considered "classic." Classic rock appeals to an older audience which has the money to buy videos. We hoped that Capitol Records would release a new Beach Boys album around the time of our release which would help promote the movie. They did, but the album flopped. Two Beach Boys books commemorating the band's twenty-fifth anniversary also came out. They, too, had little effect on our title. Malcolm Leo was an accomplished music film director, so there was confidence that we'd get a quality picture. The Beach Boys promised to support the film by doing interviews. (As it turned out, their promotional support was very limited.) The cumulative effect of the potential of the album, the book, and the Beach Boys participation bode very well and the project got the green light. The marketing folks felt there was plenty to promote and sell when the film was finished, especially in the worldwide home video and television markets. They were right. On to the Beatles.

Strawberry Fields

For three and a half years I was Vestron's executive in charge of production on STRAWBERRY FIELDS—a three-way co-production between Vestron, ITC and Computer Graphics Lab. STRAWBERRY FIELDS is currently in production and is expected to release sometime in 1989.

The project was originally a treatment for a stage production. The initial idea was weak but evolved into a feature-length animated film à la YELLOW SUBMARINE. Al Brodax, the director on SUBMARINE, would direct STRAWBERRY FIELDS. ITC, at that time, held the publishing rights to the Beatles' music and said they could deliver the Beatles' masters as well. Vestron's green light was given based on (1) the Beatles' music and songs, (2) state-of-the-art animation and effects, (3) an anticipated nostalgic audience—that "classic" group again—and (4) the film's potential to capture a young audience as well. The project was off to a good start.

It was to be a step deal. The three parties would finance writing the script, so we all read sample scripts by different writers. Henry Parkes got the job. He wrote a ROMANCING THE STONE–type plot involving Michelle and Jude, who go off in search of Maxwell's silver hammer. They hope to obtain this magical and powerful weapon before the Walrus and the evil Eggmen can get to it. On their journey they get a ticket to Rhyde where they meet Obladi Oblada and eventually end up in Strawberry Fields where they meet the Fool on the Hill. You get the idea. The script uses characters from the songs in an adventure film format. It is fast-moving, visually stunning and loaded with verbal and sight gags. The humor is designed on two levels for kids and adults.

Each of the parties put up a portion of the $5–6 million budget in exchange for various rights and profit participation. Vestron got home video and pay cable. ITC got theatrical and television. (This came at a time when it was still possible to splinter rights—ITC is now faced with the difficulty of selling theatrical without home video attached.)

All parties entered into the project knowing that "adults don't go to animated films." Of course that was before the success of AN AMERICAN TAIL and WHO FRAMED ROGER RABBIT?—two films that proved the dictum wrong. During early production it was learned that ITC would be unable to deliver the original Beatles songs; the other two partners agreed that platinum artists would be substituted to cover (rerecord) the Beatles songs.

After more than a year, many top artists had delivered cover versions of the songs: Michael Jackson ("Come Together"), Cyndi Lauper ("Across the Universe"), Stevie Ray Vaughn ("Taxman"), Billy and the Beaters ("Slow Down"), Robert Palmer ("Baby You're a Rich Man"), Crosby, Stills & Nash ("Blackbird"), etc. Epic Records agreed to advance money for the album rights, a necessary choice since all the artists are on CBS Records and Epic is one of the labels CBS distributes.

The marketing strategy went something like this: "Even though adults don't go to animated films, they will go to this one because everyone grew up on Beatles music. All the old hippies who remember YELLOW SUBMARINE will come out of the woodwork." Since the original Beatles music could no longer be obtained, it was felt that "teenagers will want to see the film because their favorite artists are doing the music." The story is contemporary and works at a couple of levels to keep kids, teenagers and nostalgic adults interested. Some of the animation is done in a 3-D style that no one has seen before, which enhances the appeal of the movie.

As of this writing the film is about 50 percent complete. Although a theatrical distributor has yet to be selected, I believe that the new music will play a significant role in marketing the film. Stevie Ray Vaughn's "Taxman" is outstanding. It's very hot. It would make an excellent single release about six weeks before the movie opens. That would give it time to climb the charts and draw attention to the forthcoming movie. Michael Jackson's song—which is also fabulous—could be the second punch in a one-two combination. It could be premiered on the radio the same day the movie opens, drawing further attention to the film.

The voices of "Michelle" and "Jude" are Debra Winger and Steve Guttenberg. Unfortunately, for contractual reasons, their names cannot be used to promote the film, but reviewers will recognize them immediately anyway. Besides, they are not the main draw—people don't go to a movie to "hear" their favorite stars. The music names on the marquee and movie poster should convey the excitement of the movie. Other platinum artists with different audience demographics are being sought for the movie. It is felt that it is important to get many different kinds of music stars who will bring their own audiences (soul, country and western, R&B, MOR, classic rock, etc.) to the movie.

An attempt was made to license the name and the toys based on the many wonderful characters in the movie, but at this late date it is unlikely to happen on any large scale. With a film that is *perceived* to be big—like WILLOW—or a television series with longevity (STAR TREK), licensing makes more sense. The products stay on the shelf longer because of the visibility and screen life of the film or program. We explored everything from board games to pajamas, but the slump in the toy business over the last two years meant that few companies were willing to take a chance on a movie perceived to have a limited release. If the movie is a hit, however, it will be too late then to take advantage of licensing opportunities. Filmmakers who think their films have merchandising potential must begin getting merchandisers and licensees in place well in advance to allow for design, tooling up and manufacturing time.

Many of the creative decisions—the programming decisions—about the movie had some basis in marketing. Things were not done because they seemed like a good idea unto themselves but rather because there was a marketing strategy behind them that allowed for additional products (and thus revenue streams) to be created.

The selection of the genre of story, the director, the music for the movie, the music acts to record the songs, the merchandising of the film—these elements all had some basis in both the programming and marketing of the film.

Without some significant marketing hooks from the get-go, all three partners would be hard pressed to shell out millions of dollars. As the film proceeds through production other marketing opportunities will be discovered, but the primary hooks and promotable elements were inherent in the project from the beginning.

Production Elements

These are only a few examples of production elements as they relate to marketing. Others may include the <u>look and design</u> of the project, which is very important. STRAWBERRY FIELDS must be spectacular and be executed in a manner that no one has seen before. ROGER RABBIT could certainly make that claim and delivered on its promise. Audiences were saying, "You simply have to see it."

<u>Music</u> may also be a key element. Remember the impact and success of the music for CHARIOTS OF FIRE. <u>Photography</u> is an element. A National Geographic video or a David Lean movie brings with it an expectation of excellence of photography. This too is an important selling point.

Exotic <u>locations</u> are also an element. Think about THE MILAGRO BEANFIELD WAR or THE MOSQUITO COAST or THE MISSION, which had great locations. Most budgets are limited. Can you create a great look with limited dollars? How much impact will this have on the success of what you are trying to accomplish? Look at the visual style that the Cohen brothers brought to BLOOD SIMPLE; they gave a unique sensibility to a well-known (film noir/thriller) genre. Even though their film was produced on a very low budget, the exaggerated visual style was one of its more memorable elements and got reviewers' and the public's attention alike.

Some productions lend themselves to <u>local premieres</u>. Perhaps the community where the film was shot can help launch the film and gain a presence in a way no other place can. Ask yourself if any benefits can come to the production as a result of the location.

What other production elements can be turned this way or that to benefit the marketing effort?

VISUALIZING THE CONCEPT

"Give the marketers something to work with."

Key Art First, Movie Second

It is not uncommon for producers to bring key art for their movies when they are trying to sell them. Charlie Band, former head of Empire Pictures, creates appealing horror and sci-fi titles and does full-color posters for them long before any scripts are written. A buyer may give the green light on a project based on the look of the poster and marketing campaign. With exploitation pictures this is possible because the concept, not the stars or story, sells the movie.

The Computer Loved It

Once, as an exercise, I took each word from *Variety's* list of the 100 top-grossing films and added adjectives of my own. I fed all these words into a computer and told it to give me every two-word combination. About an hour later the computer had printed out a report the size of a telephone book with thousands of titles. I spent a few hours going through it. Within this mammoth pile of paper were about a dozen ideas that suggested interesting movie possibilities. I selected a few and gave them to the art department and asked for some comp sketches. I wanted to generate movie posters first and see if movies or videos could be developed later. This is a technique that Roger Corman used for years. GRAND THEFT AUTO was a title that tested well. Corman asked Ron Howard to come up with a script to direct based on the title. It was Ron Howard's first movie.

Now this is an off-the-wall example of development. Not necessarily the best way to come up with ideas for movies, but it does prove a point. Filmmakers need to think about how their movies will be sold as they create their ideas. If you can marry an idea you feel is important with a good marketing concept, you have a much better chance of delivering your message when the film is finished. Many filmmakers make films only for themselves and then complain later that "the distributor didn't know what to do with it." Well, of course the distributor didn't know what to do with it; neither did the filmmaker, who didn't give the marketers anything to work with. Marketing is too often an afterthought when it can be fundamental to the creation of the idea itself.

In discussions with art directors who design key art for movies, the same theme is echoed. Create images that are strong and simple. Images that can be read quickly have greater impact. Go for single-note images. Don't try to include too much in the key art. Many films take a collage approach and try to show every car crash, every kiss, every helicopter, every actor's face. What they end up with is a mishmash of images that do not clearly communicate what the movie is about. By trying to do everything, they diminish the impact of their art campaign.

By the time a film is playing its third week, the newspaper ad is the size of a matchbook cover. The key art image and title treatment need to hold up in that kind of reduction and still communicate something about the movie. ALIEN had that wonderful egg image. AIRPLANE used that great airplane twisted in a knot. Both worked very well in reduced formats.

The title treatment is the type design that is created to enhance the image of the movie. STAR WARS used big and bold block letters; ROGER RABBIT a flowing script. GANDHI was thin, simple and elegant; DIRTY DANCING was graffiti-esque. They all conveyed a sense of the movie—even in small form.

The title treatment and key art are combined and carried through on posters, album covers, videocassette packages and newspaper ads. If it works well, the key art will remain the same throughout the release of all media for the film. Hundreds of thousands or millions of dollars are spent to bring the title treatment and key art in front of an audience. Once established, it takes on meanings and associations of its own. It is a veritable trademark of the film.

A Market Checklist

A film takes so long to develop, finance and produce that it is well worth the painstaking efforts to embody as many elements as possible with presence, heat and promotable hooks. This will give the marketers and the public something to hold on to, something to expect, something to look for when the film comes out. The following are elements that can be conceived and embellished prior to production. Many other marketing and promotional opportunities will be developed after the film is finished as well. It is important to create value in each element—if you can—as you develop your project.

How many of the following will draw attention to your film? Why?

Story
Genre
Cast
Title
Concept
Copy Line
Film Review Potential
Reputation of Director
Ability of Producer to Deliver
Music
Key Art
Exotic Location
Period-Piece Costuming
Photography
Special Effects
Target Audiences
Local Premiere
Book Tie-In
Album Tie-In
Merchandising Potential

Exhibitor's Promotions

I can't help but think that the old guys did it better—at least they seemed to work harder at it. Everything hadn't been done in the early days. A friend of my father gave me a book years ago. Published in 1937, it it tattered and falling apart, but it is a reminder of the energy and creativity of the early days. It is called *The Encyclopedia of Exploitation: 10,001 Show-Stopping Ideas*. It's fabulous even though it only has 1,001 ideas. It is a compilation of promotional stunts that two movie theater exhibitors (Hendricks and Waugh) did in the thirties when a movie came to town. They didn't just slap an ad in the paper and sit back and wait for an audience. They went out and hustled.

When I go to movies today I don't get the feeling that theater owners are going out of their way to get me into their theaters. There is a sense of apathy. And once there, they don't put on much of a show. Everything is automated. The marketing of films is left up to corporate headquarters in Los Angeles or New York. The guys at street level have no commitment to filling their theater; that's somebody's else's job: "We just show 'em and sell popcorn."

Well, not so in the old days. The exhibitors did window displays, printed fake newspaper headlines, had attractive women ride elephants through town, hired gangs of kids to deliver fake telegrams, rubber-stamped everything in sight, recorded songs for local radio stations, held contests and giveaways—and that's just from the first six pages of the book. In one stunt they led a belled cow around town with a banner that read: This is no bull, [title] is the funniest picture yet produced. The book is loaded with corny but memorable promotional stunts.

Actually, according to present-day memory experts, the more unusual or surreal the match between images and names (cow and title) better. The conscious and subconscious minds have an easier time remembering surreal juxtapositions. So what these promoters were doing really worked wonders.

The entire area of exhibitor publicity is one that deserves to be resurrected. In this era of electronic media, marketers rely too heavily on national advertising. Today's stunts are delivered in commercials. I believe that local live events and stunts can have enormous impact, especially since no one does them now. I can't help but think the guerilla approach to film exhibition offers a window of opportunity for ambitious filmmakers and exhibitors. Not only is it very inexpensive, but it provides a creative alternative to film promotion. Well-planned and well-executed stunts can create enormous returns in free publicity, newspaper articles and photos. A basic rule of promotion is that every stunt or event must produce a <u>photo opportunity</u>. So many overlook this basic tenet. I've been to dozens of launch parties and premieres where people just stood around and drank wine. With a little imagination a small stunt could provide the attendant press with photos that would generate tremendous publicity. The press must be bored to death with openings and premieres and would relish something new. Stunt production can be created for other kinds of movies besides offbeat comedies. Producers of films of a serious nature can also employ events and happenings appropriate to the image they wish to convey.

When I was at Vestron I was very proud to have made the deal that brought National Geographic into home video. The next step was to announce our new partnership to the world. For the launch party we rented the Explorer's Club in Manhattan. When you go up the

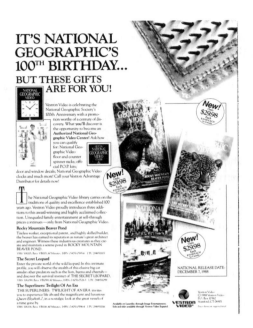

stairs to the reception area there is a fifteen-foot-high polar bear with giant claws extended to greet you. Hanging on the walls are canoes and other explorers' artifacts. We played a tape of jungle sounds in the background while waiters served very exotic foods. ("Tastes good. What *is* this anyway?") We found ways to make the event memorable and different from other press events. Specimens of taxidermy and bizarre artifacts provided numerous photo opportunities. Everyone from National Geographic or Vestron wore pith helmets and khaki jackets. It was dignified. It was fun. It worked.

MARKET RESEARCH

"Design your campaign to pull your target audience and forget about everyone else."

Market Research

Titles are very important. You can do some market research to see whether you have the right title. Cut a trailer for your film. Make several video dubs with different titles. Do focus group sessions to see which tests the best—which is the most appealing to your audience.

You can also find out which audiences respond best to your film. Men or women? What age groups? What economic or social backgrounds? Are there various audiences that can be identified? Different elements within the film may appeal to different audiences. If this is the case, you may need to design several versions of your campaign to reach these audiences. An upscale horror movie like THE OMEN may appeal not only to hardcore horror folks, but also to a more intellectual audience. AMERICAN WEREWOLF IN LONDON had a hardcore horror audience, but because it was also funny it drew people who liked comedy and wouldn't otherwise see a horror film. These were conscious, well-thought-out campaigns designed to pull distinct audiences. If you try to appeal to everyone you can end up getting no one. Design your campaign to pull your target audience and forget about everyone else.

ONE OF THE TEN BEST
FILMS OF 1987!

Vincent Canby, THE NEW YORK TIMES
PEOPLE MAGAZINE
Kathleen Carroll, THE NEW YORK DAILY NEWS
Mike McGrady, Joseph Gelmis, NEWSDAY
Sheila Benson, LOS ANGELES TIMES
Michael Sragow, SAN FRANCISCO EXAMINER
Dennis Cunningham, WCBS-TV
Pia Lindstrom, NBC-TV
Susan Granger, WMCA
Jack Garner, GANNETT NEWSPAPERS
Lynn Minton, WOR
Hal Hinson, WASHINGTON POST

TWO ACADEMY AWARD NOMINATIONS.

In this, his final film achievement, legendary director JOHN HUSTON
brings the magic of James Joyce to the screen with an evocative drama,
a profound elegy to his cinematic career. Huston leads an award-
winning production team, an acclaimed cast of Irish players, and
directs his daughter, ANJELICA HUSTON, for the first time since
their Academy Award-winning collaboration in PRIZZI'S HONOR.
Nominated for two 1987 Academy Awards for Best Costume
Design and Best Screenplay, THE DEAD is written by
John Huston's son, TONY HUSTON.

NATIONAL RELEASE DATE:
NOVEMBER 30, 1988

ANJELICA HUSTON AND
DONAL McCANN IN

John Huston's

COMEDY-DRAMA OF JAMES JOYCE'S
GREAT STORY

the Dead

A VAST, MERRY, AND UNCOMMON TALE OF LOVE.

VESTRON PICTURES / ZENITH Present WIELAND SCHULZ-KEIL and CHRIS SIEVERNICH Production
ANJELICA HUSTON and DONAL McCANN in JOHN HUSTON Film "THE DEAD" Based on the short story "The Dead" With (in order of appearance) HELENA CARROLL
CATHLEEN DELANY RACHAEL DOWLING INGRID CRAIGIE DAN O'HERLIHY MARIE KEAN DONAL DONNELLY
SEAN McCLORY and FRANK PATTERSON as BARTELL D'ARCY Wardrobe Designed by DOROTHY JEAKINS Production Designed by STEPHEN GRIMES in collaboration with DENNIS WASHINGTON
Executive Producer WILLIAM J. QUIGLEY Production Manager TOM SHAW Music by ALEX NORTH Edited ROBERTO SILVI Director of Photography FRED MURPHY
PG PARENTAL GUIDANCE SUGGESTED Produced by WIELAND SCHULZ-KEIL and CHRIS SIEVERNICH Directed by JOHN HUSTON
SOME MATERIAL MAY NOT BE SUITABLE FOR CHILDREN
DOLBY SURROUND Written by TONY HUSTON Beta ©1988 Vestron Video
STEREO ℗ 1987 VESTRON PICTURES Inc. VHS P.O. Box 10382 Stamford, CT 06901

VHS: VA6019; Beta: VB6019; Rated PG; 82 Minutes; ISBN: 0-8051-0524-7; UPC: 2848516019.

Some movies are released slowly and build. LA BAMBA and STAND AND DELIVER were both launched in East L.A. to a Hispanic audience. Both films had stars and subject matter that appealed to this market. The films went for their target audience and broadened out. John Houston's THE DEAD was promoted first on campuses to literature and film students who either knew Joyce's or Houston's work. The marketers went for the primary audience to build word of mouth, which in turn brought in others. It would not have been prudent or effective to try to advertise these films to mass audiences because they are not mass films.

Before its release, test screenings with detailed questionnaires can reveal how well a film plays. You can learn what people liked most about the movie. The marketing campaign can highlight the most appealing elements and bury the rest.

Strategy

Releasing a film in a haphazard way may prove disastrous. Too much money and effort has been put into the production to release a film without careful planning and strategy. You know what kind of film you have; study the releases of similar films. Were they released broadly or platformed city by city and allowed to grow? Or was the strategy altogether different? What time of year did they come out? What else was in the marketplace?

It is important to release your independent film out of harm's way—summer, Christmas, and the presidents' birthdays are when the studios get the lion's share of the public's attention. They will spend millions on television ads and publicity. This is not the time you want to be out there competing. You want to go earlier or later—not at the same time. This rule can, from time to time, be successfully broken. If a major studio film flops, there may be many weeks where screens *are* suddenly available. Independents can rush in with their pictures. This kind of coup takes lots of research about what the competition will be doing. A distributor is in the best position to gather this information from exhibitors, the trade publications, and his or her own knowledge of how other distributors operate.

PROMOTION TIME LINE

"The film is sampled for audiences to test its playability.*"*

Promotion Time Line

Promotion is the cheapest and most effective way to promote your film. It beats paid advertising hands down. The best way to maximize promotion is to give yourself enough time for the promotion to build. That means starting early—long before your film releases. If you don't, you will be shortchanging your film's potential.

If you are an independent with limited resources, you need all the time you can get. You will only get one chance to make your film work. When you take your shot, you want to have exploited all your promotional opportunities to ensure your film's success.

Once a release date is established you need to give yourself six months before the release date for screenings. This may seem excessive, but it's not. You need this time to play it for "influential" target audiences and the press. Long-lead magazines work three or four months in advance. If you show them your film in late January, the earliest they can get an article published is April or May. People will have a month to read the magazine. By June they may be ready to see this movie they've been reading about. That's six months. It is possible to release a film faster than this, but then you cut down your exposure in the long-lead magazines and you want as much coverage as you can get. It's rare that one article will send people into the theaters. You want to build multiple impressions. If your audience gets an impression from stories, ads and pictures about your film three times or more, they start to wonder whether they should see it. The worst thing a producer can do is be too anxious about getting the film released immediately after postproduction. Sure you want to get your film out there, but you also want an eager, informed audience that can't wait to see it. This takes time to build.

Time Line

This promotion time line chart is a general overview of the marketing for a film. Use it as a starting point in mapping your own campaign. Start with the release date and work backward.

It's a very good idea to know what will be necessary to market your film before the job is immediately in front of you and you find yourself unprepared. The time line is a sequence of activities that will come into play during the marketing of most films. This overview will get you thinking in the right direction. Embellish this plan. Modify it. Make it your own.

Development

During the first seven months the film script is written and rewritten. This is a good time for the marketers to read the script and try to find the angles, hooks and promotable elements that will help market the film later. As the film was approved for production, it is assumed that there is already some rationale for doing the picture— that the marketers have already come up with some basic strategy and understand how to approach the distribution of the film. This may also be the period where the film's title is challenged. Is it the right one?

MARKETING TIME LINE

	18 Months	Development	Pre-Prod.	Princ. Photog.	Post-Prod.	Tests/Publ.	Theat. Release	Video Release
		7	4	4	5	5	2	2
Development								
Story		■	■					
Prod. Team		■	■					
Cast		■	■					
Marketing Concepts								
Release Date, Strategy		■	■	■	■	■	■	■
Pre-Production								
Title Treatment		■	■					
Production								
Elec. Press Kit				■	■			
Stills				■	■			
Interviews				■	■			
Music			■					
Post-Production								
Interviews				■	■	■		
Trailer					■	■		
Music Video					■	■		
Art Work								
Key Art					■	■		
Ads						■	■	
Posters, etc.						■	■	
Market Testing								
Trailer & Art						■	■	
Final Cut								
Trade & Press Sceenings						■	■	■
Film Festivals						■	■	
Sneaks						■	■	
Record Release						■		
Cross Promotions							■	■
Publicity & Promotion								
Long Lead Magazines						■		
EPK-TV							■	
Radio						■	■	■
Junkets						■	■	
Talent Tour						■	■	
Giveaways						■	■	
Trailers on Screens						■	■	
Advertising								
Trade						■	■	■
Consumer						■	■	■
Premieres								
Theatrical Release							x	
Video								
Sponsorship								■
Trade Press & Publicity								■
Consumer Press & Publicity								■
Video Merchandising								■

Preproduction

Prior to principal photography, production planning is still taking place. Some marketing decisions may influence such things as casting, music, composer, soundtrack album, theme song and the like.

Principal Photography

Now the publicity people can really go to work. They usher press to the set or location for interviews. They may hire an outside video company to shoot an electronic press kit (EPK) which will include interviews with the stars, behind-the-scenes footage, etc. The video crew will shoot the most interesting scenes (action, stunts, special effects, love scenes) or whatever the publicists think they may want to compile later on the EPK. A unit still photographer hired by the production will do portraits of the actors in and out of character and costume. The unit publicist will do interviews, collecting biographical data on each star.

Postproduction

All the video footage for the electronic press kit is assembled, viewed and edited. A press kit is written which includes bios, a synopsis and other materials. Photos are selected and approved by the stars for inclusion. The press kits are sent to the newspaper, magazine, radio and TV press. If appropriate, a music video is edited using the film's theme song, clips from the movie and other shots specially taken for the music video. A marketing reel (show reel) and/or a trailer for the film are being put together and tested.

They will be screened at theatrical trade shows for exhibitors. The trailer will later be shown in theaters and possibly on television to promote the upcoming film. A poster is completed from the selected comps. It may be an illustration or a photograph from a special photo session with the film's stars.

Tests/Publicity

During this next five-month period the publicity and marketing folks are in full gear. A rough cut or answer print of the movie is available for screenings. All the press material has been compiled and sent to a "hit list" of magazines, newspapers, and television shows.

Once everyone sees the final product, the marketing strategy may be fine-tuned. New promotable angles may be discovered that weren't apparent in the script. The stars may or may not be promotable, depending on their current status and what's happening in their lives. The film is sampled before a variety of audiences to test its playability. The title may be tested. Is it the best one? Questionnaires are filled out. What do people think of the movie? Would they recommend it to their friends? What are their favorite and least-favorite scenes? Based on this research the film may be reedited. A new ending may be shot or edited. A new trailer may be made emphasizing the most-liked elements of the film. Or various trailers may be cut to emphasize certain elements for different audiences.

Depending on the kind of film produced, it may appear in selected film festivals. It will certainly be shown to press and other trade.

Advertising

A budget will be allocated for advertising. The marketers will determine the extent of paid advertising within their budget. They will try to determine the best magazines, newspapers, television and radio stations and times to advertise the movie. Various scenarios involving the sequencing of ads and costs will be presented until the most effective is determined. An advertising agency may participate in the media buy.

The release pattern will determine the most effective advertising campaign and media buy. If it is a national release, ads in the national media will appear when the film is released in hundreds or even a thousand theaters. If the film is rolled out on a regional basis, then regional advertising is bought. If the film is played as an exclusive engagement in one theater in one city, then only local advertising will be employed.

Promotional Items

There are an assortment of promotional items that must be ordered, written, assembled and distributed. These may include:

<u>One-Sheets.</u> These are sell sheets that have the key art for the film, the credits and other information. A one-sheet is usually a smaller version of the poster.

<u>Posters.</u> They are used in the glass cases of theaters and given away through record company promotions, radio stations, various sponsors, etc.

<u>Trailers.</u> Trailers are shown on theater screens before the film comes out. They may be adapted for television spots. Video trailers may appear in retail stores or sent out as part of the electronic press kit.

<u>Electronic Press Kits.</u> The electronic press kits contain interviews, behind-the-scenes footage, the trailer and sometimes a music video. Also included is a script of questions for local television stations. This way they can reedit the material to look like their local anchor asked questions of the stars, whose responses appear on the video reel. The behind-the-scenes footage can be reedited into a variety of forms depending on the needs of the news department.

<u>Stand-ups.</u> Standees or stand-ups made of cardboard are sometimes made for theaters and other retail outlets. They are very expensive, so you usually only see them on the bigger movies. Remember the full-size stand-up of Rambo?

<u>Tickets.</u> Free tickets are given away for sneak and special premiere showings through sponsors, radio stations, record companies and others involved with the film.

<u>Giveaways.</u> Other promotional items which serve as giveaways are T-shirts, buttons, visors, key chains, singles, albums, cassettes, CDs and music videos.

Theatrical Release

Activity hits a fever pitch during the weeks before the film opens. Radio stations may sponsor sneak previews to build word of mouth. Television spots of the trailer may appear. The stars may go on talk show tours. Newspapers will interview the stars and director and review the film. Television news programs may air soft news stories featuring elements clipped from the electronic press kit. The trailers will play in the theaters weeks before the film releases. There will be special contests, giveaways and stunts to keep the film in the public eye. If there is a record, it will be released and, hopefully, play on record stations before the movie opens. There may be cross-promotions with a book, an album, clothing, and other merchandising.

Sponsors may do special events concurrent with the film's release. For example, a department store might hold a special promotion. There will be "wild postering" (posters pasted to the walls of construction sites) in cities where the film is playing.

Ads and articles will appear in the long-lead magazines as well as the weekly periodicals. If this is timed right, they will be seen and read immediately before and during a film's opening. Once all this is in place—and the gods willing—the release date of the film will not be altered. Sometimes, however, a picture is so strong in an exclusive engagement that the theater will hold it over, delaying its general release.

There may be a premiere in one or more cities to garner editorial and photo coverage in newspapers, on TV news shows and entertainment programs like "Entertainment Tonight." All this effort for a few seconds of national airtime, and a well-placed celebrity picture or interview.

Then it's up to the public and the power of the film. If they like the film, and tell their friends to go, it will stay on the screen as long as it is profitable or until another movie comes along and bumps it off.

If the film is successful, the press department will no longer be soliciting publicity but responding to requests for photos and interviews. Press begets press. The press read each other for ideas. Once a film starts getting publicity it feeds on itself. But if a film does not click with an audience, it will be an uphill battle for the publicist to get any attention from the press. Then it's over and it gets very quiet.

Video Release

Most films are released on videocassette five or six months after theatrical release. The closer the video release is to the theatrical release, the more value it has because people will remember the promotion for the movie and want to see it.

The video packaging (video posters and one-sheets) will generally use the same artwork as the movie. After all, these images have already received widespread distribution through newspapers and magazines. Unless the movie died a horrid death, it is in the video distributor's interest to use recognizable artwork for the videocassette package. Promotional items may also be given away to retailers and wholesalers to help them promote the video.

HIT FILMS AT HIT PRICES!

Plus a "Buy 2 Get 1 Free" Consumer Offer.*

A $10,000,000 MARKETING BLITZ!

- MAJOR TELEVISION AD CAMPAIGN
- HEAVY CO-PROMOTION WITH NESTLÉ
- EXTENSIVE CONSUMER PRINT ADVERTISING
- EYE-CATCHING IN-STORE P.O.P.

VESTRON VIDEO*

© 1988 Vestron Video,
P.O. Box 10382, Stamford, CT 06901
Prices Shown Are Suggested Retail.

* US MARKETS ONLY

Video marketers are always looking for new ways to merchandise video. And new opportunities to cross-promote video with other products—thereby maximizing promotional and advertising dollars. A sponsor may put an ad on the video to promote a product or service. In exchange, the video distributor will get an additional marketing push through the sponsor's ongoing consumer advertising programs. There will be some tie-in between the sponsor's product and the video (e.g., the partnerships between TOP GUN and Pepsi, DIRTY DANCING and Nestle).

Video retailers want the distributors to advertise on radio and especially television when the videos of hit movies are released. They want to drive people into the stores to rent the cassettes. Newspaper and magazine advertising to consumers will be used to the same effect. There will also be special ads in the video trade magazines to alert wholesalers and retailers and support their selling efforts.

The publicist will try to get the video reviewed and find angles to get new articles in newspapers and magazines. If the film has already been well covered (or is a flop), the publicist's job will be much more difficult.

Spin-Offs

Other products bring additional attention to your film and keep its image alive in the public eye. When a film is successful, spin-off merchandising can be very lucrative. Many of the major films sell licensing rights to third-party companies that produce everything from lunchpails, beach towels and pajamas to stationery, toys and games. Most independent and art films do not lend themselves to such grand-scale commercialization because they appeal to a limited audience and because they do not stay on the screen for very long. Most films that have a merchandising component are popular among kids and teens (E. T., GHOSTBUSTERS).

It is nevertheless a worthwhile exercise to think along these lines as you develop your film and video ideas. Other communication pieces—such as merchandised products—can also carry forth your message. *Are there books, pamphlets, study guides, albums, cassettes, postcards, fact sheets, radio programs or live events to be spawned simultaneously with your film?* Do not be too fast to discard these ideas as impractical or a waste of time. The more cross-promotions you can create, the more visibility you will gain for your film.

Summary

The path for every film is different, but many of the same marketing principles apply. The sequencing may be different. The tools may be different. Studying the principles of marketing and modeling your film against other successes will give you a distinct advantage. It's akin to following the path of a sailboat—it's there for a few minutes and then it's gone. You can head off in the same direction, but ultimately you're going to have to find your own way.

You know what the questions are and how to ask new ones. You can determine what you will need to do and map it out on your calendar.

Marketing issues very quickly become production issues. The more you anticipate and understand what you need to accomplish during promotion, the more capable you will be of including promotable elements during production (without, by the way, diminishing the integrity of your film.) After a while it becomes second nature, like knowing where to set up the lights or how to frame the picture. This perspective gives you the necessary tools and forethought to expand the audience for of your film.

About the Next Section

If you are interested in the marketing case study of DIRTY DANCING, one of the most successful independently distributed films, read on. As of this writing it has earned over $170 million worldwide and spawned a television series as well.

Learn what was in the minds of the department heads at Vestron as they set out to produce and market DIRTY DANCING. What decisions were made in regard to the marketing questions and issues? How did the marketing plans shift when other realities entered the picture? And what did Vestron do about it?

Otherwise skip this section and go to the section on marketing special-interest and original home video programs. These specialty videos require their own marketing plans since they have not received theatrical exposure and are intended for entirely different audiences.

DIRTY DANCING:
A CASE STUDY

DIRTY DANCING: A CASE STUDY

"I thought the title was the most brilliant part of the script. I said go from the very first after hearing the title. It's catchy."

Introduction to the Dance

DIRTY DANCING was the most successful independently produced film of 1987–88. On an investment of $7 million the film grossed over $170 million worldwide. While luck and good timing were involved, much of the success of the release can be attributed to careful planning by Vestron.

This film was selected for the case study because (1) it was an independent film made outside the studio system on a low budget and (2) I worked at Vestron for nearly four years, watched the project mature (I left two weeks before the release of the film) and know the people who were key in marketing the film.

What follow are stories, insights and observations from many of the people at Vestron responsible for developing, producing, marketing, promoting and merchandising this phenomenally successful independent film.

The Players:

Bill Quigley, president, Vestron Pictures
Jon Peisinger, president, Vestron Video
Jimmy Ienner, music consultant/producer, "Dirty Dancing" Albums
M. J. Peckos, senior vice president, marketing and distribution, Vestron Pictures
Al Reuben, senior vice president, sales and marketing, Vestron Video
Mitchell Cannold, vice president, production, Vestron Pictures
Steve Reuther, senior vice president, production, Vestron Pictures
Pat Caufield, vice president, promotion, Vestron Pictures
Susan Senk, vice president, publicity, Vestron Pictures
Sharon Streger, vice president, creative services, Vestron

THE CREATIVE

In The Beginning There Was The Script

Quigley: "Mitchell found the script. Linda Gottlieb was producer. Jon Peisinger was the one who said OK to the film way back then. It was a great script. "

Peckos: "I thought the script fell all over itself. It seemed heavily written, but I did like the story. I thought there were a lot of things in it that audiences wouldn't get. I thought maybe it was too Eastern in flavor because of the Catskills setting. Having just moved from Los Angeles and growing up in Boston, I knew what the differences were. It's a completely different mentality and I wondered if it would translate throughout the rest of the country. I thought the character development was there. It was cute. And those John Hughes movies were doing a lot of business and all they were were cute films. And our movie had dance, which is very promotable— if done well."

Cannold: "In considering any script, the most important thing I look for is whether it makes me laugh or cry. When I first read DIRTY DANCING it did both.

I remember the Sunday at home when I first got the script. The synopsis told me that it was about a young girl's first romance and her visit with her family. It was set in the Catskills in the summer of '63. The story interested me because I myself had spent summers at a hotel that was like that, in the Catskills, and I thought I'd have something in common with the story. So I read it.

I laughed a lot all the way through and cried at the end. It seemed to me that enough of the people went through similar experiences during a summer when they had their first romance.

Peisinger: "As with most successful projects the marketing is inherent in the programming decision. You start thinking of the marketing from the time you turn the first page of the script. And that was certainly the case with DIRTY DANCING."

Reuther: "The project came in March 1986. It was sweet, had great music and everybody liked it. Linda Gottlieb brought it in. Eleanor Bergstein was the co-producer. It was a picture that was developed at MGM and went into turnaround. There was a director attached. We didn't approve that director. It was the first Vestron title and we were very cautious. Talent agent Rob Schiedlinger of ICM [International Creative Management] put the deal together. No financing or other elements were attached. Integrated Resources [a limited partnership], with Vestron, put up some of the financing. The director, Emile Ardolini, came later."

Peisinger: "Flash back to April 1986. When we first saw the project I was still president of Vestron Pictures. This was among the first projects that began to work their way through Mitchell's [Mitchell Cannold, vice president of production] operation. I remember reading the script and thinking that it had elements from a marketing standpoint that would make the job easier."

Reuther: "Unlike the whole slate of art movies we were working on, this was a national release and a really high budget for us at that time. We were looking at two- to three-million-dollar movies, and this came in at $5.2 million. It was a healthy investment—it still is. Everybody liked it. Austin Furst, Vestron's chairman, liked it, although he wasn't sure why it cost so much."

Peckos: "I was given five scripts before I moved to Stamford [Connecticut] from Los Angeles: CHINA GIRL, DIRTY DANCING, CALL ME, BAKERSFIELD BLUES and something else. I was only here for three or four weeks when we had our first meeting. We met with Linda Gottlieb and Eleanor Bergstein [producers] at the Dorset

Hotel. And we had all these other films to release like REBEL, SPACE RAGE and BILLY GALVIN, which are tough films to start off with when you are launching a theatrical company. You really have to beg for everything."

MARKETING CONSIDERATIONS

Quigley: "Mitchell and I talked a lot about the marketing issues way back then. We started calling it 'Little Chill.' We knew it would appeal to the young, but that it could also appeal to us. 'Little Chill' was our statement about the market, as well as about the type of film it was."

Peckos: "The obvious hook was the music. The problem with the music was that I didn't know what the contemporary songs were going to be. I knew the old songs and they were all great. I just kept trying to think of how to get that to work. How do you get teenagers? It seemed like a film for teenagers, which was fine because that is a very big audience; but how do you get the film to cross over? That was what we would have to decide once we saw the final product—how contemporary you could really go without mixing the message of the film."

Target Audience

Ienner: "Everyone was saying that this was a kid's movie or a sixties thinker's movie. But I said that it's everybody's movie, because a kid today will fantasize about having the ability—as the ugly duckling grows into a woman—of getting a Patrick Swayze. And a certain age group will remember when and they will relive moments. I always saw this as a 'larger than' film in terms of the demographics.

"You can't market to the general public as a whole. It's not how much you aim at one group, it's who you don't exclude. That's my theory. I don't buy the 'target only' marketing concept, not when you have a film that could hit on many levels."

Streger: "It was always a movie meant to capture a teen audience and it was always a dance movie. What we discovered after the movie was released was that it did appeal to those questionable secondary audiences we had wondered about. But it definitely hit the note that was intended, which was the teenage female audience. And the title was in line with that because it's kind of a tittering title: 'Ohh, dirty dancing....' So it worked for us."

APPEALING ELEMENTS

A Good Title?

Cannold: "For me there was never any other title than DIRTY DANCING. Anybody who ever suggested another title should get out of the movie business."

Reuther: "Most people never really knew what *dirty dancing* actually meant. The older audience, maybe, did know what dance it was. We learned that this was a mother-and-daughter movie. The mother might have remembered what dirty dancing was, but the dance in the movie was nothing like the dance she remembered. Nobody knew exactly what we had."

Peckos: "I thought the title was the most brilliant part of the script. I said go from the very first after hearing the title. It's catchy. They had a lot of alternatives but they were all ruled out. 'The Time of My Life' came up later as a possibility."

Quigley: "I was the unwavering champion of the title DIRTY DANCING because it was memorable. You have to go back to who you are selling. The exhibitors would remember the title. It would really stand out in a crowd. Having read the script I knew the title could be taken either way; in fact, at one film opening it was. There were critics who said, 'DIRTY DANCING—what a misnomer. It's really sweet and romantic,' and 'Isn't it delightful.' Then there were others who said, 'It really sizzles; it's hot; it's sensual; it's sexual,' and that was perfect. That's exactly what we were trying to do—get two audiences, two sets of expectations.

"And part of the consideration was that it stands out. It implies to most exhibitors that it's really hot. The first image is one that is a lot more sexual than the film is, but people interpreted the title that way. You don't know it in a vacuum, though. We had debates that raged literally to the week that it opened. There were hundreds of alternative titles but I would never let anybody change it. That's the only thing you'll hear me take personal credit for, because I fought the battle of the title for way over a year and a half."

Streger: "In the beginning there was caution in approaching the sexiness of it because when you think of a young-girl audience, you think of an audience of people who are uncomfortable with sex, who go to bathrooms in pairs and threesomes. Who titter about that kind of stuff. There was a concern about the title DIRTY DANCING. Is that going to be something that's hard to handle? Is that something that parents may not let their kids go see, regardless of the rating, if they hear the film is called DIRTY DANCING? But it worked."

Quigley: "There was a lot of pressure to test the title and I wouldn't do it because I was afraid that it wouldn't test well. I don't think that kind of title testing—separate from looking at the film—is worthwhile because the film defines the title."

Streger: "We thought it was a good title because it was a bit more adult than titles we could have gone with, like 'Time of My Life,' which was suggested and was very saccharine."

Reuther: "Title was always a problem from the start. We wanted something provocative enough to create something that would be talked about, something that would carry, so that even if the film didn't deliver on its promise, the title allowed more people to be curious about it: 'DIRTY DANCING, oh my god, this might be a dirty movie, but it's PG-13.' So parents tell their kids it's OK to go see it because it is PG-13."

Quigley: "If you take a title like DIRTY DANCING and test it to teenage girls, they may come up with a preconceived notion that

that's about topless dancing. If you describe a film about dance—it's hot, it's sensuous—depending on how you write the description, they are going to say it's a good title for the film or it's not a good title for the film. We knew pretty much what the film had and it worked pretty much like we hoped it would.

"The image of the movie poster is dance/romance. Or the start of a romance. Viewers take it very personally. When you explain what dirty dancing is, everyone knows what it is. Everyone remembers when they were twelve, thirteen or fourteen. They call it different things. I remember I called it the bear hug and I remember a time and a place, and that is one of the things that we recognized right away was pretty wonderful about the concept of dirty dancing. It is fairly innocent. Everybody would filter that through their own memory. Someone else called it the dirty dog, someone else called it Philly dog. "

The Setting

Cannold: "I think the Catskills setting and the strong ethnic Jewish character of the hotel was to the advantage of the picture. There was enough in common with anyone's experience whether they went to a summer resort in the Pacific Northwest or Canada or Georgia or Texas. There were enough components of what summer is always about that enabled us to market it to a very broad audience. Nevertheless, the place had its own unique character."

Peisinger: "Nobody can tell you that it would turn out the way it did. A number of us looked at the script and said here's your basic conflict-of-culture story that takes place in an interesting setting, but one that might be fraught with limitations outside of the Northeast. Non-Jews, for that matter, might not relate to that Catskills culture of the sixties. Putting that aside, you had a basic clash-of-culture story. It had elements that I found extremely promising in attracting a broad audience, because the main characters were youthful. And yet, it took place twenty years ago, so folks that were young during that period are in their forties and beyond, plus or minus ten years."

Quigley: "We never emphasized 1963 at all. That was intentional. It would be interesting if you asked kids today when it took place. They would probably say now. But if you asked anybody in their thirties exactly when it took place, they would know by the music, by the time references to Kennedy and the Peace Corps and monks burning."

Reuther: "We were looking for a national release and the appeal of this was that it was a coming-of-age story, told in a new way, that had always worked—GREASE, SATURDAY NIGHT FEVER. The company had success with Michael Jackson's 'Thriller,' so that probably had a positive effect in deciding to do a music movie."

Peisinger: "Dancing is a major element in the film. From my perspective—being involved in SATURDAY NIGHT FEVER and GREASE, having observed very closely what happened with FLASHDANCE—if we could construct a credible film with dance as the centerpiece, we had an ingredient that had consistently worked over the last fifteen years."

Music

Ienner: "Only about a tenth of movies over the past ten years really deserve to have an album released. Many movies have been smothered by trying to follow the pro forma of a SATURDAY NIGHT FEVER or FLASHDANCE."

Reuther: "The music soundtrack was always there. It was a lot harder to do than we thought. Should it all be older music or should we put in a couple of new songs? Should it all be new? The script originally called for oldies only."

Peisinger: "The way Eleanor wrote the script she actually had song titles at various points and you could see the direction she was going. We saw a soundtrack opportunity to attract the older audience that remembers the songs from that period and also the opportunity to create some new material which would emulate the sixties while still being the 'new songs' that today's young audience would like. So right from the inception this project was created with the idea of a broad audience—not the 'let's go after the fourteen- to nineteen-year-olds' knee-jerk reaction.

"Considering the project initially as a dance film, there was one factor that was so crystal clear: Films that were heavily weighted with music and dance were eminently <u>more repeatable</u> than story-driven films. As good as the story may or may not have been, the fact that we had such strong music and dance gave us the potential. The fact that it was pulled off so well allowed us to fulfill that potential. You are not bored! You listen to a record hundreds of times. There are new things to see. Whereas a film that is purely story driven, as exquisitely as that film is constructed, in most cases, you get it all the first time."

Ienner: "You look at a RUTHLESS PEOPLE and they have every hitter in the world on that album from Jagger to Springsteen to Darryl Hall. They tried to make it a music movie and it didn't do it at all. And then came BACK TO THE FUTURE, which had the hottest artist at that time—Huey Lewis and the News. The whole album ended up selling somewhere around 600,000 units. The LA BAMBA soundtrack did about 2 million units, and that was supposed to be a small movie!

"One of the rules I've learned over the years is that there are no rules. And I think that's really important. In most cases, the film people use the music as a loss leader to build awareness. They think maybe there will be some sort of residual effect from it. But there really is a very big valley between the film and the music worlds. The film people have been more aggressive in trying to close that gap in trying to hire music people. But there really is a very big division there."

Peisinger: "I would say there wasn't one key element. There were a number of factors that, when you threw them all in the hopper, gave it the potential to work. With any project you still have the problem of making this potential work on the screen. You've got to get to the point of creating the film from all these great ideas, concepts and elements."

Crystal-Balling It

Quigley: "In marketing meetings, we talked about what it would look like eighteen months later when we released the film. We made an assumption that the climate would be politically conservative and that the nostalgia of the sixties was interesting."

Putting Together The Team

Cannold: "It took a lot of guts for a company at that point in time to make DIRTY DANCING. It was a very big gamble. And ultimately the decision was awesome. The company had made a decision to make movies for up to three million dollars. This was the first real picture we green-lighted (at five and a half million bucks). It was a very big risk. When the risk pays off, the only way you can go about marketing the picture is to take the same level of risk or you've wasted your time. It just follows and if you play the safe road, you underestimate the audience.

"Vestron Pictures opened its doors in January of 1986 and we started shooting in August of 1986. The marketing staff was barely on board when the picture was shooting."

Quigley: "M. J. Peckos was hired in July of 1986. We started adding sales people like Pat Caufield, Linda Ditrinko, and we had a core group of people who were almost full time on this for an incredible length of time. We [M. J. Peckos, Susan Senk, Sharon Streger, Dori Wasserman, Mitchell Cannold] had a marketing meeting with the producers and director [Linda Gottlieb, Eleanor Bergstein, and

Emile Ardolini]. We went through a marketing agenda before they started the film: What was this film? Who are you directing it towards? What do you think the ad looks like? Do you think it appeals to this audience? We made them go through this thing that we had done internally where we had said that this is our point of view: 'We think that the marketing plan is this, and here we don't agree with you. What kind of film are you going to make? We think this is how we are going to release it.' We literally went through the whole thing. We were very close from day one."

Casting

Peisinger: "Once we green-lighted the film we started moving through the creative process, casting and marketing decisions. We didn't have a big budget so we weren't anticipating getting big stars. Ideally we were looking for someone with some recognition so we wouldn't be going out trying to build visibility for the movie and also visibility for the stars."

Reuther: "The original audience we were going after was girls—the younger female audience. The movie had to capture the heart. The lead had to have that first romance, first love. With Jennifer Grey cast, she wasn't as beautiful as everybody thought she could be, but Jennifer Grey can be the ordinary girl. That was important because the audience said, 'That could be me; it could have happened to me; it could have been my love story.' She got the impossible guy, which is what every young girl wants to do. That's who Baby was and that's why we cast Jennifer Grey.

Peisinger: "If Susan Senk couldn't solicit the cover of *Time* magazine with Patrick Swayze a year ago, she could get the teen magazines. One of the key casting decisions was, particularly with the role of Baby, was whether to go with a *strong actress* who could dance or with a *strong dancer* who could act. We took the former course, which in hindsight was the absolute right decision. It became Baby's movie. With Jennifer Grey we got an actress who made you believe, and the fact that she was not a professional dancer probably enhances the movie."

Reuther: "There was some opposition to Jennifer Grey because she wasn't 'Hollywood' beautiful and her nose was too big. But she was supposed to be a Jewish girl during a certain period in the Catskills. We did not want to take the more commercial route in terms of casting. We wanted the identification with the lead role."

Peisinger: "Patrick Swayze, on the other hand, was just a pure find—somebody who was a smooth professional dancer, had those looks, was thirty-five and could play twenty. The other marketing decision we made was to sprinkle some other recognizable names around the two fairly unknown stars".

"Cynthia Rhodes from STAYING ALIVE and FLASHDANCE had dance-movie credibility. This gave you something to talk about. Then there was Jerry Orhbach, Jack Weston and Honi Coles, who is a legendary tap dancer. There is a niche in the marketplace where he is promoted. So those all added to the mix. Nobody was there that was going to put it on the cover of *Newsweek*, but I think they were helpful in giving it a little legitimacy."

Cannold: "When Jennifer Grey first walked into the casting session, the producers, the director, the writer and I fell in love. From that moment on there was no one else who had a shot at the role. She was absolutely perfect. We had difficulty convincing senior management at Vestron because they believed that the role required a more beautiful actress. We prevailed, and convinced them that her unique look was essential and that this really was the story of a girl's coming-of-age and blossoming. You couldn't start with a beautiful girl and end up with a beautiful girl. You had to start out with somebody who looked ordinary, whom the audience would identify with, and ultimately that was very important for the marketing. The target audience would be offended by a girl who was too pretty. But they would feel comfortable with Jennifer and would buy into her story and share her experience."

Cannold: "Swayze was ultimately cast because he was a great actor and a fabulous dancer. No one came close. There were a couple of other actors who were interesting, but next to Patrick they just weren't equipped to handle the dance."

Preproduction Marketing

Peckos: "We design the campaign as early as possible. If we have a movie in preproduction or production, I meet with the filmmakers. I find out from producer, director and writers what they think the audience of the film is, so we know beforehand who they are making the film for.

"I outlined the marketing plans for them—how it would be released and how the monies would be spent. Rarely do we sit down before committing to a picture. The deals can easily fall apart.

"Once the picture is shooting, we decide whether we want a unit publicist on the film. If there is any known talent in the film, the press might be interested in going down to the set. We try to get a photo sequence done by the unit photographer.

"In postproduction we pretty much stay out of things until the filmmakers show us something they are happy with. I never rush them. I would rather not see a film until they are ready to show it to us. From that point we start to refine what the campaign will be. A couple of times we've done photo shoots on the set that haven't worked out. It's hard to see works in progress until you see all the unit photography at the end of the shoot. Sometimes there are just some brilliant things in there."

PRODUCTION PUBLICITY

Considerations

Senk: "Each movie takes on its own personality. Each one—even from the point of preproduction—takes on a different personality. You have to decide up front if your set is going to be open or closed. If you have a closed set and it's a nonunion set, you don't want the press all over the place, because then everybody gets upset. Is the talent willing to do interviews while they are on location? Some won't, some will. Can you cajole them? Can you use them later? It's important to establish relationships with the talent right from the beginning. I've been on location when it's three o'clock in the morning or when it's really cold. This helps when you have to call them later to ask them to do an interview. I think it's part of an actor's job to promote the product that they work on, but it doesn't always work out that way."

Publicity On The Set

Senk: "We decided not to do any publicity during production. We were working with a closed set and we had no huge, identifiable stars. Patrick and Jennifer really were nobody. They were both unknown people while we were making the movie.

"We pitched it a little bit and there was the possibility for a while that 'Entertainment Tonight' was going to go down, but it didn't pan out.

"Some producers like to get <u>production publicity</u> while the movie is filming. I personally feel it <u>really doesn't serve you that much because the moviegoing public doesn't remember.</u>

"The one thing you can do on certain locations, which we didn't do on DIRTY DANCING and we did do on THE DEAD, is a lot of interviews while the movie is being made. With John Houston and big stars you can get magazine writers to write profiles and to write about the filming. It will show up in *Premiere* or *American Film*. You time it. They will hold off if you ask them until it's time for the release. Robert Redford did a lot of publicity during the filming of MILAGRO BEANFIELD WAR and you are seeing it now in *Vogue*,

Glamour, Esquire, Premiere and *American Film*. They opened the set, which we didn't do for DIRTY DANCING because we really didn't have a hook.

"We decided that we weren't going to have a unit publicist who ushers the press on and off the set and whom the press calls if they see an announcement in *Variety* that something is being filmed. We had some local press coming in and out. The U.P. is the liaison who writes the production notes and does the interviews for the press kit on location."

Script & Editing Changes

Cannold: "As written, the movie actually started with the family taking a vote about whether they would go to the Catskills. What was written were closeups of the different family members writing on a piece of paper whether they'd go or not and everybody writes *yes* except for Baby. She writes *nyet* —her pencil breaks, and then we cut right to the car driving into the Catskills. It was an absolutely lackluster opening. It just didn't provide any energy."

Reuther: "The beginning was always slow. The early screenings told us how slow it was. It was very hard to get people into the movie, so we designed the title sequence to set it up and say what the movie was going to be."

Cannold: "We showed the movie to Richard Greenberg (R/Greenberg, NYC) and he came up with the spectacular title sequence opening that is now in the movie, which, I believe, next to the

Sunday *Times* article, had more to do with the success of the picture than anything."

Quigley: "Richard Greenberg did the DIRTY DANCING title sequence. He is the guy who did the wonderful babies title sequence in THE WORLD ACCORDING TO GARP."

Reuther: "It was originally an R. There were nude scenes with Jennifer that were cut. Nude scenes embarrass teenagers on dates. We made the cuts to satisfy Jennifer, our target audience and to get a PG rating."

Cannold: "There was only one partially nude scene shot, where Jennifer was nude from the waist up. We shot it with the understanding that we would show it to her when it was cut and give her the right to take it out. As it turns out, we agreed to take it out for her but had we also wanted a PG-13.

"When the film was first shown to the MPAA [Motion Picture Association of America], they indicated that it was a very tough call on whether the film would get an R or a PG rating. They encouraged us to make some judicious edits in order to make sure that it would be a PG-13. Richard Hefner and his entire ratings review board thought it was a fabulous film and so they were very supportive and helpful in guiding us to do what we needed to ensure the PG-13.

"Each picture is different. If a picture is overexploitive all the way through, they're not likely to say how many scenes you have to take out in order to change the rating. But if it's just a couple of things that make the difference, they're likely to be more specific. It's really a judgment call. They try to be as specific as they can. In this particular case, they tried to be very helpful to us. Dick and I made some relatively minor changes and we got the PG-13 rating. The picture would have never been the success that it was if it had received an R and in a sense it was destined for an R because of the connotation of "dirty dancing" and a virgin having her first sexual experience. The limited nudity and a lot of provocative dancing could have just as easily made it an R picture."

The Ending: A Critical Ten Minutes

Caufield: "What happens in a screening is that the audience is enjoying it, they are talking back to the screen, they are verbalizing and having a great time, they are in there with the characters, and they are hooked. But if that last scene doesn't pay off, when they get to the questionnaires it's the last ten minutes that they will remember the most."

Reuther: "An earlier cut by the filmmakers had Johnny in the parking lot talking with Baby. There was the big dance number, we did the lift, she talked with Daddy, and they left the room, went into the parking lot, and talked about the summer. The finale scene as a conversation just didn't work. So we cut the parking lot scene. The filmmakers didn't really object to our cut.

"We very strongly thought that we had a musical, and we had to take it higher and higher and go out on this high energy like a musical. At that point it's fantasy. We all wanted people to come out of the theater singing and dancing."

Quigley: "The ending is upbeat, a little like FAME. You dance out into the street and it's exciting."

Market Research Screenings

Quigley: "There is a term which we use called *playability*, which is how the film plays. You can't really assess how the film is going to perform in the marketplace, but you get an idea of how people respond to it, who the audience is and how they like it: 'Would tell a friend.' 'Couldn't wait to see it.' That sort of thing. There is a lot of normative data where you can correlate the results of your film against a lot of other films and that's what we were looking at.

"The raw scores get translated against all the other films that have been tested by the same company. We used the company that tests all the major films intentionally. This was really the first formal market research we did. Joe Farrell at National Research out of L.A. did the research. I thought long and hard about using them to do the test, because that would also give the majors information about our film, which was what I did not want. I wanted to find out about all the other major films in the marketplace, but you kind of also have to 'I'll show you mine if you show me yours.' That's the deal. Our data cannot be used by other companies, but the research company does separate tracking studies of all the films in the marketplace—and clearly they have an inside track on yours. They suddenly know a whole lot more about your film than anybody else.

"We do it every time there is a national release. We are pretty careful. I'm really wary of research, because historically a lot of studios have blown a lot of money. There is a lot of stuff that is really qualitative.

"Some of the production people came to me once and said that we had to edit a scene out of the movie because of the research. I basically told them they were full of it, because we weren't testing for that. Don't misapply. A lot of people get in trouble in research because you can twist it into whatever shape you want. The scene they were talking about was a scene that appeared as the least-liked scene, and I told them that was with an audience that was a specific demographic—a young audience in Paramus, New Jersey, called it the least-liked scene. (It was the scene where Baby's sister was singing her hula song at the very end of the movie.) I had to remind them that the night before they saw the scene with an older audience and they went wild for it. You don't want to make a creative decision based on what you think the research does when you are not specifically testing for that scene. If you set up a test that is legitimate, then you can use the research. My point of view is that all research is a wind indicator. You really have to use your own experience, your own professional judgement and those of other pros.

"The studios have spent hundreds of millions of dollars in research over seventy years. If it was that effective they could predict hits—and they don't. If you pull out national research, they predicted that DIRTY DANCING had the possibility of doing 10 million at the box office. They predicted HARRY AND THE HENDERSONS would be the major film of the summer. BEVERLY HILLS COP was pretty obvious. They're way off, too. The best indicator is when you show your film to an audience and watch how they react, not just how they responded to questions afterward. It's a visceral response in the theater in the dark."

Reuther: "We tested the title. We did focus groups with the artwork and the title—the couple shot. The results of the tests weren't clear. Bill's obstinacy kept us on track when the testing wasn't so great. Reviews and preliminary screenings set the stage.

"The film was tested with theater audience cards. The response cards were not that wonderful, but with the new title sequence they liked it more. Testing took place for a couple of months. Then the satisfaction levels raised a little bit."

Caufield: "I also do all the market research tests. When we do a national release and have the budget to research all the materials, we test the one-sheet and the TV and radio spots and ads. All the research and screenings will cost close to $70,000 because you are usually testing three TV spots and three different print ads. One of them is usually your one-sheet. We always test the TV spots in black-and-white, because once you go to color to finish them you've spent a lot of money with the lab.

"Audiences screen it on each coast. Once you've done that you pretty much know whether you have a movie and a campaign that are going to work.

"We can also start early and test different titles for the movies. It's easier to do when you have a trailer to work with, because then people <u>are actually seeing something</u>. When you do market research with a written synopsis and different titles, it's a totally different flavor because <u>the response could be based on how the copy is written</u>. People will use their own imagination or pick up on one word that triggers their own imagination. It's very hard. You try and take the numbers with a grain of salt and read between the lines."

Streger: "We tested three ad images. None of them tested very well. We also tested three TV spots. We pulled the test together rather quickly so the TV spots weren't really a fair test. One was finished, one was not; two were in color, one was not. So the test was a little out of kilter to start with.

"One copy line we worked on was geared to young girls: All the right moves and the wrong reputation. It was her summer vacation, it was his summer job. We tried to set up the romance approach."

Peckos: "We did marketing research screenings before they mixed the sound for the film. We got 350 people (ages fifteen to fifty-five, with more of a mix in the younger ages; male and female split fifty-fifty). We wanted to see if it worked for the older audience. We knew it worked for us, but we wanted to make sure that we weren't crazy! We recruited from Paramus, New Jersey, theaters and shopping malls. Most important is that they get people in there who go to movies. We screen the picture and the questionnaire is handed out. It asks them to rate the music. You can ask anything you want. The only two boxes that matter are 'How would you rate the movie?' and 'Would you recommend it?'"

Market Research Results

National Research Group in Los Angeles was the company that designed and conducted the marketing research for DIRTY DANCING.

In the questionnaire they asked selected audiences which scenes they liked the most. The favorite scenes (in order of best-liked) were:

> dancing (unspecified)
> ending (unspecified)
> dance at end

dance practice/rehearsal
dance lessons
sex (unspecified)
love (unspecified)
Father and Baby
Baby and Johnny
Baby and Johnny dance

The movie's strong points were very clear from these responses. These best-liked scenes indicate how the movie could be marketed and promoted to reach the broadest target audience.

The least-liked scenes (in order of least-liked) were:
Baby's sister singing
sex (unspecified)
dancing (unspecified)
sex too graphic

Other than the nude sex scenes, which were cut out, these scenes stayed in the movie but were not featured in the trailer or marketing materials.

The overall total ratings for the movie were:
excellent (43%)
very good (32%)
good (16%)
fair (7%)
poor (2%)

This was an unusually strong performance when compared to other movies.

The extremely critical word-of-mouth ratings and the answer to the question "Would you recommend this movie?" were:
>definitely (60%)
>probably (26%)
>probably not (12%)
>definitely not (1%)

This was a movie people *wanted* to talk about.

The performance ratings selected the following (in order of best elements):
>Johnny
>the dancing
>Baby
>the music
>the ending
>the setting
>the story
>the pace
>Penny

It was clear that Johnny, dancing and Baby were the favorite elements of the movie for most people. The poster and promotion emphasized them.

Some of the audience adjective selections were (in order of most frequently commented):

good dancing
entertaining
good music
leaves you feeling good

There were very few responses to the adjectives *too unrealistic, hard to relate to, offensive, too distressing,* and *too old-fashioned.*

DISTRIBUTION STRATEGY

Competition

Cannold: "We weren't looking for dance movies, but all of a sudden one came in. And it happened to incorporate all three elements (comedy, romance and dance) in a nice balance. As it turned out, we emphasized dance over comedy or a romantic drama because in terms of marketing the picture, there were lots of other comedies out that summer ... but there weren't any other dance pictures. There was one that was on the boards, a picture called BAND-STAND, later titled THE IN-CROWD at Orion. They began production at the same time and were in post production at the same time and looked like they were going to be released at the same time.

"The IN-CROWD didn't turn out very well and Orion buried it. During the time it was shot and in post, it was, from our point of view, direct competition. We thought if the movie turned out well, we'd be killed, because it was coming from Orion and we were 'upstart Vestron.'

"They were ultimately in a position to beat us because it was scheduled for August. Vestron had scheduled DIRTY DANCING for mid-July, and then three weeks prior to release Vestron made the decision to postpone the release of the picture because it would have been up against several major releases and a number of major studio sequels and it would have gotten killed.

"We did everything we could to move DIRTY DANCING just as quickly as we could. Linda Gottlieb was responsible for that. The picture was finished in record time and on schedule and it enabled us to beat the other film. Had the other film turned out any good, it would have been an issue.

"There was no other dance movie that year except for the IN-CROWD. It was a pretty good script about kids who try to break into Dick Clark's 'American Bandstand' show while it's taping in Philadelphia. So it had a similar kind of feel, it took place at the exact same time, it was about kids making it for the first time, getting on national television. It had some of the same kind of spirit to it. From a marketing point of view, we knew we had real competition for the entire year we were making the movie."

Quigley: "My background is as a theatrical exhibitor. I spent many years looking at what the studios did. I knew pretty much how they were set up. Their major 'A' pictures would come out in June, their 'B' or 'C' pictures come out in July or August. I knew we could either go in May or in August with a picture that looks like a studio picture to compete with them.

"There were other movies in the way. We were very concerned about LA BAMBA until we saw it. We thought there might be a problem for a limited-audience film. It, too, takes a nostalgic look, has music elements, is fairly romantic and idealized. We were afraid of Columbia Pictures going out there with a thousand-plus prints and spending $10 million in advertising. Coca-Cola had a tie-in where they added another 10 million to it. The double album from Los Lobos was coming out. So there was a lot of competition. You have to remember that this was in February of 1986. When we started really knowing what the competition was, it was February or March of 1987. We released it on August twenty-first of 1987."

Selling The Exhibitor

Quigley: "Originally DIRTY DANCING was to be released in May 1987. We were building a distribution system and the exhibitors' greatest fear was that this video company—whom they thought of as the big bad guy taking away all the business from theaters by selling videocassettes—was now making films. There was a lot of suspicion. They said, 'You're going to go out and screw us over and make all your money in video.' They had concerns about the windows of release: Maybe we'd open it in theaters then go to video right away, or, in other words, we would open day and date [at the same time], or we would play a lot of low-end 'C' and 'D' movies.

"It was very calculated that we went out with MALCOLM first. It was very much part of our plan. We had to get credibility. We had to establish ourselves first as an art distributor—as a specialized distributor. We did that very well. Films like MALCOLM, ALPINE

FIRE, PERSONAL SERVICES, GOTHIC and GOOD MORNING, BABYLON literally set up DIRTY DANCING. You didn't see a lot of stuff in the press about Vestron Pictures until February of '87 and that was intentional, because as a company you have to sell three markets. First, you have to sell the exhibitors that you are a real distribution company. Second, you have to sell the trade and the press. Third, you have to sell the general audience.

"As a distributor you are totally unproven until you have a hit in the marketplace."

Peckos: "There are certain films that play better at certain times. The summer is very important for films that kids are going to see because they are on vacation and you can get matinees. You can get big numbers. You wait to drop things in if you have to. We were lucky. We got delivery of the film prints in April so we had plenty of time for August. It was really optimum."

Quigley: "Exhibitors have to fill their screens fifty-two weeks a year. They know the major studios are there in force with product in June, July, August, at Christmas, Easter, Presidents' [Day] weekend in February and late September. During the other periods they look for independent product to fill their screens. They've got to be there every single day. It's one of the few businesses that operates 365 days a year.

"An art film you can play any time of the year, but a commercial release you have to put out when you have an opportunity. You have to be flexible. We knew all those things. We knew the easiest way to get credibility—and also the low-cost way—was with art films. We had to take films out. We had to show we could distribute and handle them.

"At SHOWEST, the exhibitors convention, we said, 'We've got fifteen films and this is what we are going to release, this is what we have. You can see parts of it,' because we had a product reel, 'and this is who we think we are.' We talked about DIRTY DANCING in February and showed clips of the dance sequence. We talked about it as a national release during the summer. But to get there ... we had a lot of educating and a lot of talking to do. Our point of view was basically: Judge us by what we do; watch what we do in the marketplace. We weren't going to be like other companies and say we had $100 million in production, and we had Dustin Hoffman in this one, and on and on, unless we did. We basically didn't make any promises we couldn't keep. We released twelve pictures. We would have released fifteen, but we were delayed on a couple of films, like AND GOD CREATED WOMAN."

Peckos: "We've had a lot of films which I haven't felt good about. It was difficult to get exhibitors to play them and to get critics to write good reviews about them. It was difficult to get people to interview the directors or the stars. It was difficult to get anyone to pay six dollars to go see them. That's the bottom line. You can't make it happen if it isn't there. It's got to be on the screen. DIRTY DANCING delivered. It had a schmaltzy ending that comes from left field. You feel guilty when you start to like it. You do. It sucks you in. It delivers."

Quigley: "It was literally layer upon layer. Get the confidence of the exhibitor, let them know what you were doing, stick to that ... and we delivered. The critics said, 'What's this schlock company?' and it was difficult at first. It was literally a case of less is more—just acting in a certain manner and not talking a lot about it. The process takes a lot of time. It was really a very carefully thought out strategy.

"When I was hired, Mitchell and I were supposed to make six $1 million genre films. The strategy has changed significantly since then. There's a lot of educating both ways. I didn't understand the video business and most of the video people didn't understand theatrical distribution. I had a real clear idea of what we should do because my background was exhibition. As an exhibitor I saw the distributors all the time. I was really a critic of distributors. I saw who the good ones were, who the bad ones were; and what I was really trying to do was come up with a common-sense position. It seemed to me that there was a clear opportunity, especially for a well-financed company, to capture a significant part of the middle road of the market—between the specialized distribution and the major studios.

"We wanted to look like New World or Cannon in terms of the number of releases, but we didn't want to look like them in terms of product. We want to be way north of them. If you look at our lineup, part of it looks as good as any of the studio classics divisions if not better. We have three of the top-ten-grossing specialized films last year, which is really significant for a start-up company. We have the largest independently released film in history—DIRTY DANC-ING—so we basically did what we said we were going to do. We have some small and some big, and a lot just right in the middle. We'll tailor our distribution to what we think the performance of the film will be theatrically.

"We want to distribute efficiently with fewer branches. There are a lot of differences between us and New World. We only have two offices and one guy in Dallas. New World at one time had fourteen branch offices. They're all over the place. We're in Stamford, L.A. and Dallas. Even the smallest distributors have five. It's a very different operation. The local branches sell the films to a specific theater. We've divided the country East, West and South. And that's it. We've centralized the media, co-op, marketing and creative services departments here in Stamford, Connecticut. We do buy media locally, but it's supervised from Stamford. We've set up a movie marketing network where we have eight local agencies. That's partially based on the theory that for what we're doing, given that we don't have long lead times, we have to be flexible. I've always felt that local agencies are better at buying the local markets than a national agency. Having been an media buyer I'm pretty sure I can prove that local agencies are better at buying spots."

Peckos: "It's a roll of the dice, this theatrical business. That's what amazes me about home video—you can actually guess the number and it turns out that way more often than not. I'm amazed. Theatrical is a crap shoot. Totally. PLATOON could have been a one-week movie. It's timing. I always felt that with most films you start to feel a roll and things coming together. Publicity starts to kick in and the advance word on the screenings startles you because it is so good. You start showing it to a lot of people. You start getting positive feedback. That's what happened on this picture."

PUBLICITY

Electronic Press Kit

Senk: "We decided that we were going to shoot an electronic press kit because of the music and the dancing and the choreography. We hired an outside company to do it. They research it and you give them ideas about what you want them to talk about. For example, we had asked everybody, even though we never used it, What do you think dirty dancing is? because we weren't sure where we were going with everything.

"For the first time, Patrick Swayze was coming out dancing and nobody knew that he could dance. Because it was set in the early sixties we felt it would lend itself to television coverage later. We got behind-the-scenes footage of the big finale scene—the cameras moving around, the director directing, Patrick and Jennifer kidding around.

"We had twenty-minute conversations with all the principals. We interviewed Patrick and Jennifer and Cynthia Rhodes and Emile the director. We interviewed Kenny Ortega and he did some setups for us of the dirty dancers practicing. When you looked at it, the initial hook was going to be the music and the dancing. We interviewed Honi Coles, which we never used on the electronic press kit. He's the old black tap dancer who plays the band leader. We didn't interview Jack Weston because he didn't want to be. We interviewed Jerry Orhbach. The actors talked about the music and their careers.

"The interviewer is off-camera. On the video tape you give them five minutes of open-ended questions. The question appears as a title on a black screen and the actor answers and then it goes black again and the next question comes on. It's all time-coded and the television station can do whatever they want. Then there are B-roll clips of behind-the-scenes stuff, shots of people making the movie. The questions are set up so that ultimately you can format it so some small cable stations can pretend they were there.

"We did a news wrap which we filmed later about the whole resurgence of sixties music. We interviewed Bill Medley. We went to his club in Orange County called The Hop, where people dance to sixties music. We ran around L.A. taking pictures at fifties and sixties places like Ed Debevic's. It's a little news wrap, a back-handed promotion for the movie. If you have some small station in Des Moines, Iowa, that needs some filler, you give it to them and see what happens. You throw it to the wind. The news-wrap piece was a minute and a half.

"The stations can do anything they want with the electronic press kit. Sometimes you put the movie trailer on it. You could put a music video on it, but we didn't have one then. You prepare for all of this during production.

"Sometimes it's easy to do, sometimes it's not. Some talent will allow you to do it, sometimes they won't. I've had situations where particular talent refused to be shot for an electronic press kit.

"We also brought down a still photographer at the time but found that there wasn't time in the shooting schedule to do the specials for either publicity or creative [packaging and poster]. Later you've got to get approvals. Certain actors' contracts have approvals. You either do that on location, which some people like to do, or you do it after. In this case, Patrick was the only one who had approvals and he approved his photographs later.

"We ended up bringing everybody back later into a studio to do specials which got used in some magazines."

Cost of Electronic Press Kit

Senk: "There are a lot of companies out there that can shoot an electronic press kit for anywhere from fifteen- to fifty-thousand dollars. That includes the shooting but not the tape duplication and distribution expenses. First Media was the company who did our electronic press kit [EPK]. On DIRTY DANCING we sent out about 150 electronic press kits to the major markets and stations that we knew would air it. You get research reports that tell you how many were used. On DIRTY DANCING about 40 percent were used initially, and then more later because people keep it in their files and use it again.

"The DIRTY DANCING electronic press kit included a six-minute piece, 'The Making of Dirty Dancing.' This is the length that is used in the United States. In Europe you can actually get a half-hour program on some of the television stations, like in Italy where they have a lot of TV. The six-minute piece on DIRTY DANCING was aired on HBO for two months. We don't make any money from it, but it's free promotion. It was also used all over the country."

Film Festivals

Caufield: "DIRTY DANCING is not really a film festival movie. It's commercial. It didn't play in any film festivals.

"At film festivals you leave yourself open for reviews. There is no way you can keep a critic out. And then you lose the chance of any more newspaper coverage because they won't review it again when the film finally opens. You are also taking a risk. You could walk away with a bad review.

"Sometimes you just say no because it doesn't play right. You support it in other ways—wild postering, etc. Some movies are advertising driven, much more than publicity driven. Films that don't have major talent involved are less publicity driven.

"There are lots of conversations about whether or not you should screen for the critics. Will they lambaste it? And then if you don't screen it, the critics get mad at you. And it's like this double-edged sword. You never really know what to do. Sometimes you have a movie that plays well with an audience but might not be a critic's movie. With DIRTY DANCING the critics did say that sometimes the script gets a little bit schmaltzy, but at the end of the day they had a good time. The music's fine, the dancing's fine and everybody has fun."

Quigley: "I literally had to convince Clein + Feldman [publicists] to take this because they typically did only small art films. There is no question that they wanted to do GOTHIC, GOOD MORNING, BABYLON and THE DEAD. They had been characterized as this small art film publicity agency. I knew that they would be really good on DIRTY DANCING as well."

Senk: "I put Clein + Feldman, an outside public relations firm, on to augment Vestron's staff. We were dealing with unknown actors. It's funny to say that now, because both of them became so popular because of this movie. With a lot of other people's help we made them stars. Patrick Swayze became a household name. They knew him from NORTH AND SOUTH and they knew Jennifer was Joel Grey's daughter. We were preparing for the July release date and we showed it to the long-lead magazines (*Vogue, Glamour, Esquire, Playboy*) who really need to see it three months before release. The response was really pretty good. You see, we really didn't know what we had. You get too close to a project. You don't really know how it's going to do. You know it's commercial, but you really don't know how the critics are going to react to it.

"We decided, because of the music, that we were only going to screen it in larger-size screening rooms. In New York we used MGM, which seats about a hundred. We'd fill it with all kinds of people. We'd never just screen it for critics; we would fill it with young girls, with friends, high school kids. As we started to screen it, we got an idea that there was maybe something here. What was happening was that by screening the movie we could then sell Jennifer and Patrick much more easily to the press because they saw the movie, liked them and wanted to write about them. We got positive reviews in all the long-lead magazines. We didn't really get very many negative reviews. People criticized certain things about the movie, but overall people were walking out having a very good time, singing the songs, thinking about it. We had repeaters, people who would come to the screenings because they wanted to see it over and over again. This was unusual. Regular people would call and ask if they could see it again. We were starting to create a real word-of-mouth on it."

Press Kit

Senk: "Jennifer was available in the late spring and early summer. She did a lot of photo spreads and interviews for magazines. Patrick was in STEEL DAWN, so he was unavailable. We were screening it; we were picking out the photos we were going to use, both color and black-and-white. We started working on the press kit. It was very important to me that the press kit contain some information about what the sixties meant to set the stage for the movie. There were some positioning paragraphs linked into the press kit because a lot of journalists are under thirty-five. This way they could get a sense of the culture and what was going on. It was the summer before John Kennedy was shot. It was just when the peace marches and the desegregation marches were starting. It was all that stuff which some people don't know. They don't know their history. When we were screening it, some of the older people got the jokes that were funny and that young people just wouldn't have any idea. The kids know about the music but they'd don't know about the era.

"We screened it for RCA [the record distributor] across the United States because they wanted it screened for their regional people and their big record buyers. We set up forty screenings. We screened it for the music press, for teen magazines and women's magazines from June through August. We just kept screening it. The word of mouth started to really help. The positive response from the critics helped us to set up interviews for all the talent. So Jennifer, Patrick, Emile and Cynthia were really the ones that they were really talking to. The press generated more press. At a certain point it just started to steamroll and there was no stopping it. But in the beginning I was really worried. I wondered what we were going to do with this movie. And then all of a sudden it just kicked in and came together.

"The first assignment for Clein + Feldman was to write the press kit. The first thing to do is the long-lead magazines because they will tell you what they think. They are very honest. If they don't like it they will let you know. You also screen it for the editors, the assignment editors, the feature writers, and freelance feature writers. If they like the movie they may want to talk to the actors and do interviews. In the summer we were putting all of the materials together and screening the movie like crazy in New York and Los Angeles. We had at least a hundred screenings. At the same time Linda Miller was putting together theme park promotions across the country, like Seven Flags for the beginning of August. There were visors and buttons and stuff for kids to take home with them."

Press Junket

Senk: "In early August we decided that we were not going to have a press junket because we felt we could get more mileage at less expense by having the stars travel to certain key cities where you get more special attention. We started screening for critics in all the major markets. There were radio promotion screenings which were the real test because you could tell that the real people—not the critics, not the writers—liked the movie. We got free radio time. There were dance contests and special club promotions in all the cities so that by the time the talent arrived there was an awareness about them and the movie."

Star Tours

Senk: "Patrick came back from the movie and started doing a lot of press, more short-breaking things—Associated Press, L.A. and New York City press, magazines. He was still a hard sell. He had his own publicist working as well. There was a whole team working this. It was Annette Wolf at PMK in Los Angeles. We would all have brainstorming meetings: me, Annette, Clein + Feldman, and Patrick's managers.... So for Patrick we really had a concerted effort. We sent Patrick to Dallas and Houston, because he's from Texas. And he just wowed them; they loved him to death. He did a lot of radio. He did local television. They let him play his song. This was two weeks before the movie opened. We brought him to Atlanta, and then New York.

"At the same time Cynthia went to Nashville, Memphis—she's from the south so that's where we sent her—Chicago, Washington,

D.C., and then to New York. That was a week before things started to jell. Cynthia also promoted the film later, after the fact, because we didn't release simultaneous in Canada. Cynthia was our emissary to Toronto, Vancouver and Montreal. You can send secondary talent to those areas, and she's a wonderful person and a wonderful interview.

"We were also pitching Emile as a director, which is a little harder because people want to talk to the actors and actresses. And Kenny Ortega did a couple of things. He did *Elle* magazine and there started to be some interest as well in this wild-guy choreographer who everybody adores.

"Eleanor Bergstein started to get a lot of press coverage when we started to screen the film as well. She did a lot of press. She was in the *New York Times* because people were interested in why she wrote it. It was her story, so she got a lot of publicity as well."

Publicity Efforts

Quigley: "We used the publicity, the music, the record, and radio promotions all together. We hired Spring-Green, which was a promotion agency for Jean West tie-ins among others. We did mall tie-ins, we had DIRTY DANCING parties in theme parks in Six Flags and gave away T-shirts. Linda Miller was doing promotion. The effort we mounted on this film was amazing. The PR effort was carefully orchestrated through Clein + Feldman.

"Spring-Green did the tie-ins. We had license deals. We had posters. We did music videos."

The Press Break

Cannold: "The very key piece in the success of the picture was the success of the marketing and publicity department at getting enormous coverage in the Sunday *New York Times*. The publicity department's Susan Senk and the publicists (Clein + Feldman) were responsible for interesting the *New York Times* Arts and Leisure section in doing a cover and story on the picture the weekend before the film opened. In my judgement, no single piece of marketing was as important or as influential as that.

"Why? Because every major editor around the country at every newspaper, and every entertainment editor and every critic gets the Sunday *New York Times*. Every major television station news director gets the Sunday *New York Times*. Given that this story came out on the front of the Arts and Leisure section the Sunday before the picture opened, it said something about the film that made it special and made it different. There was a half-page picture on the front of the magazine above the fold. It was a picture of Patrick Swayze and Jennifer Grey. When you open the magazine, on the right facing page there was another half-page story about Eleanor Bergstein about the basis for the DIRTY DANCING story. How it really existed and what DIRTY DANCING was all about, how this was based on her real experience in the Catskills.

"It wasn't intended to be a review. There was a separate review, but that wasn't until later.

"In my judgement, the reason this story was more important than any other marketing piece in the entire campaign-in which the company spent $15 million is because this piece told critics all around the country that a movie that they would otherwise perceive as a 'B' movie and a small teen picture was something bigger than that and something more important and special.

"I believe that Susan Jacobs simply pitched the story to the author Samuel Freedman of the *Times*. In fact, Freedman had seen the movie and wasn't really knocked out by it. It was OK, but he thought the story about what Eleanor went through and her own personal experience that led to her writing the script was an interesting story, so he went over to her apartment one day and he wrote the story. I think it had as much to do with the success of the picture as anything.

When the Sunday *New York Times* does a cover story in Arts and Leisure about MISSISSIPPI BURNING or some other important picture, it's what the audience expects and it's what the critics expect because that's what journalists write about. But when the Arts and Leisure section does a cover story about DIRTY DANCING, it says, 'Wait a minute, this isn't what you expect.' If it had come out two or three weeks into the release of the movie it wouldn't have been at all the same sort of thing. It would have had a fraction of the impact. Because it came out before the movie opened, it set a new context for this film.

If it had come out after the movie was released, at that point every other newspaper, television station and network talk show would have already done the story, and they would have done it assuming, 'Well, this is like FLASHDANCE,' or 'It's FOOTLOOSE,' or 'It's STAYING ALIVE.'

We had one very smart, very clever publicity firm and one receptive writer and we got lucky."

ADVERTISING

Title Treatment

Streger: "First thing we did was the title treatment. We did that while it was still an early script. It was developed so that Mitchell could do T-shirts and script covers for the production crew. The title treatment didn't end up the way it started out. It started with the word *dirty* set over the title *dancing*. I changed it later."

Quigley: "The title treatment was really critical. A lot of film companies make the mistake of thinking that the large ad is the ad that is going to be seen by most of the people. The reality is that the ad is often run very small. It may have an opening full-page ad, but right away it's a really tiny ad. It could be two square inches or even smaller, depending on the market and how many theaters you have in a market.

"What we like to do is design a title treatment that is really distinctive and has an image that reduces well. I call it our emblem. If you look at a lot of our ads—THE DEAD (with two people dancing) or DIRTY DANCING—there is usually one distinctive image that usually plays with a title treatment. The DIRTY DANC-

ING title treatment really identifies that original pose, that inno-
cence and romance. It's kind of like our signature."

Ad Campaign

Streger: "When it came time to open the film there was a slightly
different input to the marketing. The film was playing sexier than
our campaign and we were told that the campaign was a little
saccharine, a little too sweet. The film was playing and feeling more
MONTENEGRO-ish, which is where I started on it. We were
waylaid into this sweet, young girl's market. When we developed
the black-and-white newspaper campaign we had in mind a somewhat older audience, because that's who black-and-white campaigns are for.

"For the DIRTY DANCING print ad campaign, we needed something that had more action and movement than the poster, a prom
night two-shot, which was a little static.

"The initial campaign had three dancing shots. It was developed as
three stop-action shots to try to give the thing a whole lot more
movement than it had, to make it less static, less stand-on-the-page
posed. We wanted something that was very moving. We ended up
with our original print campaign. It started with one shot and two
others in three segments. *Dirty Dancing* was put on moveable
planes behind it. We had small- and large-size permutations of it
which had three shots, two shots and then finally this one shot
(which was taken from the film). We cut up 35-mm film for this and
we retouched it and added the feet.

"We happened to be working on the campaign at the same time that the producers were working on the main titles. And they had developed that wonderful title sequence where they did the stop-action black-and-white. Mitchell came to me and said that that was working but the lettering wasn't working .

"It's nice to be consistent and have both the movie and poster title treatment match, but it's not always necessary. It's a detail that worked."

KEY ART

The Poster

Streger: "The prom night two-shot was unit photography which we did retouching on. We retouched the background out. We retouched her face, the edge of her dress to make her shapelier, we touched his muscles, we touched his face, we took some hair off his forehead and stuff like that. When the poster came out, there was a mixed response from theater owners. Some liked it very much and some didn't like it. I don't know why."

Streger: "So even though there are three versions of campaign key art for this film, it is very consistent: (1) prom shot, (2) stop-motion threes and one, and (3) on hands and knees. There's been a consistency in the use of color, logo and stars. Pink and white, lavender ... it's always had hot pink tones to it."

Album Cover Art

Ienner: "I was the conduit between RCA and Vestron. I didn't love that [prom night two-shot] piece. I thought that the artwork was nice but that it wasn't exciting. I didn't like Patrick looking down in the art work. I felt he was a very important ingredient and the fact that he was looking down didn't thrill me. They also had three copy lines that they used on the poster art which I didn't want: First love, first something—whatever it was. I think Pam Rodi at Vestron came up with the idea of using the photos on the back of the album cover. We used a shot from the movie next to each song title which amplified it. This allowed you to relive the scene."

Promotion Vs. Advertising

Quigley: "As a strategy we look for projects that get a lot of editorial space like THE DEAD or ANNA. With those kinds of films you get a lot of editorial attention that we can't afford to buy. On a broad picture you try to do the same thing. If you can't do it by publicity, you do it by promotion or a combination of both. We emphasize publicity and promotion more than video would. You need to have the time to do it."

THE BUILDUP

Importance of Screenings

Peckos: "When the film is done, it's the big test. We already had some advance screenings in February before the film was finished. We screened our product reel at SHOWEST [the theater exhibitors convention] and everybody thought it was interesting and really fun. It was two and a half or three minutes of dancing—a shortened trailer. It was very rough. It had the editor's grease-pencil marks for the dissolves on it. There was already that recognition from them that this was a movie to look out for."

Quigley: "In May we had to convince the theaters, and by then we were fairly credible. We had a film that we knew played well, that they liked and made them feel good. We screened the hell out of the picture in May. We showed that picture constantly. As an exhibitor I knew I hated it when the distributor obviously brought a whole lot of teenage kids in and packed the audience. Universal did it on BACK TO THE FUTURE. I was just so annoyed with a high school class in there yelling and screaming while I am trying to make a decision about the film. What we did was pretty clever. We came up with the plan of inviting the record companies and their people, and radio people—a lot of people that would look roughly like contemporaries of the exhibitors. They looked around the room and were sure that they were not kids, it's obviously not a recruited audience. There are faces you don't recognize, so it looks like there could be exhibitors there. These are people who are pros. They don't go to seven screenings a week, they are not jaded and not bored and they were really into the music. So we combined the screenings with both record company executives and exhibitors present.

"If you are an independent you have to do things with mirrors."

Peckos: "The response was overwhelming. They loved it. There was only one exhibitor in the whole country who called me and told me how much he hated the movie. Most really loved it, which is unusual."

Quigley: "Instead of doing a sneak preview, which costs a couple of million dollars—which we didn't have—we did a radio promotion. We got a national sneak preview of the film, but it was through a radio promotion. We gave away tickets, we rented the theaters, we bought three weeks of radio time, which most people don't do. One of the things you need for radio is time; you need time to build awareness. Most people throw radio in for a week and it disappears and it's not effective. Because it's a frequency medium you have to pound and pound and pound. You do it for three weeks and people know the title, they know the song. We did a tracking study and plotted the awareness of DIRTY DANCING nationally. By the opening day it was way over the industry norms. Everybody knew about it."

Peckos: "The radio stations brought people into the promotional screenings and we avoided doing a sneak. Plus AMC [a theater chain], who made DIRTY DANCING a 'project picture' [a special priority throughout the chain], gave us 150 of our 800 dates. We had to rent the theaters which, cost about $800 on the average."

Quigley: "We did it all over the country. In blind-bid states you screen at twenty-four places. We screened all over."

Trailer

Quigley: "We had trailers on the screen beginning June sixth. Normally what happens is that you have a film and they put the trailer either on one of your own films or just prior to the opening of your film. We had this trailer on the screen for almost two months, which is very unusual. It's because the sales people called and followed up and kept on top of them all the time."

Peckos: "We designed the trailer to hit the target audience, which was young females. We tried to tell some of the story, make it as contemporary looking as possible and emphasize the dance. The music used was 'Baby.' In the TV spots we used 'The Time of My Life' since it was the first single. It was a fifteen-second teaser spot. We did a review spot, which was narration over picture of what the critics said about the movie.

"We then went back and did another wave of advertising for an older (secondary) audience. We knew they were coming. We just wanted to keep reinforcing that it was OK to go see this movie. And it worked. The younger audience was hooked; we really didn't have to go after them. But we did need to go after the older audience to let them know the critics were saying that this is OK to go see, even though it is about two young teenagers and it's got the title DIRTY DANCING. It's OK, it's not pornographic, it's PG."

THE THEATRICAL RUN

The Premieres

New York

Senk: "We had three. You only have a premiere if the stars are going to cooperate—and they are known enough—and you think you can get photo and television coverage. Otherwise it's just a party. It's nice to have a party, but you've got to know that at the end of the day you're going to have something.

"In the meantime Jennifer Grey and Matthew Broderick got into an auto accident in Europe. So Jennifer was out of commission. That was two weeks before the movie opened and she was in Ireland. Ultimately she decided to come in for the premieres.

"A premiere costs $10,000, $20,000 or $30,000. Some people do them for $50,000 or $75,000.

"On Monday night we had the premiere at Roseland in New York because it was absolutely fitting. It was special for Vestron because it was our first big movie and it was putting us on the map—like a coming-out party. There were 1,300 people at Roseland. The screening went really well. Jennifer flew in. Patrick was there. There was a contest through RCA where the kids who won from across the country got to come to the premiere and get their pictures taken with Patrick. The Dirty Dancers were were performing on the floor. [The Dirty Dancers have since become an ensemble group. Lucky for them.] We had tape music, all sixties stuff. We got all kinds of coverage."

Washington, D.C.

Senk: "And in the middle of it we had a benefit for the American Film Institute in Washington, DC. Cynthia and Kenny Ortega came down for that. The party was at a club afterwards. They closed off the street and they were dancing in the street when we got there. It was nice.

"I got back to my hotel in Washington at midnight, was on the phone until three o'clock booking screening rooms and then had to be on a plane at six in the morning to get to L.A. to do another premiere!"

Los Angeles

Senk: "On Wednesday night, Jennifer and Patrick flew to L.A. All hell had broken loose in Los Angeles. The party was set for Ed Debevic's on La Cienega. We took over the restaurant. The waiters and waitresses are all actors. We screened it at the DGA's 500-seat theater. This became the hottest ticket in town. As wonderful as

Roseland was, Ed Debevic's became even crazier. Word had traveled West. It was completely overcrowded. We had 700 people in the restaurant. They were outside, all over the place. We got coverage on everything. That basically was the publicity and then the movie took over.

"We were getting all the reviews and pulling quotes. The movie just took off, and the press just generated more press and more press. It kept going all through into the video release of the movie.

"We targeted it as a summer release literally from the day we went into production. We really mounted a major effort, given that there were only ten or eleven people who worked for nine months on it."

Summer Schedule

Quigley: "In 1988 the early wave will be WILLOW, another RAMBO, and CROCODILE DUNDEE II, so you have three home runs right away. That happens every summer. What the studios do is take one picture and set up a track: 'This one is going to play for eight weeks, and the next will be late July or early August, and that's a three-week picture, and then I'll have a late-August picture which will go until my September picture.' Sometimes they'll set up two or three tracks, depending on the amount of product they have. They'll try to arrange it so it's almost like mix-and-match. They try to get a theater booked for the whole summer with their product. But what I knew as an exhibitor is that typically there are thirty films which open, there are two which do breakout business and a couple which are OK, and the rest are turkeys. Which means there are one or two weak pictures. So there's usually a time, sometime in July, where if you pick a spot and pick a weakness, you jump in behind it, and for the most part the majors have all their films booked for eight to ten weeks during the summer. You come in after three weeks and you have five or six weeks of play time left. All we needed for DIRTY DANCING was three weeks, so I set a date of July seventeenth. It became apparent that this summer was unusual because it had more than two films that did a lot of business. There were seventy films that opened between Memorial Day and Labor Day, an incredible number of films.

Theater Circuits

Quigley: "We also made deals with the circuits, which was a mark of how much they believed in us. AMC made DIRTY DANCING a 'project picture,' which was unbelievable. UA Theaters gave us a lot of dates early on. We knew we had the circuits behind us. That was really a good indication of our credibility.

"I was being the hard guy about July seventeenth being the release date. I knew if I didn't insist on it, we would never make it. So I was flogging everybody to get there. It was really interesting to hear the exhibitors. My sales people were going nuts out there: 'We can't get the dates. We're banging our heads against the wall.' What convinced me was when the exhibitors were saying, 'You guys have a great film that you're screwing up because you are going at the wrong time.' Now exhibitors will always say that because <u>they want to fit you into their schedule</u> and because you are an independent—they've got to take care of the studios first. We met with a lot of the circuits on the West Coast and asked them what a good date would be. They kept saying the seventh or later. We kind of nosed around a date, so we finally said, 'OK, if we settle on this date, are these theaters going to be available?' and they said yes. I remember, we sat at the Westwood Marquis and the sales people said, 'We've got to move the date,' and I said, 'OK, let's move.' The next day we had a high degree of confidence that we had at least 400 dates, which meant—and remember that you have to commit all your advertising three weeks early—we were out there with millions of dollars and we didn't have theaters."

Peckos: "The date which we had picked [July 24] was impossible. Actually I dragged Bill Quigley out to Los Angeles to listen to the exhibitors because he was very adamant about going on July twenty-fourth, as was Jimmy Ienner [the music consultant], because they had planned the launch of the record. I was very adamant not to flush this picture down the toilet because I felt that there was too much product in the marketplace."

Quigley: "I moved it from July seventeenth to August twenty-first. It was an extraordinary effort. There are literally three people that sold a thousand theaters. There are only 22,000 screens in the whole U.S., and I think there are 13,000 play dates on this film. As of today—March 16, 1988—it's still playing in 156 theaters."

Peckos: "We didn't have a big opening week. But week after week DIRTY DANCING was consistent in its performance. Its percentage drop-off was very slight week to week to week. We never had a $7 million weekend; we had a $3.5 million weekend."

Peisinger: "When a movie opens it usually falls off over 25 to 40 percent by the second week, and then a third again the week after that. The performance curve for most movies is that they come to a dead halt the first week. DIRTY DANCING in it's worst week fell off 10 percent. There were many weeks where it went up or was dead-even from week to week. The advertising support we were doing fell off quickly. Bill Quigley was spending $100,000 a week nationally to support 1,000 prints and we were still doing a million-plus at the box office. This is a film that found its audience and the audience found it."

The Exhibition Deal: Settlement

Quigley: "The settlement for an exclusive-run art film is higher than a broad-based, mass-audience film. The distributor receives 50 percent of the box office. The average from all theaters combined should be somewhere between 45 and 50 percent. We aim for 50 percent. For an overall national release the distributor will get 40 percent of the box office, which is pretty good. It is really a function of how long the film plays in each theater. If you have a film like DIRTY DANCING that's played for six months in one theater, the weighted average drops way down over time. A typical deal will return 70 percent to the distributor in the first week, 60 percent in the second week then, 50 percent, 40 percent, 35 percent, 30 percent, 25 percent, and so forth. In some deals this is against a ninety/ten deal [distributor/theater], whichever is greater. The deals are calculated to give distributors maximum dollars in all instances—in the event of high grosses or low grosses.

"You negotiate your contracts then you settle after it's all over. My fear is, if you're in a theater long enough, you will end up with 25 percent."

Peckos: "If DIRTY DANCING would have opened in July it would have been off the screen in two weeks. The pressure on the theaters to open the studio films in August would have killed it. THE LIVING DAYLIGHTS opened in July , BEVERLY HILLS COP was going strong. There was LOST BOYS, which opened on July thirty-first. LA BAMBA came out July twenty-fourth and was doing well, which was another reason to stay away from July. In August things opened up. A lot of junk opened in the beginning of August. There was BACK TO THE BEACH. By the time August twenty-first rolled around it all surfaced out. Everyone had seen BEVERLY HILLS COP, the JAWS sequel, DRAGNET, the Bond film. There was HARRY AND THE HENDERSONS, which was predicted to be a big picture but wasn't. WHO'S THAT GIRL opened on July thirty-first and fell flat. It was a pretty crowded summer. So when we opened there wasn't much happening and we were able to get a lot of space in the newspapers for editorial pieces, which were very important. That is what got us our secondary audience, which was much sooner than I anticipated."

Opening Day

Peckos: "Picking the release dates is all part of the marketing strategy. That's why I think that distribution and marketing should be connected. Picking your release date, you not only have to think about what your competition is opening but what that means all the way down the line in terms of doing promotions and getting radios stations. Radio stations can only promote so many movies per week because of saturation. We bought three weeks of radio, we got one for free because we did the promotions with the stations. We gave away tickets and screened the film for their audiences."

Quigley: "Originally the film was set for July seventeenth. The reason was that the majors have their pictures set from Memorial Day to the Fourth of July (five- to six-week period). About thirty-something films typically open then."

Peckos: "No one was writing about the other pictures, or Spielberg. We were getting incredible responses and there was nothing else to write about. People were really eager to write about this phenomenon—that's what people were calling it in their reviews. We got pieces in the Sunday *New York Times* with that big, huge picture. There were three pieces in there: one was a whole dancing-film piece, one was an interview with Eleanor Bergstein, and then there was a capsule about Kenny Ortega. All this dominated the Arts and Leisure section on pre-opening Sunday. It was incredible. Our review was pretty good in the *New York Times*, which was amazing. That's when I said, 'Here we go.'"

Cannold: "I remember it as if it were election night, all the marketing people hanging around the office until midnight on the opening weekend to get numbers from all over the country. There were people assigned to different regions of the country to gather numbers because we had our own home-made version of what the majors would have had with a computer. And every hour people would call in to say, "How's it doing in Ohio?' It was as if it were election night. An awful lot was on the line. The marketing team is a diverse group of people,different ages and different tastes, and clearly every single one of them thought the movie was fabulous. They all got behind it and in unison fought like hell. I wish for every one of them that they have that kind of experience again."

Quigley: "The secondary audiences are us. Most people our age [thirty to forty] would just think it was another John Hughes teen film and wouldn't go. I think we all knew we would get that audience, but it takes a while for it to kick in. But because we got all that editorial space, that audience kicked in much earlier."

Cannold: "It's very hard to find fault with the marketing of the picture. I think the Vestron marketing team did nearly everything right. They had an extraordinary experience because while there were some other films that they had to devote some time to prior to this, they were relatively small releases and didn't require a great deal of their time. One of the great successes of marketing this movie is reflected in the fact that the entire marketing team loved the picture and got behind it. For ninety straight days prior to the opening of the film, they did virtually nothing else. Unfortunately, since then they have not had that kind of luxury. And they may never again in their careers."

Repeat Viewings

Reuther: "We had a lot of repeat viewings. Kids went a lot. But then we started getting into a phenomenon where women thirty years old began going. Why? As a substitute for sex. Johnny's pelvic thrust. And it reminded them who they were when they were growing up. They remembered some time in their life, when they were at their best."

AHH, THE MUSIC

Quigley: "One of the fascinating things about it is that you could see that music today—if you think about Springsteen, Hall and Oates, almost any of the white musicians that sing rock and roll, Billy Joel, they all, if not imitate, they at least have roots in the sixties imitating black men. We realized that we could take songs of the period. I saw STAND BY ME in early February as a possible acquisition—it was called THE BODY then—and, again, it was one where music had a big, big impact. One of the fascinating things that happened was that kids heard those old songs (like a Sam Cooke song) as if they were new today. We realized with DIRTY DANCING that not only could we take songs of the period and kids would hear them as today, but we could also take songs written today. I wrote a letter to Huey Lewis and asked him to do some songs. Because of his sound he could be fairly accurate about the period."

Developing The Music

Quigley: "The record was scheduled to break in early June. It didn't come out until sometime in July. It didn't get much airplay until after the movie started. The film drove the album, I'm convinced. The record company game is to get us to spend as much money as they can to promote their record."

Peisinger: "We thought we gave ourselves an enormous amount of time to actually have songs selected, if not the finished material recorded, so that when Emile started shooting he could have the scratch track of the real songs. But after almost two months we just didn't have any music. Thousands of oldies were submitted, but very few seemed to be right for Eleanor's vision. Now we were at the beginning of August and shooting was supposed to begin in two weeks and there was no music. Finally, I put the arm on Jimmy [Ienner]—who was Vestron's music consultant—to come and take over the project. One of the great miracles of our industry was that in three weeks he had made hundreds of phone calls and received hundreds of new songs. He had called up guys, told them about the scenes in the movies and said, 'Here's the feeling I want and here's the pacing I want. Write me a song, and I need it tomorrow, and you're not going to get paid very much for it.' In a few weeks he pulled the whole thing off with about seven new songs and five oldies.

"Jimmy pulled it together, pulled favors, used his experience, cut good deals for us on the oldies and did all the things that a good music supervisor should do and more. I can't think of a better success story to start off your movie."

Ienner: "I accepted a consulting situation with Vestron via Jon Peisinger. I was to watch over all projects where I could and help aim the music in the right direction. In reference to DIRTY DANC-ING, I was on as a consultant first. The original music person was fired. I was then asked to take over and try to fix it. The deals that were made were not very good in terms of the songs, the sync licenses, the master uses and in many cases the selections of tunes themselves. There weren't many original pieces. They hadn't come up with one song that was new that could be used. The intent was to mix and match [oldies and new tunes].

"My job was to try and straighten it all out. The first objective was to get a needed theme song, a 'Deliverance' piece for the finale, which was nowhere in sight. That started the ball rolling. Then my assistants and I started contacting everybody who might write something appropriate.

"We needed the music to shoot with. We had very little time. It was pure panic. In one weekend I went through about 102 compositions. Some were from well-known artists and writers, some came in as masters. But they just weren't right. On Sunday afternoon I started to blueprint things for different writers, going over what we needed: how the songs had to start, how they had to end, what they were about. We talked about what they should be thematically and lyrically and emotionally."

Quigley: "Jimmy Ienner made a contribution to this film that was extraordinary. The music is such an integral part of the film and that was him. He remixed all the old stuff and he had the new songs written, he found the people, got the artists. Everyone thanks Jimmy Ienner for Eric Carmen, Mary Clayton, Jennifer Warnes, Bill Medley. He revived all these people, called in favors. He helped us make the deal with RCA."

The Theme Song

Ienner: "I wanted the composers to speak to the director, Emile Ardolini, and the choreographer, Kenny Ortega. For 'The Time of My Life' I gave the composers a blueprint of what I and Emile felt was needed. For example, the theme song had to start slow and gain a certain momentum, but it had to have a Latin rhythm underneath it. It was almost a left-footed Bossa Nova, and yet it had to be a very traditional rock piece because that's how Ortega choreographs. (In my opinion, he was much stronger with a Latin rhythm base than with a rock base.) The composer and I talked about where the song should go in the movie. Creatively the blueprint includes theme and emotion. It's not just structural. This song had to be the climax; the music doesn't get better than this. It had to be the culmination of everything. I walked the composer through all the events that happened in the film with Baby and Johnny.

"We always knew the theme song was to be a duet; that's what we always wanted. At one time we were looking at Aretha Franklin. But if it was going to be Aretha, then I also needed a white-bread male singer. I wanted the voices to represent Johnny and Baby. Johnny being from the poor side of town who loved R & B [rhythm and blues music], and Baby who really understood and knew white-bread music. She was more from the Pat Boone school and he was from the Contours [a rhythm and blues group] school. Ultimately we came up with the perfect casting.

"Two people who really did have a lot to say about the music were Eleanor Bergstein and Emile Ardolini. They were a great counterbalance. Eleanor wanted some obscure rhythm and blues pieces, Emile wanted the white bread. I played them as Johnny and Baby in terms of taste. Emile came up with the idea for 'Wipeout' and then he hated his own idea. I had to fight to keep it in.

"The music paralleled the two character's development only in my mind. Emile went for period and emotion. For Eleanor it was the pure remembrance of songs that really had an impact on her. I felt the key to the music was that somehow you just couldn't sprinkle this film with period pieces—you had to look at how they contributed emotionally and then work it from there."

The Single

Ienner: "The single was released in June, six weeks in front of the movie. The album was going to come out the same week as the film. Actually it turned out the album didn't come out until August. It shipped a week before the movie was opening."

Peisinger: "Having a terrific soundtrack not only enhanced our opportunity for the film, but gave us a marketing hook at our low budget. We needed that exposure.

"The film and album fed off each other. What happened was, they went up together. 'The Time of My Life' was initially released in the first week of July because we had told RCA that the film was coming out then. Everybody forgot to call RCA when the film was pushed back to August, so they had already shipped out the single. Jimmy had put in place a whole promotional campaign for the record and it really threw RCA for a loop. So a month later everyone really had to regroup. But once the film opened, it was feeding off each other. The record went literally straight up the charts, taking huge leaps. At the same time the film opened well with $4.5 million the first weekend and then never dropped off. It was never the biggest film in any one weekend. I think only a few weekends was it the number two film, but through mid-December the film never dropped more than 10 percent weekend to weekend. The business doesn't work that way. In fact, a few weekends it went up."

Quigley: "What happens is that initially the film drives the record, and if the record is a hit, three months later it has an effect on the film."

Peisinger: "What has made it so enormously successful is that it maintains your interest. Every time you think it's settling down into a groove, it jerks you along and shifts to another sound. I think that's why it went to number one and stayed there so long and why now, ten months after the single was released, you cannot listen to the radio and not hear 'The Time of My Life.' It has fallen into a classic rotation."

Music Audience

Ienner: "I wasn't thinking about an audience when we made the record. I knew what I wanted to do. I wanted the strings to reflect 'You've Lost That Loving Feeling' of Bill Medley and the Righteous Brothers. To me, he was the voice of the sixties. He was one of the few successful white artists that was musically and stylistically authentically black. He had tremendous impact. And that was Johnny's music.

"I wanted the strings and the duet and the bigness of it to capture a whole other audience. I didn't want to get nailed down in terms of a reflective, nostalgia audience only. What we tried to do was subtly mix and match so many things that we would miss no one. We might not hit everybody, but we would miss no one—from Latins, to blacks, to whites, to young, to old. It didn't matter to me. I wanted a little bit of a lot."

Radio Play

Peisinger: "Because of my background [in the music business], the music was always the primary focus. That could not only broaden the sheer entertainment value and give the audience something to go home singing, but it is the promotional marketing tool worth tens of millions of dollars if you do it right. Every time that record plays on the radio you are getting three or four minutes of free airtime."

Ienner: "I'm being kind when I say that 80 percent of radio rejected it when they heard it before they saw the movie. All of radio loved Bill Medley because most of the program directors are people who either grew up with him or they are rock and roll fanatics. So they knew him. That was another [marketing] key I was using. With regard to Jennifer Warnes, they liked her voice but she wasn't a must. But when you see what the song does in the film, all of a sudden it makes sense to everybody. So the initial reaction to the record was one of, 'Gee, I really like this but, ahh, I don't know....' And there were also a few radio program directors who were very heavy hitters who didn't like it at all.

"If you think about the fact that it became the number one record, and in the beginning it drove the movie and the album, won a Golden Globe, won a Grammy, and as we sit and talk [April 1988] I am crossing my fingers that we win an Oscar [it did—for Best Song]. Very few songs have that kind of impact. This song will not go away. As we speak it's one of the two or three what they call recurrent songs on radio, which means it's getting a lot of play although it's well into 'chart heaven.'

"What charts did it hit? Everything. It missed nothing. The R&B stations played it to death, but they didn't play it as a charted record. It went AC [Adult Contemporary], it went CHR [Contemporary Hit Radio—Top 40], it got country play, it hit everywhere. Overall a lot of the thinking that went into the rest of the songs was really, 'Where is the audience?' At the initial marketing meetings you heard me screaming my theme: 'That's fine to target your advertising demographics and audience but don't limit it.' I was screaming that at everybody.

"It wasn't easy to launch. From the music marketing aspect, it was a song that begged to be done as a duet. We had to come up with some interesting names. Program directors at the radio stations would read the label and because of the names wanted to put it on the turntable and listen to it: 'Hey, this is Bill Medley, one of the Righteous Brothers!' And Jennifer Warnes, who was involved in the last two Academy Award–winning songs [with Joe Cocker—'Up Where We Belong'), and in fact has done a number of duets in recent years. She's got such a pure, distinctive voice."

Peisinger: "You want to get to the point where we eventually did get with this film where, if you go to see the movie you want to rush right out and get the soundtrack, and if you hear the song on the radio you want to rush right out and see the movie."

Ienner: "If you look at the grosses of the other records, you'll see the importance of the music. We've already passed 99 percent of them. Our music was used a bit differently, which by no means should be taken lightly. Very few of those songs were bypasses. They were all pivotal. When you think about how they were used, from 'Hungry Eyes' to 'Hey Baby' to 'Love is Strange' to 'Do You Love Me?' to 'The Time of My Life.' When you look at how pivotal they were to the visual scene you'll see there was an emotional marriage. They were not fillers. You're talking about cornerstones to scenes and flow, and I think that has something to do with the movie's success."

Record Sales

Peisinger: "We have sold more soundtrack albums than any other except SATURDAY NIGHT FEVER. We have sold more units than any multi-artist record. I remember all the things that happened with SATURDAY NIGHT FEVER—you couldn't pick up the phone without somebody being there with some scheme or angle. Here it is nine months after the film has been released and this thing has not slowed down but is picking up momentum.

"The second album will be number six on *Billboard*'s chart. It came out at number thirty, then went to six. The first album stays at number one. We are, as of this week, 6.5 million on the first [domestic] and 1.75 million on the second album. The international numbers are 3 million on the first album. Germany alone sold 1 million albums."

Ienner: "It was a real iffy situation for a while because Vestron wasn't sure when they should release the movie. Ultimately they made the right decision. I wasn't allowed to say anything. We had originally scheduled the movie for a July twenty-fourth release. Every meeting we had was geared for that date. It has become standard practice since SATURDAY NIGHT FEVER to release the record anywhere between three and six weeks before the movie."

Target Radio Audience

Ienner: "Now as RCA was planning their strategy they decided to release the single to the adult contemporary audience first. I said, 'If you do that, why don't you just confirm that Bill and Jennifer are in rocking chairs.' I was not a fan of that strategy and I could not change their minds. They wanted to go adult contemporary first and then spread it. And everybody agreed to that except me. I was totally, absolutely opposed to it.

"My thinking was that the minute you do that you set up what is a borderline adult record—nobody knows the film and you are giving a lot of emphasis to a very passive adult audience who, as a rule, won't buy many records. Adult contemporary to me is the most active Muzak around.

"I wouldn't have placed the record before any particular audience first. I would have gone for the world. Go and seek out whatever audience you can in any way you can. It's taking a risk, but the risk is worth it. Very few had the insight on the record side. That wasn't because they couldn't see, it's just that I had more input in the creation of the music. I knew what we had. I was living with the whole process and mixing the film and knew this film was bigger than anyone understood. And it wasn't because the movie was wonderful or innovative, it was just that the movie hit a chord and I felt that chord.

"When we were mixing the film I said to everybody, 'I hope you people are going to get a rest after this film is over because you are all going to be very busy.' I remember everybody turning around and looking at me and like, 'Really?' and I said, '*Really.*'"

Other Problems

Ienner: "Besides the record stopping and starting [coming out in July and then not taking off until August], RCA pressed the record off-center. So it also had a wow in it, which didn't help when you have a low voice like Bill Medley. When I first heard it, it was too late because they had already shipped the record to radio. I demanded that RCA throw the records out. The record, in my opinion, was in 'code blue.' The album was minimally pressed and shipped [40,000 copies]. And based on the reaction to the single, they weren't wrong.

"The helium had come out of the balloon. Everything that RCA was set up to do—plus the trouble they were having with radio, including the slow movement of the record, and the record being off center, and on July tenth when I had to break the news to them that the film would not come out until August twenty-first—you could physically see the helium leave the balloon. It was just deflated. Everybody had lost all the impetus, the enthusiasm, and the momentum. Everything was completely lost. So I had to do a balancing act. I thought I was Emmet Kelly and Evil Knievel. We had to regenerate some level of interest so that the album wouldn't just die. There were a few people at RCA who deserved and still deserve tremendous credit because they stuck in there. But there were very few in the beginning.

Cannold: "RCA was supportive but they weren't fully committed until they saw that the picture was going to work and they wanted to get behind it."

Ienner: "The movie opened and all of a sudden within a 24-hour period people went from the theaters to the record stores. And the rest is history.

"There had never been two albums from a film in the top ten at the same time. The only other one that ever came close was 'Woodstock,' which after three years the second album went gold. The first album was number one for eighteen weeks. It surpassed 'Saturday Night Fever' in the number of weeks it was in the top ten. 'More Dirty Dancing,' the second album, was number two for weeks.

"The first album is nearing 8 million in sales domestically and 5 million internationally. The second album is over 2.5 million domestically and over 1 million internationally.

"Private Music, Virgin and Varese Saraband are just some of the record companies that release movie soundtrack albums. Often these are just orchestral scores. In terms of sales, you are only talking in the tens of thousands of units."

Clearances

Ienner: "I had to sit on a bed with Phil Spector until 4:30 in the morning to get 'Be My Baby.' I had to get people like Frankie Vallie and Bob Gaudio and Bob Crew to speak to each other again after many years to get 'Big Girls Don't Cry.' I fought and screamed with many of the others for song rights. Each has their own story.

"We ran out of money. We had to make a deal with RCA before we were finished with the movie. Right in the middle of the process. We would never have been able to afford all the music without an album deal. At the time we made the deal, RCA did not even hear all the songs."

Remixing

Ienner: "I was busy making all the records and all the deals. Someone else mixed the film. I heard it and hated it. Eleanor was terribly depressed and she and Emile sat me down and said, 'Look, it's all the songs we have constantly talked about and dreamed of, but it is just not happening.' I said, 'Look, I've now heard this and I think it's flat and dead.' So we then went and remixed the whole film. Eleanor was in tears because all of a sudden it came to life and there was a spark.

"There was one mix for film which was more authentic to the period. And there was a second mix which was modernized for the album.

"The oldies took me forever to master because I actually remixed them in mastering. We just made instruments come out that no one had heard before. If I heard a part that was way off I found something else to cover it. I buried it, I changed it. When the mastering engineer was done he had to go on vacation, because there wasn't a two-bar phrase in any song that wasn't changed."

Album Art

Streger: "The reason why we've gotten back to using the 'popsicle' [two-shot prom pose] in trade ads is because the album became very popular and uses that key art on the album. That tie-in was there, so we started using that in our second wave of consumer advertising.

"The second album, 'More Dirty Dancing,' uses the dancing scenes from the film like the newspaper ad."

THE VIDEO

The Video Release

Peisinger: "We started planning the video release immediately after the film was released. Most major titles—the big movies—that came out in the summer the prior year will be released in video in January and February. The trick is to get the jump on them. We've done it in the past with lesser movies. Here we've done it with a movie that was clearly a major hit. And we wanted to test our theory, if it could benefit a major hit. So right from the start we had identified January fifth as the video release date.

"One of the things we've learned over the last couple of years is the value of that first slot right after Christmas. We found having that first release slot—three or four days into January—is an incredible opportunity. You have a number of factors in your favor. Retailers are flush with cash from the Christmas business, all those new VCR owners who got their first VCR under the Christmas tree immediately rush out and have an insatiable appetite to watch videos. There is bad weather in most of the country, which keeps people indoors. All that converges to create an incredible demand and market opportunity immediately after Christmas, and it continues through January and into February.

"The overriding concept was to make the video release of DIRTY DANCING an event. The release was only four and a half months after the theatrical release. Video is normally released six months or more after the theatrical run. It was a film that was clearly generating repeat viewers, which showed great promise for video because video is a medium which encourages repeat viewing. Our job was to convince the video trade this was the type of movie that it was. The trade was talking about the big studio films—PREDATOR, LA BAMBA, and ROBOCOP. DIRTY DANCING had never garnered the headlines. It had never been the number one film of the week. It was growing. We wanted to push it over the edge. There were so many things done to do that, you can't point to any one. It was the campaign in its entirety. Parties had an impact that you can't ascribe unit sales or dollars to. People were feeling good about DIRTY DANCING. I talked to a lot of people at the New York party. They were feeling part of it."

Still Playing Theatrically

Quigley: "A lot of exhibitors have a policy that they won't play through the video release, and guess what? Most of them did. I agreed to the video release sometime in September 1987."

Peisinger: "The interesting challenge here is that the movie just wasn't dying theatrically. And as we were barreling toward the end of 1987, DIRTY DANCING was still doing unbelievable theatrical business. There was a lot of questioning as to whether we should maintain our video release date. In the end it really turned on the belief that, as strong as the performance was, over the long period of time there were so many major movies coming into the market at Christmas it would be difficult to sustain the level of business we were doing for another couple of months. We did a sensitivity analysis to project what our share of the box-office revenues would be if (1) we had competition from our own video release and (2) we didn't have that competition. If the video came out, what would our total revenue picture be? We found that there would be a sharp decline in the box-office rental revenues, but having those revenues added to the incremental revenues of the video.

"Releasing the video while the film was still in the theaters was a very real concern because everyone questioned our credibility. But at the same time, we rolled the dice and figured if the movie was still doing strong business the exhibitors would be compelled to keep the film on their screens. And that's exactly what happened."

Video Packaging

Streger: "One of the early art treatments that was rejected for the theatrical campaign was used later for the video box. It's the one of Jennifer and Patrick on their hands and knees. A kind of sexy, young-love treatment."

Streger: "We had other shots of the two of them dancing, but we used different blown-up backgrounds of their faces very close together—kind of the ENDLESS LOVE approach.

"The challenge in developing a campaign for this film was that we didn't have very much good unit photography. A photo shoot had already been done and was unusable. Some money had already been spent, so we didn't want to put the stars together and do that again because it is very expensive. We had to use the little photography we had and there wasn't much. We went through several

attempts to get the shot, from blowing up the 35-mm film from the movie and doing all sorts of retouching.

"The more the art has been seen, the better it is for video. People hadn't seen the prom shot that much because it was only used in the theatrical poster—it wasn't used in the newspaper campaign. So we had to consider that the newspaper campaign had been seen more.

"Video has a different market. First, the video has the benefit of hindsight in terms of who liked the movie, who the movie has appealed to and what the movie may have grown into. So for the video there is a value that is placed on a newspaper campaign whether it is good, bad or indifferent. Just from the fact that *it has been seen*. So we wanted to use the newspaper campaign because it had been seen. But for video we also felt that we wanted to get a little sexier and a little more 'love story' because that sells better in video than 'dance movie' does. Hence we took the love-story shot and superimposed it and that worked."

Video Promotion

Peisinger: "The video promotion helped the theaters, just as the record album and theatrical promotion fed off each other. We added yet another level of a couple million dollars of video promotion simply to goose the awareness again of DIRTY DANCING.

"The week the video came out we went from 900 to 700 theaters. And that held up. As we're sitting here [April 1988] the video has been out three months and the movie is still playing in 150 theaters somewhere around this country. People are still plunking down their money to see the movie. We never made new prints—they must be held together by Scotch tape!

"We were planning the video release and putting the campaign together—we knew we had a hit movie, but we didn't know we had a mega-hit or a phenomenon, which is what it was by the time the video came out. The whole orientation was to try to make it larger than life and in this case we wanted to take advantage of everything that was available to us, not the least of which was the soundtrack

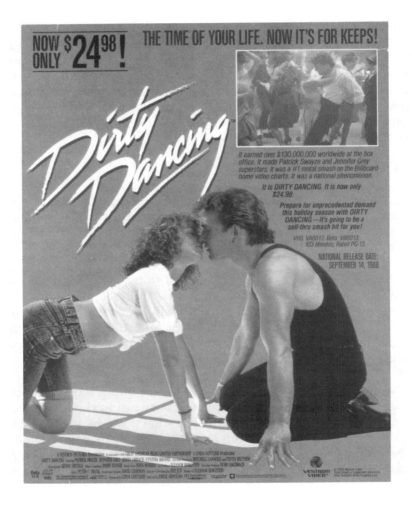

album. We solicited RCA records and added a trailer for the album at the end of the video. We had something that was valuable to them. The customer who rented the video would have heard the music through the soundtrack, and then we wanted to tell them the soundtrack was available, so we put a trailer about RCA's album at the end of the videotape."

Video Trailer

Streger: "If the theatrical trailer works we don't redo it for video. We may add to it. We do a special shoot where we show some of the P.O.P. [point of purchase] items that are going along with the video: 'You get this very special in-store stand-up with X-number of orders.' The trailer may incorporate reviews."

Video Publicity

Senk: "There was nothing more to write about once the video came out. They wanted Patrick to do some video magazines, but at that point he was tired of it. The album was taking off. Patrick was doing an enormous amount of publicity for the record because that was important to him. Jennifer was quiet at that point. Cynthia kept doing stuff. We had a lot of people to draw from. People were still interested in Eleanor. There was a little bit of interest in Linda Gottlieb, the producer, which only happens later. Producers shouldn't expect to get publicity. They want it. I can understand it. But it only happens after you have a successful movie. Because people would rather talk to the talent or the director or the choreographer.

"Cynthia went to Belgium to promote it. We didn't send anybody to Japan. Patrick went to England, France and Germany because now we had the international release to promote. We were lucky because the talent was very cooperative. They believed in it, they liked it, and it was their big break and they knew it. They worked it. You don't always have that luxury. And it has continued. Patrick just did a videotape for Australia saying 'Hi, how ya doing?' He's received all these German awards and had his picture taken for all the German magazines."

Dance Parties Promotion

Peisinger: "For the video promotion we wanted to take advantage of the nature of the film, which was fun, had dancing and great music. So for the first time, we had dance parties around the country. We got dealers involved. We got the press involved. We engaged an ad hoc network of different radio stations in every key market to participate and allow their listeners to come to these DIRTY DANCING launch parties. This had never been done before for a videocassette. You do those things for records. It was the same concept that we used for the movie. We went to key radio stations in each market and we gave them an exclusive promotion. It was extraordinary because this was taking place *six weeks before* the video's release. Again we were fanning the flames—building up interest long before the video was available. The result was that people inundated video stores: 'When's DIRTY DANCING coming out?' And the video retailer who had planned to order ten copies now ordered fifteen, and two weeks later it became twenty. Demand was reaching a fever pitch because it wasn't available.

"The radio station promotion might announce that the tenth caller from Brooklyn wins two passes to the exclusive DIRTY DANCING party at the Ritz Thursday night. At each party there was a DIRTY DANCING contest and one winner was selected. All the winners went into a pool and Cynthia Rhodes picked the grand winner, who will get a role in a Vestron movie."

Senk: "These video dance parties announced the launch of the videocassette around the country. The contest winner was going to be in an upcoming Vestron picture. That was arranged in twelve to fifteen cities. And Jennifer showed up in New York and MTV was there.

"Cynthia did radio promotions for England. She taped twelve messages for twelve different radio stations in England: 'Hi, I'm Cynthia Rhodes. You're listening to such- and-such, wait for details on the DIRTY DANCING promotion.' It just goes on. It just builds. You know, there are still articles coming out about DIRTY DANCING every once in a while."

ADVERTISING

Video Advertising

Reuben: "We did presell the video when the movie was still playing on 800 screens. It then fell to 400 screens when we released the video. We also did lots of preselling with ads in *Billboard*, *Video Store*, and *Video Insider*. Lots of publicity pieces came out. We did consumer advertising in *USA Today*, *People*, *Previews*, *Coming Attractions*, *Home Viewer*."

Sponsorship

Reuben: "We also did something very unique. We were looking for a sponsor. One of the conditions of that promotion was that Nestle do their promotion *after* the release date. The normal rental cycle ends around six weeks, but we believed DIRTY DANCING had a longer shelf life if we could find a way to extend the promotion." [Rentals fall off in six weeks because there is so much new product.]

Peisinger: "The Nestle sponsorship was an important piece because it included a DIRTY DANCING sweepstakes, national advertising and promotion, all of which were designed to kick in *a month after* the video was released. We felt we had done a sufficient job so that the video would be in high demand *immediately upon release*, and if Nestle was going to do their promotion upon initial release it would be a waste. We wanted to get the message to the retailers that there's real good news and that was Nestle's involvement in the video's promotion. They were going to help keep the video visible over the longer term.

"We were able to get this message to the retailers because, at that time, DIRTY DANCING was only the second film to have a commercial on it. This was still big news for the trade that Nestle was going to be involved. Anticipating that, we used that news as a platform for giving the rest of our message: There was going to be a sweepstakes, national promotion, and it wasn't going to start January 1 [the video release date]—it was going to start February 1 and run through March. At the time the retailers could truly benefit from the longevity. We have real proof that it worked.

"Alexander and Associates tracks the number of transactions [video rentals] from a representative sample of a thousand video stores around the country. The period the DIRTY DANCING video came out it was only number two. Then it went to number one. Then competition like PLATOON came out, so we dropped to number three overall. Look what happened to the number. In its seventh and eighth weeks sales picked up again, which is a result of the Nestle promotion kicking in later."

Reuben: "Advertising had the effect of changing the rental pattern of DIRTY DANCING so that the video rentals picked up in the sixth week after release. The title was number three in rentals at the end of six weeks. At the end of the eighth week it was back to number one because of the Nestle promotion. What happened was, it drove people back into the stores. It's a very interesting phenomenon. In our business titles don't go from number one to number three and then back to number one in eight weeks. There were waiting lists on that title."

TV Advertising

Peisinger: "What were doing here was saying to the video retailer, 'Stock up; buy more units; we are going to stand there and support you over a longer period of time.' The hue and cry from the video stores is, 'How much are you going to spend on television advertising?' The studios are looking for major units so they go out and announce to the video retailer that they are going to pull in rental customers through television. Very quickly it got to the point where video retailers are saying, 'All right, you want us to buy 200,000 units—how much are you going to spend on television?' With the Nestle promotion we found another way to get that exposure without spending millions of dollars on television advertising.

"DIRTY DANCING will come out around Christmas 1988 for the sell-through market."

Reuben: "A video would normally slow down, but promotion set in and it went the other way. Now the retail stores are starting to want more advertising after the release date. Video companies, to some degree selfishly, advertise two weeks before the order date, sending people into the stores to reserve copies. That works from a distribution standpoint but the retailer is saying, 'Fine, now you guys got your distribution [sales numbers], but do something for me—help me get it rented or sold.' We now begin to see the necessity of advertising after the release date to do that.

"We just changed our advertising plan on IRONWEED so that *People* and *Time* magazine advertising will take place after street date rather than before. That is a very major change. Another change is that the retailers are screaming for national television advertising. We are doing television advertising on our Main Muscle Promotion (STEEL DAWN and RUNNING MAN), but there is a direct relationship between the screaming the distributor/wholesaler is doing for newspaper co-op dollars and the screaming the retailer is doing for television advertising. What is happening is the small retailer is saying, 'Spend your money for television advertising,' and the big retailer is saying, 'If you do that, don't do it at the expense of co-op advertising because I want to run co-op advertising and advertise my store and your product.'

"Paramount, for example, has announced that ten titles are going to be advertised on television, and it's absolutely at the expense of co-op advertising and many people will start screaming."

Merchandising

Reuben: "There were 3-D stand-ups with a new, narrow format. We made 15,000 at a cost of about eight to ten dollars each. There was a tie-in so that, depending on how many videos a dealer would buy, he'd get a stand up. This encourages purchases and helps the retailer merchandise the product.

"We sent out 40,000 posters to the retail stores. The 2,000 audio cassettes were sent to all distribution sales people so they could play the tape in their car. This would remind them and get them excited about the DIRTY DANCING video release.

"We sent out 2,000 screening copies of the video to distributors and key retailers. There were 32,000 buttons, and 5,000 T-shirts sent to retail.

"Ads promoted the album and the video simultaneously. In the record we had a 'coming soon' ad about the video. We cross-marketed our video with RCA's album."

ANCILLARY

Dirty Dancing Tour

Peisinger: "First week in June they play at Radio City Music Hall. It will play at places like Jones Beach Theater, Tanglewood, the sheds, as they call them.

"Word leaks out and promoters start calling and throwing money at it. It has just taken on a life of its own. If anything, it's picking up. The thing is gaining momentum. When we originally considered it, it was going to be three artists, a backup band of four or five musicians and six dancers. It was going to play 3,000-seat halls. Now [April 1988] they are up to 1,200- and 1,500-seat halls because the response has been incredible.

"When all is said and done on DIRTY DANCING—and that may not be for a couple of years. Things are just unfolding. A *Billboard* article about the summer concert tours discussed every big act in the record industry going out on tour. The next day *USA Today* picked up the story and wrote an article in the Life section. They headlined the story with DIRTY DANCING, from the same *Billboard* article that mentioned that Bruce Springsteen is going to tour, that Pink Floyd, Van Halen, Robert Plant, George Michael are touring, and yet the headline and first half of the article kicked off with the May 29 DIRTY DANCING tour because it's become part of the cultural age. We've got the television show this fall. We're going to film the tour for video. The itinerary is pretty much completed, then I want to pick the date. We will film the tour for video release.

"I may be able to get some interest in the tour video from CBS to kick off the DIRTY DANCING television series. At the very least I know I can get the tour video on HBO for a license fee of between $800,000 and $1 million. We are going to record it and have a live concert album. People are throwing money at us to get the T-shirt rights for the tour. Sponsors want to get involved. VH-1 is the co-promoter of the tour. They just did a TV special on it. During the commercial break they announced the DIRTY DANCING tour. There is a lot going on."

Sequel

Cannold: "There was interest in developing a movie sequel (and that would have always been the preferred path), but Eleanor Bergstein was reluctant. From a marketing point of view a movie sequel was our logical next step. We knew that sixty days after the picture opened. We began to talk to Eleanor about writing the sequel, but she was reluctant to start on it because she believed that there was a lot of life left in this picture. Eleanor proved to be right. She felt the audience wouldn't be ready for another story about these people just yet and that the franchise could endure. She wanted to wait two or three years.

"Research demonstrates when a sequel comes out a couple of years after the original picture, the fortunes of the sequel diminish. We were trying our best to persuade Eleanor to go ahead and write the sequel. Historically, the sequel would guarantee about 50 percent of the original gross; but, historically, sequels on musicals do less well.

What made this a little bit different is, of course, the fine perform- ance of the picture. It was also an extraordinary foreign success, $110 million. In Germany and Switzerland alone it did $40 million. It did $64 million in the U.S. and Canada, so foreign was nearly double. That argued for a sequel no matter what, even if music sequels traditionally do a third of the original performance. We knew that the production cost would be higher, from a marketing point of view, there was just no question. The sequel was a foregone conclusion; it was just a matter of when.

We had the option of asking another writer to do the sequel if Eleanor turned it down, which she ultimately did in February of 1988. She said she'd be prepared to do it in January of 1989 but not before then. We then did two things—we hired another writer to begin writing the sequel and I decided it was worth proposing to the company that we embark on a television series."

TV Series

Cannold: "I thought I could sell a 'Dirty Dancing' television series and I wanted to go to a producer I was familiar with, someone I thought could get it on the air. That was Steve Tisch.

I'd known Steve for twenty years. He's done excellent work in television, including movies of the week like 'Burning Bed,' and series like 'Call to Glory.' So I went to Steve and he and I together developed it and sold it to CBS. We got an on-air commitment for thirteen weeks, half-hours, which began in September and recently went on hiatus.

"The ratings were only fair. While it was CBS' strongest show on Saturday night, CBS numbers have generally been relatively poor this season. These were, too. They were the best of the worst, but they were still weak.

"I won't affect the sequel. The DIRTY DANCING franchise seems to have nine lives. Many of us were very skeptical about the Dirty Dancing Concert Tour. We thought it was a marketing exercise that would destroy the integrity of the movie. We perceived it to be wholly exploitive and without any redeeming value, that would destroy the potential for a sequel. Many in the company, excluding me, believed that the TV series would also hurt. DIRTY DANCING is a fascinating marketing research subject because it has spawned perhaps more different by-products in every media than any other movie in history. What other picture had a concert tour? What other picture had a television series and also will soon have a sequel? What other picture is responsible for prom dresses, bicycles (Toys "R" Us) or two albums? It's spawned absolutely every single kind of endeavor, more than any movie ever has."

Dirty Dancing II

Cannold: "The script is being written, it will be shot in August. The sequel will be released in the summer of '90. Every expectation is that both Grey and Swayze will be in it. They won't commit fully until they read the final script, but they have been consulted on the story that we're writing. We've been negotiating with them for some time and I have every reason to believe that they'll want to do it.

"I suspect that one of the things that came out of it, much the result of Austin Furst's philosophy about making movies, is that at the time that we decide to make a move we also contemplate what the imagery is that we'll use to sell it. When we sit in a green-light meeting, the kind of meetings that occur in any company, we do something that probably no other company does. Before there's even any cast or director attached, we discuss what the imagery is, what the audience for the movie is, how it will be positioned, how it will be marketed, and even perhaps develop some preliminary campaign. So we're looking at what the concept is, at the audience's point of view of the film. We have spent maybe a couple of hundred thousand dollars acquiring a screenplay. This approach is probably unique in the movie business.

"This marketing technique certainly began with DIRTY DANC-ING. It didn't start there for a lot of people, but it may have started there for Vestron because it was our first picture. It's Austin's influence. It sometimes throws writers and producers and directors who may be tangentially a part of that process when we say to them early on, 'What's the image on the one-sheet? What's the image in the ad? What's the key art?' And they look at us as if to say, 'Ask me that in a year?' And yes, we will, but chances are if we don't make them think about it in the beginning, a year later they won't be any closer to a point of view than they were when the question was first asked. Now we ask it of ourselves and we ask it of them right when we begin. We may not always be right, and by the time the picture is finished it may be somewhat different than what we expected to get.

"I have a meeting to green-light three more movies this week. I have invited the head of distribution of the company to the meeting because she's read the screenplays and I'd like her to express how she'll sell each picture and what the audience is from her point of view. Because ultimately she has to sell it. She's my partner and if she doesn't join me in this endeavor from the beginning, its not a road I want to go down.

"Bill Quigley had a tremendous amount of guts. Bill's decision was truly, in some sense a $50 million call, because it was his decision to release nationally. He had the confidence in the picture. He was in way over his head. He was eager to take the risk. Just as I was in way over my head and eager to take the risk. Up until that point I had shared responsibility for $2 million movies. Up to that point we hadn't released a thing. And he just smelled it. His instincts were right. He took the risk, he fought to go national and he won. He deserves all the credit in the world for that."

Why Success?

Reuther: "It had that intangible thing. It was satisfying picture. It was a story set in a specific time period in the United States and specific cultural segment. The element of the haves and the have-nots is a universal theme—the rich girl, poor boy."

Cannold: "Beyond the Sunday *Times* article, which I consider a key launching platform for the picture; and then the cast, which satis-fied; and then the music; the next most important element was the opening that Greenberg did. It was a brilliant conceptual way to start the picture and required people to immediately get into the vocabulary of the film. It slowed them down because it was done in slow motion. It made them stare at the images, it made them forget about what was happening with the babysitter at home or whether the popcorn was any good. It immediately grabbed their attention and sucked them into the first couple of minutes of the movie, so that once we got into the story we already had the total attention of the audience. We weren't waiting for the first few minutes to gradually have people segue into joining the story of the picture. The filmmakers felt it was banging the audiences over the head, that it was coming on a little bit to strong right at the beginning.

"I think that the opening added $10 million to the performance of the picture.

"What Richard was very careful about, what he knew he had to do, was to tease the audience, not give the dancing away. That is why, first, it's in super slow motion and, second, the images are nonspecific—you never see who the cast is. You don't see the principals, you see the background dancers. Finally, it was done in a style that teased the audience with a sense of what they were going to get.

Senk: "It's become a worldwide phenomenon. We still get phone calls. People now write about the story of the phenomenon of DIRTY DANCING. *Newsweek* did a piece about the phenomenon. A guy just called one day and said this was a real phenomenon. We found this woman in Detroit who had lost all this weight because she had seen the movie so much. A guy from Boston called, some guy's daughter has watched the cassette 9 million times and he wanted to do a television piece on it. It became a phenomenon. It's hard to say why.

"Some of it is because of the film, some of it is because of Patrick Swayze. It becomes a phenomenon and it takes over.

"People from the ages of ten to ninety love this movie. They are even making trips down to the set now. It's like Mecca. People are dancing on the steps where Jennifer does 'Wipeout.' They take their video cameras and shoot home movies. It's insane."

Peckos: "I wasn't sure about it until I saw the movie. I walked out thinking it's really a great, fun, fun film. It's an audience film."

VIDEO

VIDEO

"There are really two businesses in video."

Video

For most feature films, video is an aftermarket. Films garner most of their attention and public awareness from marketing campaigns during their theatrical release. The video distributor amplifies this awareness and continues with the theatrical campaign primarily to entice video wholesalers to buy cassettes for their retailers, who in turn rent or sell them to consumers. The video campaign will focus on the video trade, letting them know the video is coming out, and the consumers, telling them to go into the stores and rent or buy it.

This section will not only address the marketing of feature films but moreover the marketing of specialty, nontheatrical titles: those videos that have not had a pre existing theatrical exposure. By this fact alone, original video programs are distinguished from films released on video.

But first, some background to give you a better sense of the market environment into which you sell your video programs.

Statistics

Half the 88 million U.S. homes have VCRs. This will increase to 70 percent by the early 1990s. In 1987 there were 54.7 million VCR households. By year's end 1988 there should be 59.4 million VCR homes.

221

Remarkable as it may seem, only 30 percent of all VCR owners have ever purchased a tape. Most use the machine to time-shift: record their favorite programs for playback later.

The Two Businesses

There are really two businesses in video. There is the rental business where tapes are rented to consumers. And there is the "sell-through" business where, like books or records, consumers buy tapes for ownership. At the wholesale level in 1987 the sell-through business was $2 billion.

PRERECORDED HOME VIDEO
Ratio of Rental to Sales Dollars at Retail

Year	Rental	Sales	Total (Billions)
1986	68%	32%	$ 5.4
1987	61	39	7.2
1988	58	42	8.7
1989	55	45	9.8
1990	54	46	10.5

Source: Vidmar Communications Inc, Hollywood, CA

The video business is a two-step transaction. A manufacturer/supplier (e.g., CBS/Fox, Vestron) sells to a wholesaler/distributor (e.g., Commtron), who in turn sells to a video retailer. There are twenty-five to thirty independent wholesalers selling to 25,000 video stores. The wholesalers get 40 percent off the list price. They resell at 28–30 percent off to the retailer, keeping 10–12 percent to cover their overhead and profit.

Most video programs released on cassette are <u>in search of a market</u>. Many never find their audience and are returned to the supplier by the retailers and wholesalers for credit.

Total retail sales have grown from $810 million in 1985 to $3.3 billion in 1987. In 1987 combined rental and retail sales were $7 billion. Some think this will reach $10 billion in 1990. By 1992 it is expected to hit nearly $11 billion. By this time the studios share of revenues will be a tad under 40 percent.

At the wholesale level in 1987, 60 million units were sold worth $1.1 billion. In 1988, it is anticipated that 87 million units worth $1.5 billion will be sold. And in 1989 total sales are expected to be $1.8 billion.

Sell-through represents only 27 percent of manufacturer's revenue. This is expected to rise to 35 percent in 1989, representing a growth of 55 percent.

The mix of programs is 70 percent theatrical features, 16 percent specialty video and the 14 percent balance is adult, music video, etc. Of 25,000 video titles listed, over 40 percent are from smaller video suppliers (who publish one to five titles). Most reach institutions and consumers through direct marketing.

The Fairfield Group, a Connecticut marketing research firm, reported that in 1987 the average VCR family made fifty-six trips to the video store.

Of the 40,000 to 50,000 new book titles published each year only a few are successful. The home video industry publishes about 6,000 new theatrical and nontheatrical titles per year or about 500 per month. The genres break down accordingly:

Category	1987 Share	1990 Share
Features	65%	70%
Children's	24	15
Exercise	6	6
Music	1	3
Other	4	6

Seventy-five percent of all video specialty stores are independently owned mom-and-pop stores.

Forty percent of prerecorded video unit sales are to non-video specialty retailers such as mass merchants, toy stores, grocery and convenience stores, drugstores, bookstores and record stores. More units will sell in the future through these outlets.

Other new markets for videos include over 6,000 public libraries. Here, over 50 percent of the video collections are nontheatrical. The average purchase is about $8,000 per year.

VIDEO ISSUES

The Rental Market: Breadth vs. Depth

One of the major issues in the video business today that affects everyone from the retailer through the video supplier and producer is the *breadth vs. depth* issue. Most video stores buy multiple copies of a hit title like BACK TO THE FUTURE or E.T. so that they will have enough copies on hand to meet the demand of all their customers who want to rent these tapes. This is called "depth"—they stock a title in depth. The limited dollars they have to spend go to a few new titles because they buy them in depth and not breadth.

The main competitors to the video rental stores are the burgeoning new outlets of drugstores and 7-11s and other convenience stores. They also buy in depth. They, in essence, have the same hit titles that the video rental store has, the only difference being that they rent their tapes for significantly less. Their logic is that once they get people to come into their stores (once to rent the tape and once to return the tape), they may also buy a loaf of bread and a carton of milk while they are there. The convenience store can afford to rent tapes as loss-leaders in order to build customer traffic. Because of their lower prices and because they have the same titles, the nearby video store starts to lose customers. How can it compete?

The answer is with "breadth"—the video store can stock more titles so that the customer has a greater variety to choose from. The convenience store does not have the space to stock a great number of titles. Here's where the video store can find a competitive edge.

The new "superstores" carry 12,000 to 15,000 titles. This breadth is significant and is great news for the video customer who has seen all the hit titles and now wants to see something else.

Depth of copy is having enough copies for rental. Breadth of copy is having more different titles (like a library) to compete with the 7-11 down the street. Depth of copy only works for the short term. Because most video stores are concerned with having enough copies of a single title (depth of copy), the wholesaler's sales force focuses most of their attention on selling the blockbuster titles. And even though there are 500 titles released each month (including many nontheatrical titles), most retailers deliberate over thirty or forty titles and buy far less. This phenomenon has given rise to the increase in sales of the "A" hit titles and a great falling off of sales on the "B," "C" and "D" titles. Consequently many suppliers of these low-end titles are losing customers and profits. The result is that the suppliers of "A" titles (the studios) are gaining market share and clout while the smaller guys are losing their toehold. Without a market for "B" titles, smaller producers and suppliers are in trouble.

There are various new schemes in the works which allow video retailers to buy videos in depth and then return them to the wholesalers after a few months for credit. It is too early to know whether these attempts at getting more product into the stores at lower cost will actually work.

Hopefully the video stores will realize that they must carry both the hit titles and lesser titles (depth and breath) in order to keep hard-earned customers returning to their stores. If the video retail stores try to go head-to-head with the convenience stores on the "A" titles, they may very well lose.

Video Sales

There are two markets: rental and sales. The video stores are "rent-ailers," not "retailers." They do not really put much effort into selling videos. Consequently, when people decide they want to own a videotape they go to where they know they can buy it—the book store or mass merchant. Since their local video store has gone to little or no effort to let customers know that it sells tapes, customers go elsewhere to buy them. The video store loses a sale. This should not be happening, but video stores have failed miserably in participating in the sell-through business—something that should come very naturally to them.

Are there other businesses that a video store could learn from? Yes. The tuxedo shop. When I go to rent a tux I know that, should I ever want to buy one, I can go back to the same store to do so. Why? Because the salesperson tells me that, because there are brochures on the counter, and because there are tuxedos on display with price tags. In the video store one is hard pressed to find tapes that are priced to sell. In my local video store the only tapes that are priced are the handful under the glass counter. It is very strange that a video store will go to enormous lengths with posters and newspaper ads to let customers know their rental prices, but most people would never suspect that they can also buy tapes there as well. This is a lost opportunity for the video store.

Shelf Space

Even with video stores sitting on the sidelines and not selling video, the sell-through market is growing enormously. In 1988 about 42 million tapes went into the rental pipeline and another 87 million into the sell-through market (thanks to E.T. and CINDERELLA). According to Paul Kagan's Report, videos that came into the marketplace by nontraditional (non–video store) means accounted for $62 million. It is anticipated that by 1992 nearly 200 million videos will be sold. While the volume of product increases, the money per tape returned to the supplier will decline from $11 average to about $8.72 average.

With more and more activity at the sell-through level there will be greater competition for shelf space. Already more than 30 percent of the sell-through product is priced at $19.95; prices will continue to drop in the rush to compete. More tapes will be sold, but each tape will return less profit to the supplier and everyone else down the line.

Special Interest

Most small video stores carry very little special-interest video. The larger superstores do carry video. It is really the other sell-through and alternative markets that handle nontheatrical programs. National Geographic Video, for example, ships fifty percent to the video market and fifty percent to the alternative markets during a tape's initial release. Within six months, however, the mix becomes seventy-thirty or eighty-twenty because the alternative non-video

outlets continue to place orders. Why? Because they are selling tapes and need more. The video retailer no longer pays attention to backlisted titles and is onto the next batch of hot "A" titles to be rented.

MARKET TRENDS

Fewer Wholesalers

With the number of video stores holding steady (or even falling somewhat), the video rental store market has plateaued. As a consequence of this and other factors, many suppliers have cut down on the number of wholesalers that service their product. This cutback gives the remaining wholesalers more power and a greater territorial reach. The wholesalers who have been dropped must either find other lines to carry or go out of business. This lack of strong product for smaller wholesalers may suggest that nontheatrical product will begin to get more of their attention. If wholesalers cannot get movie product, they may opt for specialty video. The future will tell. This still doesn't mean, however, that they can sell it to their video store accounts who are still focused on "A" movie titles.

Pricing

On major "A" titles, the pricing has headed upward to $89 and $99. Why? Why not? The video stores want the "A" titles and buy them in depth. The suppliers figure they can sell the same number of copies at a higher price. Because of the fixed number of video stores (and few new store openings), the number of units shipped on an "A" rental title has plateaued out at around 250,000. By raising the price, suppliers can capture more dollars; although this takes more money out of the market for other "A" and "B" titles. It is expected that the trend toward higher prices for rental titles will continue.

Advertising

Retailers are demanding that video suppliers commit to significant consumer television advertising to help pull people into the stores to rent. There is also greater emphasis on in-store merchandising (posters, stand-ups, special offers) to push "A" titles, which the suppliers must provide if they are to continue to get the stores' support.

Sponsorship

TOP GUN, PLATOON and DIRTY DANCING all had major sponsors participating in marketing and cross-promotions. Other major sponsors will follow with titles that are perceived as appropriate.

Alternate Retailers

Specialty video has been the little brother to features in the video store. There are now more and more retail outlets that carry specialty video. Hardware stores, drugstores, gardening stores, maternity shops, gift stores and health food stores are just a few of the kinds of retail stores that now carry video. Videocassette sales to video stores (by the wholesaler) on a single title last for only about six weeks. This is the period when the suppliers and wholesalers are really pushing it. Once that period is over, their marketing effort moves on to other product. Specialty product, by its very nature, has a longer life and is back-ordered by the new alternative outlets.

Video Clubs

Video clubs continue to do a brisk business. CBS, Time-Life, and Reader's Digest have sold through clubs for years. National Geographic has just begun to sell its line of videos directly to its membership in a video club format. More video clubs will spring up.

VIDEO PRODUCT

There are two markets for video product. Each market can have different program content and price. Each market also has a very different definition of the business. The two markets are the <u>rental market</u> and the <u>sell-through market</u>.

The rental market is designed for quick turnover. Tapes are sold to the video stores at high prices. The consumer only wants to see these tapes once and then return them. The focus is on movies.

The success of the sell-through market demonstrates that people want to own *some* tapes. The old adage about a tape having to be "repeatable"—that for people to buy it a tape must contain information or exercises that are to be repeated—no longer holds true. The retail price for video tapes now approaches that of records, CDs and books. People want to buy tapes because they want to own them. They want to have them and be able to watch them whenever they like. They want to collect them. And like books, they may be watched once or twice or not at all. There is a pride of ownership and the thought that "I'll buy this tape because someday I *may* want to watch it."

The markets where tapes are sold are video rental stores, mass merchants, bookstores, toy stores, convenience stores, sports stores, through direct mail and direct response television.

Home videos are packaged goods like soap. Sales are affected by pricing and advertising like packaged goods. Tapes have a perceived value. Unlike books, you cannot preview a tape. So the sales promise delivered through packaging is vitally important.

PROGRAM GENRES

Like books and movies, videotapes also come in various genres, cover different themes and are intended for different audiences. In special-interest video, the most popular genres are:

Kids

There is a resurgence in children's video (and children's books as well). The baby boomers who grew up in the TV generation now have kids. It's not surprising that they are willing to buy great numbers of tapes to both entertain and educate their children. Prices are generally $29.95 and less. Lorimar tried low pricing (in the $10–15 range) a few years back, but it didn't work. There was not enough margin for the seller. The result was that high volumes of tapes were pushed into the market but then came back as heavy returns. Lorimar posted a $31 million loss as a result of returns from the mass market retailers.

In the children's video field the top players are Disney, Disney and Disney. With such a wonderful franchise and respected name this is no surprise. They are also very good at marketing. The other players who are trying to get a foothold and have children's lines include A&M (distributed by Crown Publishers), Best Film & Video, Celebrity Home Entertainment, Family Home Entertain-

ment, Kids Klassics, Price/Stern/Sloan, Random House, Scholastic, Sony, Vestron and Western Publishing.

For a while in the children's video business the push was toward recognizable, licensed characters drawn mostly from off-network television. However, the acquisition costs for such well-known characters as Barbie and Captain Power (Mattel) were exorbitant ($2 million) and didn't pay off. The trend has been a return to well-known, classic stories. It is mostly children who recognize the names of the hot television characters. But it is parents and grandparents who make the purchase decisions. Classic names and well-known hosts or narrators are more likely to capture parents' attention and dollars. Videos that are presently in the marketplace, and rely less on hot, licensed names are Raffi (a concert tape), Bible Stories, tapes with holiday themes (Christmas, Easter, Halloween), animal themes (dinosaurs), Velveteen Rabbit, exercise for kids, Paddington Bear, Aesop's Fables, Mr. Magoo, Berenstein Bears, combined book and video series, animated features (with narration by Robin Williams, Meryl Streep, etc.) and Beatrix Potter stories. These classic characters have a much longer shelf life and are better known by the purchasing audience.

The best environment for licensed characters are toy stores which are visited by kids and parents alike. Most licensed characters tend to die in about eighteen months. It's a video buyer's nightmare to predict who the hot new characters are going to be and put up six- and seven-figure advances. The toy companies have been in a slump over the last two years, in part because they have misjudged the marketplace—spending millions on development, production, advertising and marketing, only to find their best shots didn't work.

The industry leaders of just a few years ago—Coleco, Mattel and Worlds of Wonder—have been particularly hard hit.

In 1986 about 9 percent of the wholesaler's video dollars came from children's video. In 1987 it went up to about 13 percent. Most tapes sell for $19 and under and are generally one hour in length.

Golf

Golf is the new hot category. By the time you read this everyone who has ever taught a golf workshop will have a tape out. Unlike most categories, golf tapes are not price sensitive. A dedicated golfer will pay almost anything to knock a few strokes off his or her game. Nearly half of the tapes released are at $29.95 or higher. Even the comedy tape DORF ON GOLF from J2 Communications sold 200,000 units. A golf sequel is in the works.

Exercise

Exercise represents 3 percent of all videos sold and 2 percent of the wholesaler's dollars. Seven Jane Fonda tapes sold a combined 1.1 million units in 1987. Four million Fonda tapes were sold through early 1988.

Many thought that Fonda's domination of the exercise category would keep out all other competitors, but JCI Video committed an extended marketing push to newcomer Kathy Smith. Her three tapes sold nearly half a million units, grossing over $8 million. CAL-LANETICS, based on the best-selling book, also sold nearly half a million units.

Documentaries

Everyone always speaks highly of documentaries, but when it comes time to watch them on television, those who spoke the loudest are always watching something else. This mentality carried over to documentaries in home video. In the beginning, only exploitative MONDO CANE–like documentaries were released. No one thought quality documentaries would sell.

When I was at Vestron I spent over a year trying to convince National Geographic and Vestron to release these television specials on video. The marketing folks' opinion was reflected in the question: "Who would want to rent or buy these programs when all

they have to do is tape them off television?" The sales and marketing people projected 3,000 units per program. My feeling was that
National Geographic was something special and that if packaged in
the familiar yellow box, people would want to own them. Think
about the magazine—it's impossible to throw issues away. People
collect them. (I actually think collecting *National Geographic* magazines is genetic—part of our DNA!) I thought people would collect
the videos as well. After all, here's a name that we've all grown up
with, that implies quality, and that leads the viewer to an expectation of outstanding photography, music and narration. As of this
writing nearly thirty National Geographic titles have sold over a
million units. It is the most successful documentary video series
ever. The best-selling titles are in the 25,000- to 50,000-unit range, a

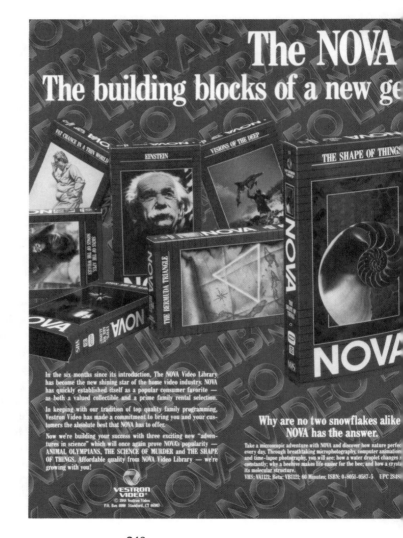

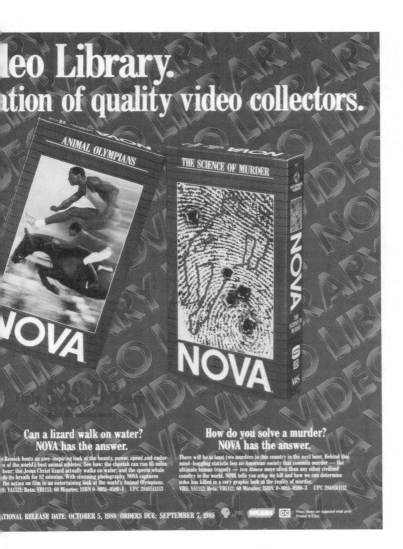

leo Library.
ation of quality video collectors.

ANIMAL OLYMPIANS

THE SCIENCE OF MURDER

NOVA

NOVA

Can a lizard walk on water?
NOVA has the answer.

Remick hosts an awe-inspiring look at the beauty, power, speed and endur- e of the world's best animal athletes. See how; the cheetah can run 65 miles hour; the Jesus Christ lizard actually walks on water; and the sperm whale ds its breath for 82 minutes. With stunning photography, NOVA captures the action on film in an entertaining look at the world's Animal Olympians.
S: VA1113; Beta: VB1113; 60 Minutes; ISBN 0-8051-0589-1   UPC 28485I1113

How do you solve a murder?
NOVA has the answer.

There will be at least two murders in this country in the next hour. Behind this mind-boggling statistic lies an American society that commits murder — the ultimate human tragedy — *ten times* more often than any other civilized country in the world. NOVA tells you *why* we kill and how we can determine *who* has killed in a very graphic look at the reality of murder.
VHS: VA1112; Beta: VB1112; 60 Minutes; ISBN: 0-8051-0588-3   UPC 28485I1112

TIONAL RELEASE DATE: OCTOBER 5, 1988 ORDERS DUE: SEPTEMBER 7, 1988

long way from the 3,000-unit projections. Nick Noxon's National Geographic special: THE SECRETS OF THE TITANIC—which *premiered* on home video before television—sold 150,000 units the day the video shipped.

Because of the success of this "quality programming," I also acquired the TV series NOVA, Smithsonian Video and Audobon Video. Other suppliers have been scooping up whatever else is available. Pacific Arts and Warners had Cousteau, but now it's with Kodak, which is also producing a new Smithsonian series and a new Audobon. Lorimar has NATURE. Vestron recently picked up COSMOS. NOVA has sold about 10,000 units each in its initial three-title release, with half that amount going to Walden Books for sell-through.

The advantage to these series is that they are kept alive through ongoing release and promotion, something that cannot happen to a single documentary. Most other non-series quality documentaries lacking a promotable trademark or cachet are lucky to sell 3,000 units.

Mythologist Joseph Campbell's THE POWER OFMYTH with Bill Moyers, from Mystic Fire Video, was first broadcast on PBS. Campbell's books *Hero with a Thousand Faces* and *The Power of Myth* sprang onto the bestseller lists. As a video consultant for Mystic Fire I tried to interest video companies who marketed quality programs in handling the series. No one was interested. Old theories echoed: "No one knows who Campbell is." "It's free on PBS." Mystic Fire ended up selling the six-volume series themselves through print and a direct mail campaign. They are approaching sales of 30,000 units of the $149.95 set. A very respectable number.

Sports

There is a burgeoning market for collectible sports tapes—not how-to's, but compilations of highlights and big sports events. One of the most successful releases was for a videotape which was given away as a sales premium. If you signed up for a subscription to *Sports Illustrated* you got a tape. They gave away 600,000 cassettes or more (with new subscriptions). With a promotional giveaway, the producers of the tape never needed to go through any of the traditional

channels. Assuming they sold the tapes to *Sports Illustrated* for $2 per tape above duplication cost, they grossed $1.2 million, less their production budget. Not bad for home video. Although these deals don't come along every day, it's certainly a marketing approach that can be replicated.

Sports tapes can also sell very well on a regional basis. Since local fans are the prime buyers of these tapes, a producer need only

market them regionally to have a hit. THE CHICAGO BEARS SHUFFLE (a music video featuring the team) started the trend by shipping over 200,000 units in the Chicago area in 1986.

Vestron followed with LET'S GO METS—a music video and behind-the-scenes documentary (structured like Michael Jackson's THRILLER video) and sold over 60,000 videos and 10,000 copies of the record in New York, New Jersey and Connecticut alone in 1986 as the Mets made their climb to the World Series.

The same year a Mets compilation from Rainbow Home Video sold 120,000 units and grossed $1.5 million. The 1988 Redskins Super Bowl video was sold a few weeks after the game and sold 70,000 units. The 1988 Dodgers tape was also sold everywhere and certainly garnered big numbers.

By now the teams have come to expect greater participation and up-front payments than before. The deals are becoming increasingly difficult to make. Still, every year there will be one or two teams worthy of a best-selling sports video. The only question is: Who will it be this year? The investor who doesn't answer that question right is going to go belly up.

Comedy

When I joined Vestron my mandate was to find new programming areas for home video. Comedy was a natural. Very entertaining tapes could be produced for very little money. They were good rental fare and we hoped, like albums, there could be some sell-through revenues. HBO (and occasionally Showtime) did comedy specials and showed no interest in ancillary home video rights, so I frequently made deals with HBO or the comics' agents to acquire the video rights in these comedy specials. For about two years Vestron was the comedy leader with tapes from Robin Williams, Whoopi Goldberg, Billy Crystal, Joe Piscopo, George Carlin, Father Guido Sarducci, Robert Klein, Bob Goldthwait, Steven Wright,

Steve Martin, Richard Pryor and many others. Vestron sold the tapes to the rental market at $59 retail.

It didn't take long for Paramount and then the newly founded HBO Video to go to school on these successes and compete with me in the marketplace. Prices began to escalate now that there were more suitors for the programs. It became much more difficult to do these shows. At the same time, retail prices for tapes were falling and Vestron's competitors were selling comedy tapes at $29 instead of $59. This made it more and more difficult to make the economics work and Vestron acquired fewer comedy tapes. Now the leaders in comedy are Paramount, Warner, HBO and Vestron.

The video business is very competitive. Whenever anyone has a nontheatrical hit, the other companies are quick to follow with their own versions within that genre.

Music

Music is a very difficult area because the record companies hold very tight reins on any audio or video product their artists may create. Unless the video company and record company are related at the corporate level, it is very difficult for an independent video label to get the video rights to music videos. The record companies are particularly cautious about licensing music video rights to a hot act when they have the record rights. They are afraid that a video may cannibalize on the record revenues by drawing attention away from the audio-only product. Even when an independent (non–record company associated) video supplier did get the rights and come out with a music video, there was usually little coordination between the record company and the video company at a time when—for both their sakes—they should have been working together. (This has begun to change somewhat.)

Equally frustrating is that the largest consumers of music—teenagers—do not have ready access to VCRs (they are usually under the control of their parents) nor do they have the money to plunk down for videos, except perhaps the current big acts. Then there is MTV: You can see videos all day long for free. Why buy them?

Many of the video companies that advanced large sums for the hot new acts lost money. The only music video format that began to gain sales success was classic rock and MOR (middle of the road) music video. This music appealed to ages 30 and above who also had the money for nostalgia programs. Vestron successfully sold music videos from Neil Diamond, Dick Clark (BEST OF BANDSTAND) and Liberace. Other suppliers also packaged their own compilations of classic music.

The genres above are generally the most successful in home video today. My book, *Home Video: Producing for the Home Market*, goes into much greater detail about video genres and programming opportunities than is possible here.

THE BUYERS: THE VIDEO FOOD CHAIN

"Your video has to make it through the bottleneck of the hourglass."

The Video Food Chain

The problem with specialty video is not that there are too few good ideas, but that there is too much product in search of a market.

A little visualization to prove a point: Imagine an hourglass. At the top you have thousands of video producers and suppliers pouring in product. In the middle you have wholesalers, telemarketers and retail stores each selecting a small percentage of tapes for sale to the next buyer in the chain. At the very bottom of the hourglass you have millions of people with VCRs picking out a very small percentage of the total number of tapes released. If you want your tape to be successful, you must understand the psychology and methods by which tapes are bought and sold in the video food chain. You have to make it through the bottleneck of the hourglass.

Most producers do not stop to think about this. <u>There is more than one buyer.</u> The consumer is only the buyer at the end of the chain. Yes, these people need to be identified. Yes, you need to know their tastes and what they'll spend on a video program. You need to make a list of all the potential classes of customers and get a real feel for whether there are enough buyers to warrant spending production money on a program. But there are also several other buyers between you and the consumer who can make or break you.

CLASSES OF BUYERS

First is the video trade. The manufacturer/program supplier acquires or produces the program and sells it to the wholesaler/distributor, who sells it to the retailer, who in turn sells it to the consumer. If you don't get to the first buyer—who sells it to the next buyer—you are dead in the water.

The video supplier/manufacturer has very specific needs and an agenda that is unknown to producers. More often than not the supplier/manufacturers (CBS, Vestron, Paramount, Lorimar, J2) have some sort of strategy and idea about who they are, how they want to compete in the market, what kind of product they plan to release and when, etc. There are specific markets that they have decided to target and other markets they are just testing. There will also be markets they've consciously decided not to pursue, and other markets they are overlooking. Although this is information they will not readily give you, you somehow have to sort through what they tell you, what others tell you about them, what you read in the trades, and what you can glean in meetings to get an overall perspective on the appropriateness and effectiveness of the supplier/manufacturer.

To be successful in licensing your program to a program supplier it is vitally important that you know <u>who they sell to</u>. Without this knowledge you have no real way to evaluate them. <u>Producers love to think that their manufacturer will sell to "everybody." Not so.</u>

A consumer will only buy your program when he or she knows about it. To get them to that point, they must receive several positive impressions about your program so that it reaches their awareness and they want to rent or buy it. You must create some kind of buzz and excitement about your program through advertising and publicity. But prior to that you must produce and package your program with elements that will entice the potential buyer and provide some perceived value. Your program must fill some need in the consumer. There must be some reason why they want your program and it must deliver on their expectations.

It would be time well spent if the producer prepared his or her own two-step marketing plan that addressed potential buyers—a kind of strategy on setting out. The first step is to identify the program suppliers who would be right for a specific program. The producer can look at the current release schedules of program suppliers (which can be found in wholesalers' monthly catalogs and mailers) as well as their backlisted product. After this research, a question well worth asking is: *Does my program fall into the category that they manufacture and sell?*

The second step is to strategize how the program can be sold to the retailer and consumer. This, of course, is not your job; however, this mental exercise will help you pitch ideas to manufacturers—your prospective buyers. It may just push them into making a decision to finance or buy your program. Of course their job is to enhance, modify and then execute a marketing plan that gets your product into the marketplace. Anything you can do to make their job easier will pay off dividends when it comes to pitching and selling. You will also learn, by their response to your ideas, about how they would approach the selling of your program. It gives you something which will elicit a conversation that will give you insight into how they think and operate. You will leave with a more substantial impression of the job they might do with your program. That's why it's so important to have some insight into how video programs are sold within the trade itself.

The Mechanics and Mystery of Selling

As much as you may like to, you won't be holding your video's hand through every level of distribution. Since you won't be there to explain, the program's accompanying sales material must be strong enough to survive the inevitable reinterpretation along the selling path.

As you work with your concept and begin developing your ideas, find the most appealing elements (genre, title, stars, story, etc.) that will <u>entice all buyers</u>: the video distributor/wholesaler and the consumer. Find the most compelling way to design and present these ideas. It could be through artwork, copy, a verbal pitch or a combination of all three. Video distributors don't have a lot of time to spend with you or your program to "get it." The program must grab them immediately. (This is even more true of the consumer, who may glance at a video magazine ad for a few seconds! How are you going to get their attention?)

There are elements required to sell each level of buyer. Video companies are looking for broad appeal. Exercise is now a broad genre. The broad appeal may come through the inherent quality or name of the program's producer (e.g., National Geographic).

Three video companies are now interested in financing and distributing the following program. It takes about three minutes to hit the most appealing elements and give them a handle on the program. Notice how most of the items have more to do with marketing than programming. (The pitch is *less about* the program's creative potential and *more about* how they can sell it.)

Here are the notes that I used in my pitch. (I try to engage them in a conversation about the program and elicit questions and their response. I do not simply blast through these topics but use them as jumping-off points for discussion. The more your buyer participates, the more interested they are, and the more interested they are, the more involved they get. Then the idea becomes theirs and you are on your way to a sale.)

HOME PLANET: Pitch Notes

• A thirty-minute video which compiles U.S. and never-seen-before Soviet space footage and gives the home viewer an experiential trip to space and back. The viewer is joined by the world's cosmonauts and astronauts via their reflections and reenactments of the actual words they spoke on their space travels.

• Program is based on a book (edited and created by Kevin Kelley) which will be released Christmas 1988. The book was produced with the cooperation of the Association of Space Explorers—men and women from seventeen countries. The program engenders goodwill with the Soviets, glasnost, opportunity and international cooperation in the exploration of space.

• HOME PLANET is featured on the cover of *Life* magazine's November 1988 issue, which includes an eight-page pictorial feature with text. The video packaging can utilize the book cover and graphics which have already been widely seen on *Life* and on the book.

• The book is a co-publishing venture between Addison Wesley and a Soviet publisher. It is being published in seven countries. It is their big Christmas book. In the U.S. they've printed 360,000 copies and are going back to another printing. In the U.K. there were 54,000 pre-orders, which is a huge number there.

• The video will be structured like a space flight—beginning with preflight anxieties, moving to the launch itself, then moments in space, reflections and finally the return home. The narration will consist of the actual words of international astronauts reenacted in voice-overs. There will be approximately seven selections of space music to underscore the dramatic content. The program promotes peace and an appreciation of the planet we live on. There should not be a dry eye in the audience at the end of the tape.

• Besides the international book push (and worldwide home video marketing tie-ins) there are numerous other opportunities. Several major U.S. museums want to present a HOME PLANET exhibit. This will expose HOME PLANET to another 5 million people.

(Tapes can be sold in museum gift shops before, during and after the exhibition.)

• HOME PLANET could be this decade's video equivalent of FAMILY OF MAN. It is an evergreen video—perfect for gift-giving, families and young explorers. It can be priced at $14.95–19.95.

• There are various television opportunities in the works which can boost awareness of the program.

• A possible release date might by December 1989, when the U.S. is planning to send the space telescope into orbit. Cosmonauts and astronauts are available to do talk-show tours, etc.

• Cousteau wrote the foreword for the book. His participation is being discussed but cannot be guaranteed.

The pitch to the manufacturer/supplier presented a title tie-in with an international book, product positioning in terms of audience and collectability, exhibit and television tie-ins, potential star host, tour opportunities, an appealing dramatic structure, a potential music album and a video release tie-in with a highly visible space launch.

I pitched these elements in bullet-point fashion, with just enough detail to let them know it was well thought out, yet not so much that they couldn't contribute ideas if they had them. I did much of their work for them. I wanted them to see that this program could be long lasting and have international appeal—they could make money with this video. I then followed up with the details: a copy of the book, a budget, schedules, sample footage, etc.

Results: Now the bad news. After pitching this project to four video suppliers they all passed. The first was interested for two months and then lost interest. They had overbought. The next two passed, one in two weeks, the other took a month. The first one, who had lost interest, called back all excited about the possibilities—then after another go-around passed again. The fourth was a two-day pass. If you're going to get a pass, I'd rather they come right away. The project did not have enough "heat" or appeal to interest these major and minor distributors. Other projects took my attention and I stopped pitching it for the time being. Meanwhile, the book continues to climb as a best-selling Christmas (1988) book. Obviously, the best time for the tape would have been right now. Often it may not be the idea itself—only bad timing. It's therefore useful not to close any doors. I suspect someone will come back and want to do this project.

About the same time, I was also consulting with a friend in marketing the Joseph Campbell series. Two major suppliers passed almost immediately. They didn't get who Campbell was or how to sell the tapes. They couldn't see that the fascination with his books would translate into tape sales. Now that the series has sold 100,000 units, I've had calls from one supplier saying, "Remember that tape you had a few months ago? We're very interested. What's happened to it?" What's happened to it is that they are too late—Mystic Fire, a tiny supplier, has a hit on their hands. So timing is also a factor you cannot predict.

Producers need to remember that they are pitching to marketers— not other producers. More of my pitch had to do with marketing since marketing is how the program will be sold. That's what they want to hear about. An unproduced program they like but cannot sell remains an unproduced program.

MANUFACTURER/SUPPLIER AS BUYER

There is some mystery to selling your programs. The mystery is: Who is the buyer? What company? Which person at that company? Who really makes the buying decision? How is it made? When you know these things you can tailor your pitch accordingly. You won't emphasize the wrong things or play down what might be the most appealing aspect of your project.

The Acquisition Maze

Here's how it usually works. First you call the receptionist at the distribution company and find out the name (and correct spelling) of the program development or program acquisition person. (Write down the name of the receptionist or secretary, so that the next time you call you can use his or her name. Establish a connection because that person is your link to everyone else. When you need help, guess who's going to either be there or not. (My secretary always told me when someone treated her shabbily. And believe me, that influenced how I felt about that person, regardless of how courteous they were to me.) Next, you ask to speak to the acquisition or development person.

The good news is that acquisition people want to buy product. They are predisposed to buying. That's their job. To keep their job they must buy. However, many are afraid to say yes (they don't want to make an expensive mistake), and they are also afraid to say no (for fear that your project will be the next "Jane Fonda"). In either case, and regardless of how busy they are—eventually—they'll talk to you.

This is your moment to establish a connection with the buyer. Even when they don't buy, if you are professional, courteous and leave a favorable impression, they'll be open to hearing from you again. If you are ill-prepared, waste their time, or your project is absolutely dreadful, you'll find it more difficult to see them next time around.

If they like your project and get enthusiastic about it, they'll meet with their sales and marketing department, who are rarely enthusiastic. But that's natural as it's much easier to buy product than to sell it. Every new program is another new problem for the sales and marketing staff. They're going to have to pull out all the stops to sell it down the line and, frankly, they'd rather have big movies, which are much easier to sell than original programs.

So now the going gets tough. The sales and marketing people will kick your idea around and try to answer the "how many" question. How many will it sell? What will we have to spend to sell it? Do we have any time to spend on this new product? Will it take time away from more lucrative and productive programs? If the sales staff determine that after all their effort there will be a profitable return, then they might recommend that the program be acquired. But wait…that's not all.

Their tempered enthusiasm about your program may be passed on to the president of the company. Even though the acquisition person and the sales and marketing team are behind the project, the president may be the final arbiter of whether the program is produced or acquired. After all, the president is responsible to a chairman or owner and possible stockholders for the bottom line. He or she will not want to make a mistake that will cause embarrassment or loss of profits.

So given the precarious journey your program has to travel, how do you get a yes? You must have something hot to sell.

The supplier/manufacturers are the most powerful of the buyers because they supply and control the product. The ten major companies or labels that dominate over 70 percent of the business are Paramount, CBS/Fox, RCA/Columbia, Warner, HBO, Disney, Vestron, MCA, MGM/UA, and Lorimar. Another 10 percent is controlled by Orion, Embassy, IVE, Nelson, Fries and Prism.

Okay, you've sold your program to a manufacturer/supplier. (See the chapter on "The Deal" for a breakdown of distribution contract terms.) Now it is their job to sell it to the wholesaler. Here's how it works.

WHOLESALER AS BUYER

First the manufacturer will have a sales staff meeting to determine the key marketing hooks and sales strategy for the program. They may or may not consider any marketing ideas that you have presented, depending on how good they think they are. After all, marketing is their job, so they will more likely come up with their own scenarios. Once the sales plan is worked out, they will put together a presentation and arrange meetings with their numerous wholesalers—the next buyers in the video food chain.

The meeting with the wholesaler may last twenty to forty minutes, during which the manufacturer will pitch the big movie titles first. This pitch may include eight to ten titles, a special promotion (like special pricing on a set of movies or kids programs), etc. The presentation will be less focused on individual titles (unless it is a major promotion like E. T. or CINDERELLA). Because time and attention are limited, the presentation will generally address an overall marketing campaign in which the wholesaler is being asked to participate. *The wholesaler is always listening for the answer to this question: How are you going to help me sell it?* (Interesting, isn't it? Everyone wants the other guy to help with the selling. Behind the initial buyer is another buyer with another buyer behind him.)

The wholesalers need selling materials and a supporting promotional campaign to implement your video's marketing plan. The message the supplier has to deliver to the wholesaler is that the sales campaign also includes trade and consumer ads, point-of-purchase (P.O.P.) displays, celebrity tours, in-store appearances, an attractive video package, sell sheets, ad mats, etc. This is all part of the supplier's marketing plan. By five o'clock, who knows whether the wholesaler will even remember your marketing plan. That is why it must be very strong and appealing—the wholesaler will present this plan to their sales staff in the next day or so. The wholesaler will remember the overall promotion and marketing campaign well after they've forgotten the specific title.

Let's say the wholesaler really liked the overall marketing and promotion campaign that the supplier laid out and said that yes, they'll support it. This is a different kind of yes than we've heard before. In essence, the wholesaler needs the supply of product from the manufacturer, so they're really not going to say no and cut off their supply. But they're going to be more enthusiastic about some programs than others, because they must resell this product to their own sales department. The supplier sells the wholesaler's management—people who aren't going to sell your product directly. That's the job of the wholesaler's sales staff and telemarketers.

To recap, the manufacturer/supplier sold the wholesaler buyer, who must now sell their own sales people and employees on how they can best move your product. (Remember also that the wholesaler handles hundreds and thousands of titles—mostly movies—from other supplier/manufacturers whose needs are the same as yours.) Other suppliers are also competing for the wholesaler's attention and sales effort with sales programs of their own. The wholesaler's sales staff are telemarketers who get on the phone and sell your program to retailers. The wholesaler/distributor is buying the program to resell to the retailer, which is done through telephone sales and by sending out thousands of sell sheets.

Wholesale Margins

Wholesalers buy at a 40 percent discount from retail list, which leaves them a 10–12 percent margin, often less. Book wholesalers have traditionally had a much greater discount (50–55 percent). At some point video publishers will need to offer greater discounts to compete with other kinds of products (books, toys, etc.). As duplication costs drop this may be more possible.

Who Are The Wholesalers?

There are about twenty major wholesaler/distributors such as Commtron, Baker and Taylor/Sound Video, Video Trend, Source, Win Records, Ingram, Artec, East Texas Periodicals, SBI Video and Metro, which serve 20,000 to 30,000 video stores. (See Appendix for addresses). Some of these also distribute to alternative outlets like bookstores (Walden Books), record stores (Tower, Wherehouse) and department stores.

Commtron is the largest video wholesaler with nearly a dozen branches around the U.S. They send a non-movie video catalog to 25,000 retailers and 15,000 non-video stores like sports stores and mass merchants. Video Trend sells to bookstores and libraries. East Texas Distributing has many branches and distributes to 200 supermarkets, bookstores and drugstores. Baker and Taylor, the parent of Sound/Video and VTR, are traditional video distributors and also one of the largest book distributors. They sell to bookstores, drugstores, video specialty stores, convenience stores and discount and department stores. ZBS is a traditional distributor and sells some nontheatrical product. Ingram's is the largest independent book distributor in the country. They sell to bookstore chains like Walden (and B. Dalton until they folded their video operation).

Distributors can also be "rack jobbers" who distribute to giant discount and mass merchant chains like Fedco, K-Mart, Walmart or Sears. The rack jobber comes in and sets up displays, stocks titles, refreshes product, provides promo material and P.O.P. material and generally tries to turn over and sell as much product as possible. These rack jobbers buy from wholesalers and sometimes have their own line of product.

The two giants are Handleman (Clawson, Michigan) and Lieberman Enterprises (Minneapolis, Minnesota). They do not manufacture or package but distribute finished goods with P.O.P. materials.

Special-Interest Distributors

There are also special-interest distributors who handle non-movie or alternative specialty video programs. Special-interest distributors who use catalogs to sell product are Videotakes in Red Banks, New Jersey; Video Collection (formerly Video School House) in Monterey, California; and Greenleaf Video in Santa Barbara, California. They distribute their catalogs widely. They stock videotapes and take orders. Some require that you pay to be included in their catalog, as well as offer them a healthy discount and supply them with the finished goods.

Videotakes sold 75,000 special-interest cassettes in 1985 and had revenues of $2.75 million. They sold 100,000 units worth $4 million in 1986 and doubled that the following year to 200,000 units worth $6 million. They have 2,500 titles from more than 200 different supplier/producers. They send their catalog to over 20,000 retail stores; about 80 percent of those are video specialty stores. They advertise and list an "800" number consumers call to get information on the nearest store.

The Retailer

There are many kinds of video retailers. The video specialty store is a retailer, or actually a "rent-ailer." They rent rather than sell videotapes. This retailer is usually an independently owned mom-and-pop video store. It could also be a retail chain of video stores. They are besieged by not only your wholesaler but at least another dozen or two. Most make sales calls. They all make phone calls and send sell sheets. Sometimes the retailer receives sell sheets from two or three or four different wholesalers all selling the same product. The only differences may be the price, the payment terms and promotional support. Wholesalers are very competitive with one another. Retailer buyers are being hit almost daily with different product. They don't have enough money to buy even one of each of the new 500 titles released each month. Their money must be spent trying to satisfy the rental customer. They gamble that every tape they buy customers will want to rent. Any tape that is not rented or that is rented infrequently is a loss of the retailer's investment.

There are big video chains such as Wherehouse, Erol's, RKO Warner Video Theaters, and Video Library which dominate the wholesale business regionally. The national chains are National Video, West Coast Video and Blockbuster Video. Convenience stores like Circle

K and 7-11 rent tapes to build traffic and do so at a loss. They offer lower rental prices than video stores.

There continue to be new outlets outside the traditional video channels opening all the time. They include department stores, gourmet shops, sports stores, health stores and others.

Toys "R" Us, a major retail chain, buys children's video directly from the manufacturer. By not going through a wholesaler they can pass along greater discounts to their customers. This gives them a big edge on their competition.

Record Stores

Wherehouse and Tower are the two largest chains that sell video. They do good cross-promotion and merchandising on video which they've learned from being successful record merchandisers. Because they are big and powerful they want generous margins and return privileges. They use lots of posters, banners and aisle ends to sell product. Video stores can take merchandising lessons on how to sell product from their cousins in the record business.

Bookstores

Bookstores sell features but they also sell many non-feature and alternative programs. Prices are at $29.95 and below. They do a good job of selling videos along with books of the same title. Many video titles are bought as gifts in bookstores. Walden carries a healthy stock of video. Independent bookstores are also starting to carry videos in limited numbers. Many sell video to their customers by direct mail.

Bookstores' book inventory is 10 percent fiction and 90 percent special interest. Walden Books says that 60 percent of bookstore purchases are made for gift-giving. The end-user is someone other than the buyer. It is much easier for a customer to buy a gift for a friend that addresses his or her special interest (sailing, golf, bridge, gardening) than it is to know their book tastes in fiction. It stands to reason that many special-interest video purchases will be for gift-giving.

The video Walden carries is now relegated to a "video ghetto." Customers who may be interested in special-interest video are not finding it on the special-interest shelves (where I believe it should be) because it is in a separate video section. As a customer, I'd be much more likely to notice a video I might like to buy on a special-interest shelf than in the video section. Walden and other book-stores are apparently about to place videos throughout the store. That would make more sense.

Drugstores

Drugstores primarily rent videos to increase traffic in their stores. High-traffic retailers sell many other products as well. Kartes, a video supplier, sold 120–200 titles via L'eggs (hosiery) who did the rack jobbing. It was an innovative idea at the time but failed to sell enough tapes to be profitable.

The customer base in drugstores is very consistent. They are more loyal than grocery store customers. If you can pinpoint who the customers are, then the retail buyer can stock videos that address their interests and tastes. Prices do not have to be as low as in the mass and chain outlets.

Retail Margins

Video retailers get 28–30 percent off the list retail price. As video is a new business, many accepted these margins. In other businesses, like books and toys, the retailer is accustomed to 40–55 percent off. As both video wholesalers and suppliers hold on to greater margins, retailers try to make up for their slim margins by buying and selling the fast-moving product—the "A" titles.

It becomes a vicious circle. Until video suppliers get their manufacturing costs down and give up some of their extra margin (which they have been accustomed to since the early days of video) to wholesalers, who in turn can pass some of it along to retailers, video product will be unlikely to get into the retail outlets that are used to higher discounts. This is an ongoing battle throughout the video business. Everybody wants more.

Giving all the stumbling blocks at every level, it's remarkable that tapes actually get through this maze and are rented and bought by consumers. I imagine that's why direct mail video has created an alternative distribution system. But more on that later.

WHAT DISTRIBUTORS WANT TO KNOW

"The best way to do this is to climb inside the mind of a distributor."

What Distributors Want To Know

Let's go back to the top of the video food chain and examine what can be done to improve your tape's chance for success. The best way to do this is to climb inside the mind of a distributor. (Now there's a frightening thought!) A producer's concerns are radically different from those of a distributor (a supplier or a wholesaler). As a producer, you think about how to produce the program, what the content will be, how to finance the program and so on. Put aside those concerns momentarily and try to understand the needs of the buyer before you pitch your program. Here are some questions that the supplier/manufacturer, wholesaler and even retailer will want to know before taking on new, untested product:

1. **What is it?** Is it an original video? A television program which is just now finding its way to home video? A movie? A specialty program? What length is it? (Films are 90–120 minutes; original and specialty programs are approximately one hour long.)

2. **What's the genre?** Is it horror, thriller, drama or comedy? Is it a how-to, compilation or documentary? What can you compare it to that was already successful in the marketplace? Are the title and packaging immediately recognizable?

3. **What can I sell it for?** What is the price? Can it be repackaged to increase its sales potential? For example, when we created AR-NOLD PALMER: PLAY GREAT GOLF we originally set out to make an hour program to be priced at $39.95. We quickly realized that for a little more money we could shoot some more footage and create two tapes at the same time ("The Fundamentals" and "Course Strategy"), each 45-minutes long. The retail price would stay at $39.95 per tape. The sales staff could pitch both programs at once and create more revenue for everyone with the same amount of effort.

4. Does it have a great title? The title is the first thing any buyer will see or hear, so it better be good—descriptive, exciting and right to the point.

5. What are the promotable elements? Above all a tape must be promotable. Does it contain one or more elements that bring with them a presold audience? Does it have a recognizable trademark? Is it based on a best-selling book with the same title? Does it contain larger-than-life people or events, have vast television exposure, or a tie-in with national magazines?

6. Who is the intended audience? If a producer has thought this through, he or she can present a program so that a distributor will immediately recognize its value. The intended audience should be easy to reach through existing distribution channels.

7. What will it cost me to get it there? The distributor will quickly assess whether the tape can get to its market—through normal distribution channels. If special marketing is required, additional funds and staff time need to be expended and it will be harder to turn a profit.

Unless there is great upside, a distributor will not want to go the extra distance to earn a dollar. Many producers do not understand this. They may have a tape with a presold target audience. But it may be so expensive and difficult to reach that market that distributing the program wouldn't be worthwhile. Before you stomp off criticizing the distributor for lack of vision, consider that the real lack of vision may lie with the producer whose job it is to create product that can be successfully distributed.

8. Is there any other publicity or promotion that the video can capture when it's released? Because original videos have no preceding public awareness, it is important to create programs that can capture free publicity when released. This is easier if a celebrity or national event is involved to help amass wide newspaper and television coverage.

9. Why will someone want to own the video? The trickiest thing of all is determining if people will want to own a tape. Why would they want to own it? Will they perceive some personal value in the tape? Will it make them richer, smarter, more attractive to the opposite sex, better in business, better in bed or better with a golf swing? Will it enhance their self-image somehow? Is it something they will want to collect or preserve? Will they want to view it again and again?

Market Requirements

The economics of video publishing vary considerably between a big company and a small company. A big company with its burdensome overhead will have to sell a lot more units to be profitable than a small company. A big company must move product month after month. If a large company takes on your program they will expect to make their profit on large numbers of units during the tape's initial release; their sheer overhead is so great they cannot wait for the program to earn out. Besides, they have a lot more product coming out that they must make way for and won't devote too much attention to your tape after the initial sales effort. A small company, on the other hand, may not have as much clout and leverage to push a program out; but they will, by necessity, promote the program over a longer period of time. The title will not be backlisted as quickly. A small company can make a profit on fewer units, and they must continue to sell your tape month in and month out because of their lack of resources and access to other product. These differences can be very important, depending on the kind of program you are making.

Many specialty videos do have audiences but never get distributed through major companies, who see them as having too narrow an appeal for the market. In these cases you have to look to other markets and other marketers.

Going Direct to Wholesalers

Why not go directly to the wholesaler and cut out the manufacturer? The thinking here is: You'll make more money because you won't be giving a healthy percentage away to the supplier/manufacturer. You could duplicate your own tapes. Do the packaging. Print the one-sheets, posters and point-of-purchase displays. Call on the wholesaler yourself. Maybe it would be worth it.

On first glance this seems to make sense. However there are several things to consider. First, how low can you really get your manufacturing costs? If you are a very small independent supplier it may cost $4 or $5 to duplicate and package a one-hour cassette. You can get the price down somewhat by duplicating several titles or by making a volume output deal with the duplicator for future product. But it is rare to get your price down to what the big suppliers who manufacture millions of cassettes can command. And during those periods when the duplicators are up to their gills manufacturing product, it is easy to see who will be pushed aside in the battle over duplication time. The big guys have enormous clout and their work will come first.

Second, you will have to design and create all the packaging. You certainly could hire third-party companies to design, do color separations and print for you. The packaging and design of one-sheets will have to be competitive. If you are going against the big guys, the quality of your promotional materials and packaging will have to be as good or better.

But none of this is impossible. With some research you can find competitive prices and good graphic designers. You may even be able to raise the money necessary to get into business. That's the easy part. Now you still have the job of selling to the wholesaler. How will you do this? You could call on them yourself or find a sales agent.

If you have only one or two tapes this method probably won't work (unless it is a tape that everyone is dying to have). Why? Because wholesalers are interested in <u>lines of product</u>. They work primarily with multimillion-dollar companies that supply them product every month. They want a stream of product. They don't want to deal with lots of suppliers. They want the kind of product that will have predictable sales. They want product that the supplier will support with reams of sales, promotional material, advertising and publicity tours. Okay, let's say you're real good and can deliver all this.

Let's say the wholesaler likes your product and agrees to take it on. What kind of deal can you strike? They may tell you that they need a greater margin than the big guys give them just to take you on. That it will be more expensive for them to set up and handle your account. You have no leverage. If they get 40 percent off from the big guys, they may ask you for 50 or 55 percent off or even more. (There goes most of that margin you were trying to hang on to.)

What about terms? The first issue will be returns. They will demand return privileges. The onus of risk shifts back to you. If they don't sell it, you get it back. No risk on their side. If it doesn't sell in the stores, it will come back to you. When will they pay? The big guys have credit departments that stay on top of their wholesale accounts and make sure they pay. If they don't, they hold back product. How will you make sure they pay? You are at the bottom of the pecking order. You don't have that much product and it doesn't sell as well as the "A" titles. You get paid last regardless of what the purchase order may say. Paramount and Vestron and CBS get paid first because wholesalers can't afford to alienate the big suppliers. You, they can. They don't need you; you need them. And if they don't pay at all, what can you do? Small claims court? Life is too short.

The feasibility of this scenario changes if you have a program or line of product the wholesaler perceives as being highly profitable. Several programs from small companies were very successful: J2's tape DORF ON GOLF sold 200,000 copies. Now DORF ON MT. OLYMPUS, the follow-up, is in the market as well. Small producers selling directly to wholesalers—it's not impossible, just very, very difficult.

And there are a dozen or more wholesalers you will need to work with to cover the whole country. Even if you find a few to work with you, you may still not get the coverage you need to sell the thousands of units necessary to recoup your production, marketing and manufacturing costs.

I know a small supplier with several dozen titles. After a few years, he has acquired enough good product to induce a handful of wholesalers to carry his line (or at least some of it). Acquiring product on very little money has been difficult, but the attention some of his titles have achieved is attracting other product to him. Besides working with a few wholesalers, he also sells to several hundred video stores directly.

At some point you have to ask yourself if you want to be in the distribution and marketing business.

Selling to Wholesalers

If you want to give it a try, find out who handles new accounts and acquisitions at each wholesale company and send an inquiry letter directly to that person along with screening copies with good packaging, examples of one-sheets and other promotional materials. Include a marketing plan. Follow up with a phone call.

Discuss terms. When will they pay you? They will offer 60, 90 or even 120 days. The majors get 30 days. You also will want a letter of credit from the wholesaler's bank. This is usually for 50 percent of the credit limit you extend based on their anticipated orders.

You will be asked to grant them a healthy discount off the retail price. They usually get 40 percent, but some ask for 45–55 percent to take on new accounts. This is always negotiable—if you grant too much you jeopardize your business.

Try to get a sufficient number of copies out in the initial order, but beware of the return policy. The norm for returns is usually 18–22 percent, but it can be even higher on unknown product. They may ask for a 20–25 percent return privilege or even more.

Some suppliers offer a greater margin or discount in exchange for a no-return guarantee—once they take delivery of your program, it doesn't come back. The rack jobbers, bookstores and toy stores are the toughest. They will require 100 percent returns. Here's where you can really get killed. The record industry in the late seventies was decimated by high returns. A video example, AUTOMATIC GOLF, shipped great numbers but had significant returns. One error in marketing and the next stop is bankruptcy.

To soften the blow, some wholesalers allow the retailer to exchange 10–15 percent of returns for new product. This way the wholesalers are at least able to replace the returns with some of their other product and don't lose the sale altogether; this doesn't help you, however, unless they are exchanging your product for other product of yours. Of course, if the product isn't sold, some retailers and wholesalers will try to renegotiate the deal to not paying at all.

Presenting the program is not enough. You will also need to lay out a marketing plan for the wholesaler that discusses how you will advertise and promote the tape. They will want to know what kind of point-of-purchase materials you will provide, what posters, sell sheets and ad mats. They will try to get you to pay for shipping. They will request in-store appearances by your host or celebrity. They will ask about star tours with television and radio appearances.

By now you may be thinking that the percentage that you give to the manufacturer/supplier to do the job is worth it. Depending on your adroitness in business, you may be right.

Retail Chains

What about selling directly to retail? You skip both the manufacturer and the wholesaler, do the work yourself and collect the loot. The first step is to find large chains to sell to and save running around, making phone calls or mailing sales material to many individual stores. One chain can buy a lot of product. Toys "R" Us buys children's product directly from manufacturers. However, because large retail chains have great clout they expect greater discounts. You will also find yourself waiting in line for payment, being asked for extended payment terms, paying for advertising and promotion and all the other things discussed above. Toy and bookstore accounts require 100 percent return guarantees and want 50–60 percent discounts. What you save by cutting out the middlemen, you may have to give back to the retailer. This doesn't mean it can't work. With strong, desirable, promotable product you can gain leverage; but if you only have a single title, it will be very, very difficult. And if your program is successful, what leverage do you have to collect?

If a retail chain doesn't have its own internal distribution system, you have to ship small quantities to their many stores. This is expensive. They also will expect you to check inventory, provide and dress up the point-of-purchase materials, and function much like a rack jobber.

A well-capitalized, well-organized person can try to enter this field, but market realities cannot be ignored. If you're thinking of jumping into the skillet, you should know where you are going to land.

If you are a video producer of specialty product and cannot find a major supplier/manufacturer to handle it, you may be forced into doing it yourself. You will have to manufacture tapes, prepare point-of-purchase materials and launch an advertising campaign if you want to go directly to video store retailers to sell your product.

You can buy mailing lists of the 20,000 to 50,000 stores than sell and rent video. You might want to target chains like Tower, Wherehouse and Toys "R" Us initially. Mailings lists can be purchased from trade magazines like *Video Insider, Video Business, Video Store* or *Video Software Dealer.* You can call the Video Software Dealers Association (VSDA) in Washington, D. C., to inquire about these lists.

If you are selling special-interest tapes to video stores, find or make a list of the video stores that sell—rather than rent—videos.

A few days after your mail reaches the stores, follow up with a phone call. Be prepared to offer posters and point-of-purchase materials to help the retailer sell your tape. Be sure to let them know the extent of advertising and publicity you are doing. Perhaps you could devise a "spiff" program—if they buy so many units of your tape they get a free tape, free shipping or a gift of some sort.

Determine your discount rate and keep it standard among all retailers. In fact, it is illegal to give different discounts to the same class of trade. The discount schedule could be 30–55 percent off retail across the board, or you could have a sliding scale where the discount increases with multiple-copy orders.

Schools & Libraries

For many years the so-called nontheatrical business sold and rented film prints to schools and libraries. It was a lucrative business. Prints sold for as much as $700–$800 per hour. Nowadays feature films on cassette sell for $29.95 and the bottom has fallen out of the nontheatrical business. Many nontheatrical distributors are doing their best to reposition themselves and supply their school and library accounts with lower-cost videocassettes.

These videos—while they may look the same to you and me—are really not. They are intended for "institutional or public performance use" and not "home use." If a school or library wishes to show the video to a class or group of people they must pay a nontheatrical institutional rate. These prices are significantly less than they were for 16-mm films, but they are still higher than the normal home video price. For example, a nontheatrical tape might rent to an institution for $10 to $100. The same tape could sell as a home video for between $29.95 and $125. For institutions these prices are still much lower than they use to be. While schools and libraries are not as price sensitive to video as everyday consumers, the difference between video intended for home use and institutional public performance use is creating a lot of confusion in the marketplace.

Geography Teachers

After I concluded the National Geographic video deal for Vestron I was invited to Washington, D.C., to meet with president Gil Grovesnor. He said he had a "few friends he wanted me to talk to." They turned about to be a couple hundred geography teachers who were attending a National Geographic seminar. Even though the first three National Geographic videos had not been in the marketplace very long, I wanted to know how many teachers had heard of them and I asked for a show of hands. Nearly all the hands went up. When I asked how many had rented the videos, about 80 percent of the hands went up. When I asked how many had bought them, I was really stunned. About 75 percent of the hands went up.

What I learned was remarkable and indicative of where the nontheatrical market was headed. The tapes had not been advertised in *National Geographic* magazine, nor had there been a direct mail campaign; the tapes had not been advertised to the educational community at all. Even so, all the teachers knew about the tapes. They saw them in their video stores. And, even though these tapes were being rented for "home use only," very few teachers really understood the distinction. For $5 and $6 a night, they were renting the tapes and showing them in their classrooms which, apparently unbeknownst to them, is illegal. They needed an "institutional or performance license," which a home video store cannot grant. Now this directly undercut the efforts of National Geographic Films, a nontheatrical distributor, which was renting the same titles to institutions for as much as $125 (their special reduced price).

Even more surprising, most of the teachers bought these tapes using their own money. They were not reimbursed for these purchases. Unbelievable! These were not wealthy teachers from private schools; these were ordinary elementary and high school geography teachers from all over the United States.

The reason these teachers were reaching into their own pockets to buy tapes for their classes was that it "was easier" than going to their media center or library and reserving a film for such and such a date. Once a film title is requested, the media center or library fills out a purchase order and sends it to the distributor, who sends the film for the requested date. The teachers told me that inevitably they didn't get the film on time. Many said their local media-center librarians were very protective of the films and didn't want them out of their sight. Teachers also don't like noisy projectors, having to request an audiovisual person to run them, and having to darken a room. It's too much trouble. Besides, their schools had VCRs and monitors and kids like watching television more than films.

These teachers were circumventing what is a very cumbersome educational distribution system. The ordering, the logistics and the fact that they usually don't get the films when they want them are obstacles. Video is easy. You plunk down $29.95 and walk out with

your National Geographic video. You can use it whenever you want, year after year. None of them expected to get reimbursed because they knew it "wasn't in the budget." (Most of them told me that they spend hundreds or even a thousand dollars a year of their own money for supplies that the schools cannot afford to buy. And some teachers are paid as little as $13,000 per year.)

We should be supporting and applauding these people. Their personal commitment to education is truly phenomenal.

These teachers took the shortest route to getting what they wanted <u>even though the product was never advertised to them</u>. This is happening throughout the country regardless of the laws about institutional use and performance rights. It's an enormous and very real problem for distributors who have paid for these rights. Home video is making a prosperous end run around an antiquated and outdated distribution system while traditional nontheatrical distributors are going under.

Nontheatrical vs. Home Video Issues

Home video has thrown a curve ball into the game which is still a source of frustration and revenue loss for the legitimate nontheatrical distributor, who has bought and paid for the institution and public performance rights to lease videos to schools and libraries for group showings.

In direct conflict with this right is home video's "first-sale doctrine." This means that a manufacturer can sell a tape to a wholesaler and the first-sale doctrine allows that wholesaler to sell it to whomever he or she wants. So <u>even though the manufacturer did not have performance rights to the program, by selling it to a second party the tape can make its way into the school or library arena</u>, thus siphoning rentals and monies from the legitimate owner of those performance rights. I don't know the extent to which the legal ramifications of this dilemma have been tested, but it is apparent that these conflicting licensing terms and conditions are taking income away

PAUL GAUGUIN
THE SAVAGE DREAM
National Gallery of Art · Washington

from many nontheatrical distributors and putting it into the pocket of home video manufacturers.

Public Library Market

There are 16,000 public libraries in the United States. About half of their collections are made up of non-feature programs. Libraries order their videos from distributors' mail order catalogs. They are highly selective because of their limited budgets and buy from a number of different sources. The average library will spend about $8,000 per year on videotapes. Libraries are less sensitive to price because in the past they had to spend hundreds of dollars for one program. Many of these libraries are in small towns (where there are few video stores) and have populations of less than 100,000.

Schools

Most schools have VCRs and buy their tapes from distributors' catalogs and direct mail. They may have tens or even hundreds of tapes in their libraries.

Distributors that specialize in the school market are Listening Library, Films for the Humanities, Library Video Company, Coronet/MCI, Pyramid Films, Churchill Films and Films Inc.

The nontheatrical distributors advertise in school and library publications to announce new film product to teachers, media buyers and librarians. Many of these publications run reviews of these films and videos. The primary publications are *American Educator, Educat's Curriculum Product Review, School and College Product News, American Libraries, NEA Today, Booklist, Children's Video Report, Library Journal, Media and Methods, Parent's Choice, Publishers Weekly,* and *Video Librarian. Bacon's Publicity Checker* (which you can find in your library) will give you a list of other appropriate publications for these and other markets.

The nontheatrical school and library distributors buy mailing lists from various list companies and solicit teachers, media buyers, principals, schools, libraries, colleges and universities directly with sales catalogs and order forms. Some send out field reps to their largest accounts. Films Inc., a longstanding nontheatrical distributor, in an attempt to move into the home video business, began Home Vision a few years ago. Home Vision sells upscale cultural and performing arts videos to consumers, schools, libraries and museum gift stores. It is one of the first to successfully straddle both worlds—nontheatrical and home video—with specialized programming.

SPECIAL MARKETS

The traditional video market is primarily rental and it is an uphill climb for most original home video programs. The traditional video rental market has also reached a plateau in terms of growth. This is not the case with the sell-through markets, which are continuing to expand. Beyond the video wholesale and retail outlets we've already explored are niches that if penetrated can yield significant returns. There are dozens of special markets ranging from catalogs to specialty stores to premium sales.

A Word About Splintering Rights

Alternative markets offer other opportunities for producers and their product. They provide options to traditional video store distribution. It is sometimes possible to negotiate with traditional video distributors—whose primary market are the video specialty stores—to retain some of the special market rights (such as premium, sponsor and mail order rights). This is called splintering. Obviously many distributors will not want to give this away. On the other hand, some distributors—particularly the large ones—do not aggressively seek these opportunities. Why? Because they have a large quantity of product to work through well-honed traditional channels. They don't have the energy or inclination to try to individually sell every tape to every niche. That leaves lots of room (with some product) for the smaller entrepreneur. There's no reason, really, that you shouldn't ask to retain rights to these markets when they clearly will not exploit them.

Premiums

Premiums are a $10 billion-a-year business. Premiums can be all sorts of items that are given away free to promote sales of other products and services—pens, coffee mugs, notepads, clocks, paperweights and thousands of other items, sometimes imprinted with the company or product name. There is a whole industry devoted to selling premiums to corporations, charities and other sponsors. A leading magazine in this market is *Premium and Incentive*. Video has arrived as a premium.

Sports Illustrated used a video as a premium to sell subscriptions. New subscribers received a video of sports highlights. With premiums you sell thousands and thousands at very low margins. The volume makes up for the low profit per tape.

Credit card companies may give away tapes for upgrading to a "gold card." A financial institution may give you a tape if you open an account. Dan Markim, director of special markets for Vestron Video, says, "Remember that video is an expensive item when compared to other premiums like coffee mugs, pencils and napkins.

So it probably only makes sense as a premium in support of a high-ticket item: Buy a car, get a video, etc. No one else will want to give away a five- to ten-dollar item. Premiums are a real long shot but worth pursuing. A minimum premium order should be at least five thousand units."

Catalogs

When a video program is initially released, the traditional video stores sell about 40 percent of the sell-through product and catalogs sell about 20 percent. However, those percentages are decreasing rapidly for video stores and increasing rapidly for catalogs.

Dan Markim's position at Vestron as director of special markets is very unusual because few major distributors have established separate sales divisions entirely for special markets. Markim reflects, "It's a very labor-intensive process to sell catalog accounts and feed them product. In the three and a half years I've worked at Vestron the nontheatrical department acquired some two hundred programs in music, comedy, sports, documentary, how-to, and quality series areas. At that time there were no catalogs carrying video." Dan now has hundreds of special-market accounts that buy millions of dollars of tapes each year. It's remarkable because these are non-movies.

Markim very specifically pinpoints a large buying segment of catalog market. "Many mail order catalogs are geared towards women ages forty to sixty. Their buyers are educated, have high incomes, are collectors and most frequently buy video for gift giving. I call it 'grandmother video.' They buy videos for their kids or their kids' kids. The most popular product is children's video classics like Beatrix Potter, BABAR, LITTLE PRINCE, HEIDI and other traditional, well-known classics. Contemporary titles like CAPTAIN POWER will be bought by the parent when urged by the child at the video, toy or mass merchant store. The grandparent is not familiar with the faddish characters."

Traditional stores need fifteen or more copies of a hit movie to satisfy rental customers. In contrast a catalog store sells product but typically has little inventory. They order product from the suppliers as they get orders. Catalog companies usually receive a 45 percent discount from the retail price.

The merchandise manager is responsible for product selection. Once it is in the catalog an inventory clerk buys. If the supplier receives a call for twenty copies it means that twenty copies have been ordered. The catalog must supply the buyer with product within thirty days by law unless otherwise specified on the mail order coupon.

The catalog business is made up of many small orders. The good news is that there are no returns. Catalogs prefer higher-priced videos—$29 or $39 and frequently higher. Sometimes they will package several videos together for $79 or more. ABC/Vestron's 45/85: AMERICA AND THE WORLD SINCE WWII is popular. A four-volume set is priced at $99. There is a trend to "bundle" product into gift-giving sets. Some catalogs will even mark product up. The McEnroe/Lendl tennis tape from Vestron was released at

$29, but Sharper Image was charging $39 to their catalog customers and getting it.

Catalogs are on the rise because video stores do so poorly actually selling video. It's a question of letting the customer know that videos are for sale as well as rent, but video stores have overlooked the sale market for the most part. If you want to buy videos you go to a bookstore, K-Mart or order through a catalog.

Large libraries have resource books such as the *Publisher's Source Book* which list catalogs. Within the world of catalogs there are several classes: general merchandise, video catalogs (such as Book of the Month Club, Publishers Central Bureau and Crown), specialty (which can be sports, camping or erotic like Mellow Mail) and high-priced (like Sharper Image or Price of His Toys). Camping and gardening are new areas of growth in the catalog business.

How to Sell to Catalogs

Markim describes how to make a sales presentation to the catalog market:
"First make a hit list of catalogs that you think are appropriate for your video. Send an introductory letter about your video product along with a four-color brochure or sell sheet and a sample if they request it."

Video is new to many catalogs so you may have to pitch them on the concept. In your letter you can talk about the video industry, the size of the market, recent sales successes and why they should want to handle video as a product. Markim suggests stressing points like, "Sales have risen X percent, here's who's buying it, it is a multibillion-dollar industry and VCRs are in over 50 percent of America's homes. Only after this setup should you discuss your specific product. Emphasize why people will want it, what the various sales and promotional points are and, finally, state your price and terms."

In time you will receive a form letter either rejecting the video or accepting your terms. If they accept your video they will then request a color transparency and copy for the catalog.

Space is the biggest issue with catalogs. They have to make so much money per square inch of catalog. They must earn out their page cost, which is enormous because they may print 200,000 to 2 million catalogs. For example, if a page or part of a page costs $10,000, they must earn more than that to keep the product in the catalog.

Markim says, "Generally if a catalog sells less than 200 copies of your video, then it's most likely that it will be dropped from future catalogs. This just isn't enough sales to justify the printing and mailing costs." Let's assume that your tape retails for $29.95 and the catalog gets it for $16.47. Their profit is $13.48. If the catalog sells 200 copies the gross is $2,696. If, on the average, a catalog page costs $10,000 (and your video got a third of a page), the gross doesn't cover the approximate cost of $3,333. If your tape doesn't do better than this, you are out of the catalog in the next printing. Or the cataloger will try to renegotiate the margin with you and leverage that against you to stay in the catalog.

A medium-range catalog may sell 500 tapes, with 1,000 tapes being the upper end of the sales spectrum. There have been tapes that have sold many thousands of units through catalogs. National Geographic's SECRETS OF THE TITANIC, ARNOLD PALMER, LIBERACE and LIBERTY WEEKEND are all examples of tapes that have sold extraordinarily well through catalogs. This would indicate that bestsellers must (1) be collectible, (2) have a big name associated with them, (3) be perfect for gift-giving and (4) have a long shelf life. *Reader's Digest's* catalog—which mails to more people than anyone—finds that a strong title will sell 10,000 tapes. This is expected to double for 1988.

Catalogs do not allow suppliers to put any direct response message on the end of the tape or on an order blank within the video package. They obviously do not want their customers to be able to order directly from the supplier. Their business is customer names and they do not want anyone else to capture valuable names for their own use.

It's important to find out how many times a year a catalog is mailed. Small catalogs will mail to 200,000 people twice a year. Other catalogs batter consumers with catalogs relentlessly. Publishers Central Bureau (PCB), for example, mails a million pieces every other week! Large catalogs have staffs that are always on the lookout for the next hot product. A new trend in catalogs is the "magalog" or catalog/magazine. The *Whole Earth Catalog* is an early example of this genre. A magalog mixes editorial, reviews and advertising. You can read about product and then order it. *Video*

Marketplace and *V* are magalogs that sell videos. The orders from their readers are usually for multiple tape purchases.

Markim explains that there is an advantage to being in the hot catalogs first. "Catalog buyers keep a close eye on what other catalogers are doing. Some catalogs, like Sharper Image, take a leadership position. If they carry something then the other catalogs play copycat and carry the same or similar items. Therefore, if you get in the leading catalogs, other catalogs will track you down and want to carry your videos. For example, the Nature Company catalog carried National Geographic video. From that exposure, other catalogs called Vestron hoping to carry the line. Being in a catalog carries with it a secondary value of exposure to other catalogers."

Like other classes of distributors, catalogs are also interested in dealing with suppliers with lots of product. They have large product needs. If you are small and don't follow up with more product, you may be the last to get paid. The catalogs make payments to their major suppliers first to stay in their good graces and not be cut off from product.

Airline Catalogs

Airline catalogs reach upscale audiences. Many major catalogs place ads in the airline catalogs themselves. They take pages out of their own catalogs and reprint them. Sybervision, which has a line of sports fitness and business tapes, advertises this way. Sometimes the catalogs will ask the program supplier to pay or help pay for the cost of being in an airline magazine. You never pay to be in regular catalogs. Sometimes you can exchange free goods (videos) for advertising space. This is obviously a cheaper way to go than paying cash. If you have a strong product it's to the advantage of the catalog to advertise in the airline magazines for you, but if your product is weak you may have to pay to be included.

DIRECT RESPONSE

"Get recognition for your product any way you can."

Direct Response

Direct response is another way to go to reach very specialized markets with specialized product. Direct response includes direct mail catalogs, ads in newspapers and magazines, and also television direct response ads with "800" numbers. Direct response also drives retail store sales. People are exposed to your product through television ads and even though they may not order it then, they may see it in a store and buy it later. You need to get recognition for your product anyway you can.

Direct response TV ads are a tough way to sell video. Very sophisticated selling formulas must be followed. Buyers <u>have to understand what the product is immediately</u>, which may be one reason that rock and roll compilation records do so well. You hear the music, see the titles of the songs and artists roll by, are shown a product shot of the album and audio cassette. This is followed up with information on how to order.

Video, without stars, is a tougher sell. Direct response television experts say you need 90 to 120 seconds to sell your product. Sixty seconds is not long enough. You flash the order price, address and phone number on the screen for a long time. You must give people enough time to get a pencil and write down the ordering information. Some "800" numbers are selected because they are clever or easy to remember. ("Dial 1-800-BUY TAPE or 1-800-333-3000.")

Some ads leave the phone number up the entire time. Most direct response ads are run in the late evening when rates are lower.

Sponsor Tie-In

Besides making a deal for use of your video as a giveaway premium you may also entice sponsors to assist with the production financing or marketing of a tape by offering: (1) product placement and use of their product in the video, (2) their logo on the package and in the titles of the tape, (3) an ad at the beginning or end of the video or (4) all of the above.

A sponsor's primary interest will be in reaching as many of the people as possible who make up their target audience. You can get a sponsor's attention by demonstrating that you can deliver a new audience via your video, introduce their product to a target audience that they cannot reach any other way.

The Fairfield Group announced in 1987 that the video rental market can provide advertisers with 2.8 billion exposures. They figured that the total advertising value of the rental market was nearly $43 million.

The demographics of the typical renter was equally male and female, 37 years old, income of $41,000, and some college education. The household had 3.5 people (2.2 adults, .44 teens and .74 pre-teens). The renters went to the store 56 times a year and spent 20 hours a year at the rental store.

The real obstacle to finding the worth of a home video rental tape to advertisers is that there has been no formal study or standardization of measurement. The cost per thousand (of impressions) is thought to be very high because a rental tape with a long shelf life will have more impressions than a tape that goes directly into a consumer's home. On the other hand, a home video impression is valued greater than television because a tape requires the consumer to go through an extraordinary effort to rent or buy a video. The selection process is far greater than simply turning on the tube—that is, video is a very "focused medium" because consumers pay to watch tapes. Therefore, the home video viewer is far more prone to take action and buy than the average television viewer.

Movies and other highly visible entertainment forms are the best vehicles for advertising, but that does not rule out how-to's and some event programs. The Fairfield Group also interviewed consumers to find out the most acceptable genres of video for ads and came up with action/adventure films (21 percent), drama 15 percent, kidvid (13 percent), sports (8 percent) and comedy (7 percent). These interviews also showed that the ads should not look like tv ads and that consumers would object to more than 2 ads on the same tape. Interestingly enough, other studies showed that only 10 percent of people fast-forwarded through the Pepsi ad on Top Gun even though 68 percent of people said they would fast-forward through ads on tapes. They just don't seem to be doing it to as great a degree as was feared.

How to Figure Impressions

To date there is really no generally accepted formula that can guarantee the number of impressions a sponsor's ad will make on its video audience. Because sponsors are used to thinking in terms of impressions, you must come up with logical scenarios they can understand. Since advertisers like to talk in thousands of impressions, video producers have come up with various formulas for figuring impressions to help them convince potential sponsors of the reach of a video program.

For example, an "A" feature film (grossing more than $30 million at the box office) will sell at least 200,000 copies. Multiply this by the number of rentals in each tape's lifetime, say 50, and multiply again by the number of people who will see the tape each viewing, say 3.5. Using these assumptions the "A" title video will yield 35 million impressions. What is the worth of 35 million impressions? Let's make another assumption, that a targeted mailing list costs $50 per thousand. So 35 million is 35,000 thousands. Multiply this by $50 and the value is $1.75 million. You might then take these numbers to an advertiser and ask for $1.75 million (in cash and/or advertising barter) to put their ad or message at the head of this hot "A" title. This also assumes that your title and their target audience match precisely. They will not want to put their ad on a video they perceive as too sexy or violent or contrary to the image they wish to extend.

Let's drop down to a "B" title. Let's say it will sell 50,000 units. Since it is a "B," it will rent only thirty times in its lifetime. Keeping all other assumptions the same, its value is $262,500.

Now let's examine <u>sell-through product</u>. These tapes sell to one consumer and may be viewed by two people. Unlike rental product these tapes will not have large numbers of people viewing them because they are owned and not lent. If an exercise tape sells 100,000 units, then you have 350,000 impressions. Its value is $17,500. Even so, you might be able to go to four non-competing sponsors (a shoe company, a sweat shirt manufacturer, a soft drink manufacturer, and a vitamin company), offer to promote their product within the tape, and give them ads and on-package advertising. That strategy could yield $40,000 ($10,000 each) toward your budget or in advertising and promotion from the sponsors. Every little bit helps. It will certainly give your tape visibility that it wouldn't be able to get any other way.

Direct Mail Pieces

With the right single product you can do a direct mail piece. This is extremely expensive but if, for example, you had aeronautic tapes and a very narrow mailing list of interested targeted buyers (private plane owners) who were willing to buy your tapes at a high price, it might be cost effective. National Geographic sells single issues of their books to their 10.5 million members through mail order promotions. These books are rarely marketed in bookstores; nevertheless, the response rate that National Geographic gets from their loyal membership is staggering. Their recent Centennial book, *100 Years of Adventure and Discovery,* quietly sold more than 200,000 copies through bookstores and more than 500,000 through direct mail to the membership.

Direct Sales Expenses

When you sell direct you are asking the consumer to buy directly from you. Advertising and promotion is aimed directly at the consumer. This sales strategy works well for highly targeted programs to highly targeted audiences. It is very expensive for the seller to communicate directly with the buyer (through magazines and newspapers, catalogs, coupons, "800" numbers and cable television).

Direct Mail Costs

Direct mail is very expensive and should only be used when the seller is confident of reaching highly motivated customers who will take action on the mailing piece and buy tapes. Conventional wisdom says that you should <u>test various lists to establish which ones yield the best response</u>. You should also test different pricing.

Start-up costs include ad preparation and design ($2,000 to $5,000 depending on size, illustration, color, copy and design fees). The total might break down to $1,000 for the copywriter, $750 for typesetting, $1,000 or more for the design work, $500 to $1,000 for the artwork and $250 for mechanicals. In addition, you may need an ad agency to produce commercials and print ads and to design coupons and freestanding inserts (FSI) for newspapers.

Media Buys

The next expense is the media cost. Say you select a magazine which has a circulation of 500,000. The cost of a black-and-white ad is

$12,000 or, viewed another way, $2,400 per 1,000. In some maga-zines it is possible to do a split run—test two different price points to the same market. You could also test two different promotions or offers to see which draws the best. (The return coupons are coded so you can tell where the response came from.)

Fulfillment

Another expense is for the services of a fulfillment house to handle telephone orders, mail orders, recording the order information and customer info, product ordered, price, credit card confirmation, banking of payment, preparing labels, packing the product and shipping. They handle customer service, "white mail" (inquiries and non-orders), returns, complaints, and charge the customer for handling and postage charges. They also do the preparation of accounting, sales and inventory reports.

Fulfillment charges vary greatly from facility to facility. Here is a sampling of some of the costs you can expect:

.10–.20	per shipping box
.02	label of any type placed on package, price stickers, etc.
$1.25	processing an order
$1.25	packing list/bill of lading return freight and UPS charges plus 15 percent
.50	per item on split orders
$1.25	credit invoice
$1.50	each handling of white mail

$4.50–8.00   per pallet monthly storage charge
$2.25   checking pallet in or out

There are also additional charges for the "800" number telephone line, UPS account, post office box, and the shipping charges from manufacturing plant to fulfillment house. When setting up fulfillment systems most first-timers significantly underestimate costs.

You might end up paying $1.50–6.00 per tape, depending on the number of handling services and the reporting required, plus the shipping zone. When multiple tapes are shipped the price can be reduced significantly. Some distributors will take their own orders and fax them to the fulfillment house. Others will have the fulfillment house do everything.

Usually, some portion of the shipping and handling costs is passed along to the customer. In many instances the seller ends up paying about 20 percent and the buyer 80 percent. Tests have shown that buyers are not price sensitive to an additional shipping fee up to 10 percent of the cost of the item. So if a tape costs $29.95, adding a charge of $3.00 or less is acceptable. It may actually cost as much as $4.50, however, to send out a tape, in which case the seller will pick up the difference of $1.50. Nevertheless, the seller is still getting an undiscounted $29.95 for the tape by selling to the consumer direct. There are no middlemen with direct sales marketing.

Video Clubs

Video clubs sell directly to their members, offering enticing entry programs with great discounts in the hopes that they will stay in the club long enough to generate profits. Many clubs sell on a negative option plan. They send tapes to members automatically, who must buy unless they utilize their negative option—just say no. These clubs generally carry tapes that have broad appeal. There are some book clubs that carry very special interest books, so it shouldn't be long before small, specialized video clubs spring up as well.

DIRECT SALES ANALYSIS

"It may take many impressions on your potential customer before a purchase is made."

Direct Sales Analysis

INCOME

Price		29.95	39.95	59.95
Shipping/handling		3.50	3.50	3.50
Gross		33.45	43.45	63.45
Returns %.05		-1.67	-2.17	-3.17

Net Revenue		**31.78**	**41.28**	**60.28**

COSTS

Cost of Tape		6.00	6.00	6.00
Royalty	.12	-3.81	-4.95	-7.23
Order Processing		-2.50	-2.50	-2.50
UPS		-2.00	-2.00	-2.00
Credit Card Cost	.03	-.95	-1.24	-1.81

Net After Costs		**16.51**	**24.59**	**40.74**
Ad Design Costs		3,000	3,000	3,000
Media Buy		15,000	15,000	15,000
Total Marketing		**18,000**	**18,000**	**18,000**
Gross Units to Recover Marketing Cost		1090	732	442
Magazine Circulation		500,000	500,000	500,000
Gross Order needed per Thousand		2.18	1.46	.88
Response to Circulation		.22	.15	.09

Explanation of Direct Sales Analysis

This analysis is purely hypothetical but it gives producers and marketers an idea of what expenses may be in store for them through a direct mail campaign.

The analysis looks at three different price points. All other costs—shipping, duplication, credit card charges, design and media buy—are constant. The only exception is the royalty, which is tied to the net revenue.

A shipping charge of $3.50 is paid by the customer. There will be some returns and bad debt (checks bounce, etc.). Assume 5 percent. There is a net revenue of $31.78.

The costs involved are assumed to be $6 (including duplication, tape stock, labels, cassette packaging and a box to ship the cassette in). This is a relatively high number and could be reduced to $5 or $4 with larger volume. But let's assume that only a few thousand tapes are being manufactured. Let's assume that a 12 percent royalty must be paid to the producer. (It could be higher or lower based on the actual retail price point used; the higher the price point, the higher the royalty.) The fulfillment house charges $2.50 to process the order and get it out the door. The UPS shipping charge is $2. (It will vary depending on the zone. Also, the shipping cost per tape is reduced for a multiple tape order.) If the customer uses a credit card to make the purchase, the fulfillment house charges 3 percent. (This charge varies from as low as 2.9 percent to as high as 5 percent). The net after costs is $16.51.

We now must deduct the costs of design and preparation of the advertisement and the cost of buying ad space. Our media-buy budget of $15,000 is to be spent on magazines. The designer charges $3,000 to make an ad(s), which includes the design work, any illustrations and photos, and the mechanicals—everything we need to send to the magazines. Assuming a 500,000 circulation, and depending on the magazine, this probably buys a full-page color and a half-page color. Or we might spread the money out and buy a series of smaller ads, or substitute black-and-white ads. The total marketing outlay is $18,000.

In order to break even on our marketing costs alone, we need to sell about 1,090 cassettes or 2 cassettes per thousand subscribers—a response rate of 2 percent. Depending on the product, the effectiveness of the ad, and the economic profile of our consumer, this could be a pretty high number to hit via magazines.

Looking at a higher price point we need less than 1 percent to break even. Is a higher price point possible? Will the consumer pay $59.95 for this program?

Use this format or expand on it by adding your own real numbers. Analyze the performance you must achieve. Perhaps it's all right if you do not recoup the full direct mail expenses. Perhaps in addition to direct mail sales, you want to buy awareness of your program among a target audience. After all, it may take many impressions on your potential customer before a purchase is made. Analyze the sales levels other video programs have achieved in the same magazines by contacting marketers who've advertised there before. The advertising manager of the magazine should be able to give you names of past advertisers. Think about running split ads (to test two different price points) before buying a series of ads. You might find the higher price point more profitable.

Keep in mind that this analysis does not take into account the acquisition or production cost of the tape itself, which must be recouped from all sales revenues before real profits are generated.

DIRECT SALES TIPS

"Don't let them get away. These customers will buy again. "

Direct Sales Tips

1. Advertise more than one product per ad. Advertising is very expensive, so compile a "line" of programs that will appeal to your target audience.

2. Small suppliers frequently join together to do co-op mailings to reduce costs. Each supplier makes up his or her own sales sheets with order information. This is added to a mailing packet with other sales sheets. Each supplier fulfills their own orders.

3. Test different lists. Use a large enough sample of names to be representative. If good results are obtained with a specific list, do a full mailing. Code the order form so you know where the order came from and can tally the results.

4. Once you've sold one tape to a customer, try to sell another. You know that the customer is interested in your tapes, that they have a VCR, that they can afford it. You know what subject they are interested in. This is valuable information. Don't let them get away. A substantial percentage of these customers will buy again. When they call in, have the telemarketer make them a "special offer" for a second tape. If they've ordered by mail, include a sales sheet about other tapes when you fulfill the order.

5. When you sell direct you are communicating directly with one person. You want them to take action. You want them to buy your product. Design an ad (magazine or television) that is clear, direct and personable. Don't be too clever. <u>Your customer must quickly understand what the product is and what you want them to do.</u> They have to get your message immediately or you will lose the sale.

6. Publicity is free and can be very effective. Try to get the newspaper or TV show that reports on your program to give a telephone order number or address.

7. As your fulfillment house takes orders, they capture customer names in their computer's data base. Reuse this valuable list for soliciting similar product. You can sell or exchange this list with other video suppliers. You can also buy their lists.

Direct Sales Dangers

The higher the price, the more credibility your program must have. Five dollars is not very much to risk through a direct mail purchase. But, as a consumer, are you willing to shell out $29, $39 or more for something you haven't seen? Maybe. It depends on how you perceive the tape and the company that is selling it, and whether the risk of ordering through the mail is going to pay off. Many direct mail ads do not pay off directly but rather indirectly. They make consumers aware of the product so that when they see it in a store they are more disposed to look it over and perhaps purchase it. It's very easy to convince yourself in direct mail that "we only have to sell to .5 percent of the magazine's subscribers to become filthy rich!" Keep that enthusiasm in check and evaluate your options carefully.

Direct Response TV

Promote your tape on television when you know you have the appropriate viewership and demographics. Sell a golf tape during a golf tournament. Or a boxing tape during a boxing match. Television is a good medium because potential buyers can actually see what they are getting.

It is very expensive. The commercial must be a least 60 seconds long and preferably 120 seconds. Once you design one spot it is not difficult to cut three different versions, a 60-, 90- and 120-second spot. Then test them. Two minutes is the best. The consumer needs time to get a pencil. During the last thirty seconds of the commercial flash the "800" number. Include credit card information, price and address. It could cost $5,000 to $25,000 to write, produce and edit a commercial. There is also the cost of buying the time itself. These ads solicit large numbers of orders in a very short time period, so the fulfillment house's answering service must be set up to handle calls 24 hours a day or whenever your ads are running. Most calls will come in immediately after an ad runs on the air. Make sure your fulfillment house is set up to handle lots of calls simultaneously; busy signals can mean lost sales.

The correct media buy is very important. Ad agencies can help design a strategy and campaign. It is very expensive. Usually you buy late-night time or what is called "preemptible time" for the lowest rates. If someone else comes along who will pay more you get bumped—but that's okay because, when the spots finally do run, you'll get them at a much lower rate. The "800" number is the terminal for calls and you can easily tally where the orders are coming from. Once the ad starts running you can check <u>which stations and time slots produce the best results,</u> rerunning them while dropping the time slots and stations that are least productive. Watch what happens, revise your strategy, and make your media buys accordingly.

Testing a campaign might cost $20,000–30,000, which would buy about 100–130 two-minute spots in eight to ten markets over a week or two.

Per inquiry (PI) deals can be made with both magazines and television stations. You get charged (usually 10 to 30 percent of the price) for every inquiry about your product, even if there is no sale.

Cable

Cable is similar to magazine advertising in that it reaches a very specific, special-interest audience. The demographics are much narrower, so you can better target your message. You know that people who like sports watch ESPN. Teenagers, who like music and pop culture, watch MTV. Women watch Lifetime's programming. Culture buffs watch Arts and Entertainment (A&E). Black audiences watch BET (Black Entertainment Television). Match your video or film ad to the demographics of the cable network and its programs.

Radio

Radio is also a narrowly focused medium. It reaches a specific geographic location at a specific time. This means that you can market your film or video on a regional basis. Unlike most magazines, you can target a specific area of the country. If you had a business-oriented tape you might advertise it in Los Angeles and New York during drive time on a news program. Radio stations can tell you who is listening when. Their ad sales departments can help design a campaign for you. It is difficult to give ordering information over the radio—especially since many people are listening while driving and cannot write down phone numbers—but radio can be very effective in introducing programs and getting people into retail outlets.

Magazines

Magazines are good for certain special-interest tapes because their demographics are very narrow and focused. A few years ago, many video suppliers made the assumption that people who subscribed to print magazines would buy video magazines of the same titles, but for the most part subscriber interest did not carry over. Many magazine and video publishers co-produced dozens of tapes with the magazine's name on them. Some were very successful—*National Geographic, Esquire, Playboy* and *Penthouse.* But many performed very poorly—*Weight Watchers, Pro Wrestling, Consumer Reports, American Health, Business Week, Parents* and *Black Belt*—and did not meet expectations. This is not to say that video magazines will not work, but simply that the format and marketing has yet to be fully developed.

Magazines are, however, an excellent medium for advertising special-interest tapes and continue to be exploited as such.

New Channels

New opportunities for the sale of video are occurring wherever there are captive audiences. For example, hotels and sports and music arenas are new venues where tapes are being sold. Vestron sold copies of LET'S GO METS at the stadium during Mets home games. Many music videos are sold in the concession stands along with T-shirts and posters when rock and country-and-western artists tour. Tapes are popping up as premiums everywhere: at banks, insurance companies, car dealers. These are just some of the areas to think about when developing an idea for a video.

SPONSORS

"The manufacturers of the products in your audience's shopping bags may be your next sponsor."

Sponsors

Sponsorship is the big buzz word in home video. Everyone's talking sponsorship. Outside of a few well-publicized marriages of corporate sponsors (Pepsi, Nestle) with movies on video, there's a lot more talk than action. It took years before cable television could sell advertising to sponsors. Home video is a world neither sponsors nor their advertising agencies understand. This will change. Some ad agencies have formed home video groups to act as marriage brokers between their clients and video companies.

Eavesdropping at a recent Billboard/AFI American Video Conference, it was clear that manufacturer/suppliers are more interested than ever in video sponsorship. However, they are looking more to producers to deliver the sponsors along with their program ideas. It's not that the suppliers are unwilling to finance productions, it's that they want the reassurance that there will be more marketing clout behind the program when its release date arrives. <u>The job of soliciting and landing sponsors is falling more and more into the lap of the producer.</u>

The best way to approach sponsors is to know that you have something to offer them—<u>from their point of view</u>—that just can't be passed up. That means you must have some understanding of their needs (and not just your own) to get their financing and

marketing support. Your program must address their target audience and have no negative baggage that could soil their corporate
image.

As you develop the idea for a program think about sponsors who
would be the most likely and appropriate partners. Once you've
identified the candidates, study what they do and how they do it
before approaching them. Make it very clear to them what benefits
could be derived from sponsoring your project.

Getting money may be your need, but it's certainly not theirs. And
their value to you may lie beyond production dollars. Think
marketing. <u>A link with your potential sponsor's marketing, promotion and distribution resources could give your video a tremendous
push.</u> You must study what resources they have at hand before you
suggest such a deal.

One way to determine the feasibility of a tie-in is to look at sponsors
who do a good job of promoting their products or services. See if
they use premiums, giveaways, proof-of-purchase offers or coupons. If so, your tape may make a good premium. It will be easy to
pitch because they are already dealing with premiums and understand their value to their own products.

They have a different agenda than you have. They are not interested
in selling your video. They want to sell their service or product and
your video must help them accomplish this task. This is where the
thinking of most producers falls short.

Don't sell your program only on what a great idea it is, but also on how well it ties in with your sponsor's product and marketing plan. Audience demographics and the penetration your tape can make into new markets for their product or service are most important to them. Let them know all the ways the tape will be distributed; if you don't, they may think that they are doing all the work to get distribution for your program. (And that may be true.) Come in with a national video distributor in your pocket. That gives you more clout. Don't come with your hand out—you have to bring something to the party.

Get multiple, non-competing sponsors for a tape if you can. An exercise tape could have a shoe manufacturer, a soft drink company, a sportswear manufacturer and vitamin company as sponsors. If they all cross-promoted and marketed your tape through their own outreach, public awareness could be significantly greater than you'd normally get through traditional distribution channels. What if you tied in a large national magazine as well? Maximize resources. Create some synergy by combining powerful third and fourth parties where everybody wins.

What is Sponsorable?

What is your tape about? Who is the primary audience? What is the income range of your audience? Where do they live? What are their interests? If you were to follow them around for a week of shopping, what would they buy? The manufacturers of the products in their shopping bags may make up a hit list for sponsorship! This is, of course an oversimplification, but gives you the idea. You want to get inside the lifestyle of the consumer as much as possible to see which products and services they use and if a video-to-sponsor match is possible.

Recently I consulted on a video for teenage girls. Not knowing too much about them, about their buying and living habits, I immediately went to teen magazines to get an overview of the potential sponsors who sell cosmetics, food, clothes, and records to teenage girls. A whole universe opened up. Knowing full well that most teens don't themselves buy the videotapes they watch—the purchases are made by their mothers and grandmothers—I did a similar study supplementing the potential sponsor list significantly. The tape's packaging, then, had to be designed to appeal to the teens and the moms. And then matched to a sponsor.

Let's try one example. You want to do a rock concert or a comedy concert. OK. Your audience: probably ages twenty-five to thirty-five; income around $20–35,000; urban—they live in cities or large towns; probably 40 percent female, 60 percent male. Let's go shopping with them on the weekend. It's summer. They're having a barbecue and then going to the concert. They've bought beer, hot dogs, relish, chips. They're wearing clothes from The Gap. They drive Jeeps. They buy lots of records and tapes. And read *Rolling Stone* magazine. There are your sponsors. Your rock concert or comedy concert tape could be of great interest to a beer or soft drink company, a fast food chain, a magazine, and a car or clothing manufacturer. Think of the subject of your tape only in the sense of whom it reaches. That's what sponsors want to know.

STARS&BARS

STARS & BARS MEDIA BLITZ!

TELEVISION	OCTOBER	NOVEMBER	DECEMBER	AD DATES
NBC			■	11-23-88 to 12-19-88
CBS			■	11-23-88 to 12-19-88
abc			■	11-23-88 to 12-19-88
USA NETWORK			■	11-28-88 to 12-23-88
VH1			■	11-23-88 to 12-19-88
NIGHT FLITE			■	11-23-88 to 12-19-88
RADIO National Spot Radio (Top 40 Mkts.)		■		11-7-88 to 12-3-88
CONSUMER PUBLICATIONS				
TV GUIDE		■		11-19-88
USA TODAY		■		11-18-88 (Life Section)
Rolling Stone		■		12-1-88 (Holiday Shopping Issue)
PREMIERE THE MOVIE MAGAZINE		■		October, November
Coming Attractions		■		October, November
Previews		■		October, November
Prime Time Video Guide		■		October, November
NEWSPAPERS FREE STANDING INSERT			■	12-4-88

That's a total of 265,000,000 impressions! PLUS—heavy trade advertising, co-op funds and extensive promotional and merchandising support!

325

Vestron did a deal with Wheaties. Here's how it worked. The tape was LEARNING FOOTBALL THE NFL WAY. Phil Simms was the host and a dozen other superstar football players taught how to play offensive and defensive positions. A player appeared on the Wheaties box. That's in keeping with Wheaties strategy; they are, after all, the "breakfast of champions." The tape was loaded with champion players. The marriage worked. Wheaties put a special videotape offer on the back of 10 million Wheaties boxes with a coupon that granted you a discount on the tape with proof of purchase. Wheaties also mailed a promotional sales flyer to 150,000 high school and college coaches and athletes. Vestron supplied the art and paid for the printing. The Wheaties logo was printed on the videocassette jacket and there was a brief commercial spot on the cassette. Everybody won. Vestron got enormous marketing support from Wheaties. Wheaties reached an audience of football enthusiasts from kids through adults—an audience interested in sports and nutrition. The image of the tape further reinforced Wheaties corporate message. It was win-win.

The big sponsorship deals happen with the "A" movie titles. Disney did a promotion with MacDonald's and got a LADY AND THE TRAMP promotion into 65,000 fast food restaurants. This, combined with Disney's superb marketing, moved over 3 million videos. Both Disney and MacDonald's speak to families: Disney for entertainment, MacDonald's for food. It was a great match.

A more unlikely but also successful match was Nestle and DIRTY DANCING. The video sold 375,000 units. Nestle's promotion kicked in after the video release and extended the normal selling period for a video. The tape returned to the number one spot on the charts six weeks after its release, which is very unusual. Nestle got a commercial on the videotape and their logo on the cassette package and promotional materials. Vestron's tape was promoted in Nestle's magazine and TV ads. The movie's demographics are very broad. So are Nestle's. They promoted white chocolate to a new audience through a new medium.

Crystal Light sponsored a Championship Aerobic Workout which Lorimar released as a video. The tape gained additional credibility by being tied in with a national aerobics organization. Not only did the organization lend a stamp of approval to the exercise method, but it gave the sponsors visibility before their national membership.

The tape had an exclusive "first window" of sales through Crystal Light. The only way to get the video was as a premium when you bought the drink. Crystal Light and the tape were distributed by General Foods. They did freestanding inserts in 46 million newspapers. Not bad for a humble original program. That exposure gave the tape a presence so that when people saw the tape later in video stores they were more likely to buy or rent it (even if they weren't moved to do so in the initial Crystal Light release).

An advertiser can help a tape get tremendous exposure—way beyond the resources of a video distributor. Their support in the marketing of a tape is far more important in the long run than having them pay for its production. They don't care about the production—they care about the tape's outreach. And so should the producer and the distributor.

327

One of the first and most successful video sponsorships was the TOP GUN/Pepsi promotion. A special TV commercial featuring Pepsi that looked like a scene out of the movie (but wasn't) was shown with a tag that let people know the video was available for $24.95. This ad made it look like the price was so low because Pepsi was involved. Pepsi was a hero for getting consumers a break on a hot tape. Pepsi spent several million dollars on the TV spots and of course got an ad featured on the tape along with their name. Over 2.5 million videotapes were sold.

The Exchange

What can you offer a sponsor? Here is a checklist of ideas that may serve as an outline for a deal that you can propose.

1. A terrific program that specifically meets their product or service demographics.

2. A means to distribute their message in a new environment to a new audience.

3. The ability to associate their corporate image with _____ (fill in the blank).

4. An ad or "info-mercial" at the head or tail of the tape.

5. Their corporate logo on the packaging.

6. A presentation title. (This will make it look like they had a whole lot more to do with the creation of the show than they really did.)

7. An opportunity to put coupons inside the videocassette packaging.

8. A vehicle to show their product (e.g., exercise equipment in an exercise tape) or service in the context of the tape—a soft-sell approach.

In exchange your sponsor may provide:

1. Production funds.

2. Goods or services during production.

3. Magazine or newspaper advertising for the video.

4. A special promotion for the video.

5. A national tour for the tape's host, celebrity or spokesperson.

6. Their national spokesperson's appearance in the video.

7. A well-known trademark which may bring credibility and additional perceived value to the program.

8. Many other innovative and valuable resources they may have in their corporate coffer.

Keep in mind that the sponsor's primary use of a video program will be as an advertising medium and perhaps a promotional premium.

It may take some research to find the right person to pitch your project to. Corporations are large and it can be difficult to determine who has the authority to make the decision you want. You may have to shuttle between their advertising agency (which will want to take credit for this great idea if they like it—or trash it if they don't) and an internal product manager. Or you may have to work through the promotion or corporate communications (public relations) department. At some point you may have to pitch their sales and marketing group. Always address each group with a presentation on the benefits to be derived through their association and participation in your project.

Sponsorship can take an unbelievable amount of time. A year or more. It's not a quick pitch where everyone says, "Yes, let's do it," and you're off and running. There are committees and corporate strategy. Corporate officers are very cautious—no one wants to make a mistake—so decisions are frequently made and remade and second-guessed. Megalithic corporations plan strategies years in advance. By the time you talk to them, they are already a year or two down the road in implementing what they will do.

Once in a while you get lucky. I sold 500 copies of a new board game called GOIN' HOLLYWOOD to *Premiere* magazine in July. It just so happened that the day I walked in, the marketing director was looking for a Christmas gift idea for her top advertisers. And the game offered the solution. I didn't know that coming in; I thought I was already too late.

Vestron's sponsorship deal with Nestle also came along through serendipity. Nestle had a promotion already lined up with another product that fell through. Vestron was there with DIRTY DANCING as a replacement in the final hour. Previously many other sponsors had turned down what turned out to be one of the largest-grossing independent films of all time with a record-breaking soundtrack album. Many sponsors were afraid of the title and the image they might get by association.

Video is a highly competitive business. Sponsorship brings significant clout to the marketing effort and increases a program's chance for visibility and for success. A sponsored video deal would be very interesting to just about any video supplier or manufacturer. It would give them considerably more resources to work with. <u>It will be very difficult, however, to get a sponsor without a distribution company in place.</u> Sometimes producers have to be creative and juggle deals with distributors and sponsors at the same time until a ménage à trois can be arranged.

National Organizations

A national organization carries its own kind of endorsement. The right name can bring quality to a tape. For example, a first-aid tape with the name Red Cross adds tremendous punch. A stop-smoking tape without an endorsement from Smoke-Enders would be a missed opportunity. Magazine names offer an awareness as to the quality, scope and subject matter of videos; however, they haven't always performed as well as expected. A magazine as sponsor may be useful in providing advertising space, coupons, and helping with other cross-promotions.

Home video is not at all understood by sponsors and advertisers. But then the advertising and corporate sponsorship world is not understood by producers. Looking across the table at each other can be pretty strange sometimes. But there seems to be a mutual desire to understand the other's needs. To help bridge the gap between sponsors and distributors, a new kind of agent has sprung up. These people usually have a background in both worlds and serve as marriage counselors for advertisers, sponsors and producers with good ideas. Sometimes they know sponsors who are looking to enter home video. They also consult with producers, helping them shape and position their programs to be more appropriate for sponsorship. They may also make the presentation, alone or with the producer.

The some of the best-known consultants and deal makers with a foot in both worlds are The Howard Maier Group, Melissa Hoffman of Polaris (the program supplier who did the Esquire GREAT BODY series), and Jay Coleman of Rockbill—all located in New York City—and Fred Johnson in Ridgefield, Connecticut.

VIDEO PACKAGING & P.O.P. MATERIALS

"It needs to cry out, 'Pick me, pick me!"

Video Packaging & P.O.P. Materials

Videotapes are packaged goods. Believe it or not, sales and rentals are greatly affected by how good the package looks. Consumers not familiar with the title or the stars put their trust in what they see. Videos with good package design, point-of-purchase displays and promotion reach out and grab audiences.

Independent producers do not have the moviemaking resources of the major studios. They can't spend mega-millions to make their movies. When it comes to good packaging, however, independents have every opportunity to compete with the big guys. Good artwork is expensive but not out of reach. Good design is good design and it needn't break your bank. With a little forethought, low-budget movies and original home video programs can be made to look like studio product. The key art for the package, poster, one-sheets and advertisements should be conceived and executed by an art director well versed in package design. Independents should make every effort to produce covers, packaging and promotional materials at least as good as the studios. <u>This one strategy alone will give independents the edge they need to be competitive.</u>

The important thing to highlight in the packaging is the film or video's most promotable element. This could be the star or the title. It could be a high concept or the genre itself. Each genre has its own look which will draw genre-specific audiences. Never do an upscale campaign for a horror film, for example. Since consumers do put their trust in what they see, the packaging must build expectations that will be paid off. If it doesn't, the retailer and consumer will be confused and sales will suffer.

Once upon a time, manufacturers went to extremes to make themselves immediately identifiable on their video packaging. Warner Bros. always used the same basic orange label and dropped in artwork. You can always tell a Warner's box—but so what? The viewer is interested in the show, not the producing label. Other manufacturers (especially the porn-mongers) designed oversized cassette packages. They stood out all right, but their size caused problems for retailers, who had trouble fitting them on standard-sized shelves.

The video package's artwork has to stand out. It needs to cry out, "Pick me, pick me!" The title should be large and the key art (painting or photo or graphic) should be a single image. A cluster of images gets lost at a distance. Since cassettes are displayed both face-out and spine-out, the spine must also have large, readable type. Sometimes the key art is reduced and displayed on the spine to create more interest.

The manufacturer's name (RCA/Columbia, CBS/Fox) should not be too large. Many first-time video publishers—who want to establish their company name—put a huge logo on the box. Other than ego gratification, this is a waste of space. Consumers care about the program, not the program supplier. Have you ever heard of anyone going into a video store and asking, "Hey, what's the latest RCA release?" If you want to establish your name as a video publisher, get a hit. Then your name will appear on the bestseller lists. Consumers don't care about your company now, and they won't later. Ask the man on the street who released the Jane Fonda or Michael Jackson cassettes. He won't be able to tell you.

The color of the package is very important. Think about your target audience. What colors will appeal to your audience? It sounds ridiculous, but it will get you thinking about how to graphically position your program. WEIGHT WATCHERS featured an attractive pink box with scriptlike typography to appeal to women. For NATIONAL GEOGRAPHIC to use anything but yellow would be a walk down death row; it didn't take a rocket scientist to decide what color the box should be.

First develop an overall design—one you can live with as it acquires a life of its own, one that will hold up for years. Create a trademark that will outlive you. Use the same typeface throughout the series; drop in different artwork for each program. The design of the back of the package can also be standardized.

My first book cover (*The Independent Film & Videomakers Guide*), used key graphic elements that could be carried over onto future books. My goal was a hip design that wouldn't become dated. Filmmakers are very visual, so the cover had to be very visual. My target audience was students and professionals. (When I was a student, I wasn't the only one who liked to carry around books that let the opposite sex know I was a filmmaker. "Oh, are you a filmmaker?") I wanted covers that would identify the owner as a film- or video-maker.

In 1981 when the book was published, I was very concerned that it appeal to both filmmakers and videomakers without alienating either so we combined visual elements from each field. For filmmakers we used the camera lens and film icons. To appeal to the videographers we *screened* these images to achieve a video monitor effect. It worked very well for both—the result of a <u>very conscious effort to determine the psychological make-up of the audience and to design the cover to address their tastes</u>.

A second benefit to a consistent look in packaging is that you can capture more shelf space. There are now five books in my mini-line with a similar look. When they are displayed on a shelf—often right next to each other—the consistency of the line-look gives them an advantage over the competition. Several books with similar covers pack a punch that a single book cannot. The line-look implies credibility, continuity and scope. Potential buyers think, "Hey, it must be a good company. They must know what they're talking about. They've got all these books." Getting this initial attention and selling one book opens the door for additional sales of the other titles later. And the reorder pattern seems to bear this out.

These book-publishing principles hold true for video publishing—maybe even more so, because you can't flip through a video. Videos are packaged goods like soap, perfume or cereal. Since you cannot see the contents when you pick them up, covers are vitally important. Your only impression comes from the package (or from any promotion you may remember).

The Power of Packaging

A very interesting thing happened after the release of Michael Jackson's THRILLER. Everyone at Vestron was very concerned about piracy and off-air taping. After all, the video was aired on MTV repeatedly; if people taped it, sales could suffer. But the broadcasting of the video did not seem to affect the sales (1 million units). Sure, you could tape it off the air, stick a typewritten label on it and give it to a friend for their birthday. But no one did. (At least not enough to affect sales.) It's too tacky. It looks cheap. <u>People seem to want the packaging too.</u>

Many special-interest tapes are given as gifts. Why? Because when shopping for a present you think about what the person likes to do, what their hobbies or other interests are, and try to find something that matches their interests. It shows that you were really thinking about the person when you bought their gift. You might buy a golf or fishing or exercise tape, depending on the recipient's interest; and when you must decide between two tapes in the same genre, the one with the most attractive packaging will often win out.

The video HALLEY'S COMET had a 3-D holographic cover. At a distance of 70 feet the mirrorlike cover threw off a rainbow reflection. "What in the world...?" You had to walk over and take a look. And when you picked it up and turned it over you saw a 3-D image of the comet streaking through space. Now that's a package that involved you. Once the cassette is in the buyer's hands, you're halfway there. The holograph wasn't cheap to produce (about 25 cents each), but it made the tape stand out in an ocean of video. Callenetics packaging graphics

What to Put on the Package

Any cover design should hit the high note of the program. It's this one note you want people to remember. Don't try to cram too much onto your cover. A single image will always have more impact; it's easier to take in and leaves a greater impression.

Why reinvent the wheel? There is already an established format for videocassette packages. Next time you are in a video store note the similarities. Examine the cassette jackets carefully before you design yours. The standard elements are:

1.   Title. Use a strong, evocative title. Select appropriate typography to strengthen its meaning.

2.   Subtitle. It may redefine the title or increase its punch.

3.   Segment headings and highlights lists. Like magazine covers, the key segments or highlights of a tape may be listed on the front of the package. (I think this clutters the cover and prefer to see the contents described on the back.)

4.   Reviews and endorsements. Well-known individuals or reviewers can write reviews or endorsements before the cassette package is manufactured. Put the best quotes on the front or back of the video jacket. A movie that has played theatrically will already have reviews to draw from.

5.   Strong photo(s) or key art for the back of the video jacket. (The cover image may also be used on the spine of the video.)

6.   List of Credits. Star, host, director, producer, writer and any other primary credits. Usually there are just two or three credits, printed very small. Only star credits have any meaning to consumers.

7.   ISBN number. Used on all books and videos, this number assists libraries and bookstores in ordering and cataloging.

8.   Program length (running time). If a tape is under sixty minutes it will read "approximately one hour." Length is important to retailers and consumers alike.

9.   Copyright notice.

10.   Manufacturer's address.

11.   Program synopsis. Written with a marketing slant to make the program as appealing as possible, it may appear on the back cover.

12.   Bar code. Used for inventory control and cash register sales.

13.   Sponsorship credit, burst or blurb (if any).

For a video movie the box art will probably echo the theatrical campaign since the public has already been exposed to it, making the selling job a bit easier.

<u>The cover, title and text have to be great.</u> They're the first things a consumer comes into contact with. You want a quick read—a single image that jumps off the shelf. I've seen shoppers pick up a video, look at the box and say, "Hey, this looks good." Often the tape is dreadful, but since it comes in a hot-looking box...

Esquire's GREAT BODY tape packages are very well designed. They use a slip-in cover sheet which you can read through a transparent clamshell image, and when you open the cassette box you see a sponsor's advertisement which is printed on the backside of the cover. It's very clever and unusual.

Develop a list of concepts for your packaging before production. Do sketches. Have an art director work up some storyboards. A photographer can shoot what you need on location or in a separate photo session later. Spend the time necessary to create something that is visually very strong and well executed.

Know Your Audience

Know your audience and what they respond to. Are they teens or adults? Men or women? Each group responds differently. The education, earnings and geographic location of your audience are important considerations. Be aware of these things as you develop your marketing campaign.

Specialty video requires a different marketing approach than theatrical video. If you have a theatrical feature to be released in video, at least you know how well the campaign worked for the movie's target audience. You know what age groups liked the movie. You know what worked in newspaper advertising. You know who to go after for the video release and how to get to them.

Original video programs are different from movies in terms of what sells. Titles and packaging that sell sexy, romantic love stories do well in video. Art movies don't sell well in video or theatrically. Black and white graphics are the kiss of death because they look like old or classic movies. Upbeat, silly comedy does better than oblique black comedy. The stars are one of the key selling ingredients in home video.

Packaging Examples

Here are some examples of titles and the thinking that went into the key art and campaign designs.

SPACE CAMP had unfortunate timing. It was released right after the Challenger space shuttle disaster. This tragedy was so strong in people's minds, it was difficult to market this movie without immediately drawing associations to this real-life event. The campaign used the shuttle in a documentary-style ad with small photos of Kate Capshaw and the kids at the bottom. This was the theatrical campaign. For the video release, Vestron redid the campaign entirely. They used a painting of the kids floating around inside the space capsule having fun. This worked much better, did not evoke painful memories and sold a lot of cassettes.

THE UNHOLY was sold as a sexy thriller. THE EXORCIST's campaign was very dark and very successful. THE UNHOLY followed a similar strategy with horror-oriented TV spots to reach the kids and horror fans and with arty newspaper ads to reach older audiences. Radio is a good place to sell horror movies because sound can be so evocative. THE UNHOLY campaign sold on two levels. To the kids it sold horror and monsters; to the adults it was sold as a thriller.

POLTERGEIST delivered to an older audience because it was about a normal family trying to hold it together under incredible odds. Kids remembered the movie and told their friends because of the horrific ending—the last ten minutes.

Cost of Artwork

There is a great cost range for finished artwork for film or video because the key art material can come from many sources, some more expensive than others. The key art can be an illustration or a photograph and each has its own specific costs. Generally artwork can range from $8,000 to $100,000 including comps, photography, layout, and mechanicals. An excellent job could cost $25,000. You could do even better with $40,000. The movie studios often ask several different art studios to submit bids and sketch comps of visual concepts for a film title. This is called double vendoring and gives the movie studios a greater variety of concepts to choose from.

Once a comp is chosen it is turned into a rough illustration. Color may be added at this point. When the rough is approved a finished illustration is commissioned. One artist may do the comps and a second artist the rough illustration. A third artist might be brought in to do the finished illustration. (A top artist gets $25,000 to create a piece of finished art for a major motion picture.) The art house that gets the job will then add the copy and tag lines, go to mechanicals (which include the color separations) and oversee the printing of posters, one-sheets, ad mats, or videocassette packaging.

For a video movie the preexisting key art is incorporated into the cassette package, which saves considerable money. But if the video is an original program, new art must be created. Since the expense

MAN FACING SOUTHEAST

"AN E.T. FOR ADULTS...IRRESISTIBLE."
DAVID LIDA, *WOMEN'S WEAR DAILY*

"ONE OF THE FINEST MOST ARTISTIC AND THOUGHT PROVOKING WORKS..."
WILLIAM WOLF, *GANNETT NEWS SERVICE*

A man named Rantes suddenly appears in a Buenos Aires psychiatric hospital expertly playing the organ. But who is he -this man with no recorded identity? Doctor Denis dismisses Rantes' claim of being an alien visitor as a simple case of paranoid delusion. Beatriz, his only visitor, sees him as an intimate and knowing companion. And the other patients, intrigued by his mysterious intelligence, see him as their only source of hope.

$79.95
SUGGESTED LIST PRICE
(Priced slightly higher in Canada)
CATALOGUE NO. C40101

FILMDALLAS PICTURES

Released Theatrically in 1986.

345

cannot be amortized over a theatrical campaign, <u>the art production costs should be kept in the area of $3,000 to $5,000 for an original program</u> depending on the sales projections.

Producers frequently prepare artwork before making their films and videos. They use it—often in poster form—to help get financing for their projects. For about $5,000 an illustration can be created for a comp poster. Some producers add stars' names to a poster, even when they are far from casting their picture; of course, getting those particular stars later may be a problem. A poster gives the impression that the film is done and is a real attention-getter.

As mentioned earlier, some producers will create a list of titles, have artwork done for them and then decide—based on the response from financiers, distributors and exhibitors—whether to go ahead and have scripts written. This demonstrates the importance of a strong concept—one with a title and key art that can be executed visually in an advertisement or poster. These are the elements (with casting) that sell most films and videos.

Same Movie: Different Campaigns

Sometimes after a movie is released you'll see a change in the look of the ad campaign. This is usually an attempt to hone in on a specific audience by trying to find what appeals most to them. If you can select the emotional, intellectual and visual elements that most appeal to your target audience, there is nothing that says you can't redefine your campaign as you go. Especially with art films that are rolled out on a regional basis—there's plenty of time for testing. As reviews come in, quotes may be incorporated into the advertisements.

Note that DARK EYES had two different campaigns; one romantic in nature while the other highlighted Marcello Mastroianni.

COPY ELEMENTS

There are two primary copy elements: the copy line, which comes before the logo, and the tag line, which comes after.

The copy line is used on ads and one-sheets for a film before it opens and before reviews appear. <u>The copy line sets up the picture</u> and grabs your attention: "Seduction, submission, murder ... tonight he goes over the edge." Right away you know what you are in for and what kind of movie it is. Once you get reviews you can replace it: "Seduction was never so dangerous ... kept me on the edge of my seat until the final fade-out"—*New York Times*.

Here are two examples of actual copy lines:

"You think they're people just like you. You're wrong. Dead wrong."—THEY LIVE.

"The last neighborhood in America"—TALK RADIO.

When the reviews come in, the best quotes from reviewers can replace the copy line in the ads.

<u>The tag line comes after the title</u> and accentuates it. Here are some examples:

BEACH BOYS: "The true story of the legendary group that created the California sound."

THE UNHOLY: "You haven't got a prayer."

TEQUILA SUNRISE: "A dangerous mix."

INTO THE FIRE: "When the passion is this hot, you're bound to get burned."

MISSISSIPPI BURNING: "1964. When America was at war with itself."

COCOON: THE RETURN: "Journey to the most wonderful place in the universe ... home."

A CRY IN THE DARK: "A true story of conscience, conviction, and courage."

AMSTERDAMNED: "This city is murder."

MYSTIC PIZZA: "A romantic comedy with the works."

THE ACCUSED: "The case that challenged the system and shocked a nation."

TIGER WARSAW: "Years ago he shattered his life. Now he's back to pick up the pieces."

HARDWARE WARS: "An incredible space saga of romance, rebellion and household appliances."

The tag helps define the movie, create a mystique about it, give you something clever to hang on to. Study the movie advertisements in newspapers. Clip out what you think are the most successful campaigns. Build a file. You will see that there are certain graphic conventions used again and again. Why? Because they work. Build awareness for your film or video based on these conventions.

P.O.P. (POINT OF PURCHASE)

P.O.P. is a term that encompasses all kinds of merchandising tools that help draw attention to a product. What these tools have in common is that they are all displayed at the point of purchase (usually the counter)—where the buy takes place. P.O.P. material can be a counter display, a tent card, a "take one" (where customers can take a small flyer), a banner, a poster, a mobile, a button or a bumper sticker. Sometimes it is a big cardboard stand-up advertising the video or film.

Sell Sheets

Sell sheets are usually a single page promoting one or more titles, but they can be large posters that fold out with a small poster on one side and ad mats and other information on the other side. Sometimes a sell sheet will be a brochure with many pages. A one-sheet is usually just that—one sheet of paper which promotes one title.

The supplier/manufacturer creates and prints an ample supply of sell sheets for wholesalers to send to retailers. Just in case the wholesaler doesn't do the job (the wholesaler is busy selling other suppliers' goods as well), the supplier also sends sell sheets directly to retailers, even though the supplier will not be selling directly to the retailer (in most cases). This way the promotional material is sure to get to the buyer. Often the retailer ends up receiving duplicate sell sheets from several different wholesalers as well as the supplier. Suppliers don't mind this, however; they feel that the more material a retailer sees about a title, the better he or she will remember it the day orders are taken. Overkill is better than not getting any material to the retailer at all.

The wholesaler also gets ad mats from the supplier for use in the wholesaler's catalog. Since many different wholesalers sell product from the same supplier, retailers will receive several catalogs containing the same titles (although the layouts will differ, of course). Some retailers go through all the catalogs trying to find the best deal and pricing. Others let a wholesaler sort all the product out for them and go by their recommendation. (Only after retailers have already bought all their "A" titles will they go for specialty product. In many cases they'll buy another copy of an "A" feature before buying an original program.)

Stand-Ups

These big cardboard P.O.P. displays are unfolded and set up in retail stores near the cash register or the end aisle, or they may be put in the window. ROBOCOP had a life-size stand-up. Sometimes they are very well designed and attract attention for a video. Other times they fall over and crush customers (only kidding!). Worse yet, retailers may not put them up at all. Or they may get damaged in shipping and not be usable. And some stand-ups never leave the warehouse of wholesalers too busy to ship them. To circumvent this a supplier might send stand-ups directly to retailers. Basically, many wholesalers find it inconvenient to handle point-of-purchase material—even though it helps them sell product. For this reason, some suppliers have their regional managers make sure that stand-ups are in the stores. Stand-ups are expensive—$10 each or more depending on the quantity manufactured.

Product Displays

As a book publisher I supplied counter displays for the parody *Hollywood Gift Catalog* to one of my wholesalers. We offered retailers a counter display with every purchase of ten copies. This, of course, encouraged multiple book purchases. When I checked to see how sales were going, I was puzzled to find a tremendous number of backorders. The books and counter displays had long been delivered to the wholesalers, so I couldn't understand why they weren't getting the books out to the stores. What had happened was that the wholesaler misplaced the displays and their computer inventory system said that they were still waiting for them to be delivered. The books that had been ordered were just sitting there waiting to be packed in the counter displays—which were already there! This is the the kind of thing that drives suppliers crazy. You do everything right and then a small foul-up keeps your product in the warehouse. It also illustrates a point I made about P.O.P. when I was describing stand-ups: Although the purpose of these displays is to help sell product, they're an additional item that wholesalers have to keep track of.

One National Geographic promotion included a shipping carton that held about two dozen programs. All the retailer had to do was open up the carton and unfold it—instant display unit! It included a header that could be attached to the top of the display. As the number of titles grew, a small, and then a large, floor spinner (rack) was provided to hold product. This gave National Geographic videos a <u>permanent</u> display in the stores, which was quite a coup. Usually a promotion in a retail store only lasts a few weeks unless there is advertising support for a more extended period. The permanent racks gave the line its own floor space, which is extremely valuable in an environment where cassettes are literally pushing each other off the shelves.

PUBLICITY

"Different facets of the program may be promoted to different audiences in different media."

Publicity

The difference between publicity and advertising is that you don't have to pay for publicity. You do have to find exciting ways to interest magazine, newspaper, radio and television writers and interviewers in your video.

Your publicity and paid media campaign are designed for your target audience. Publicity, promotion and advertising are the means through which you reach them.

Create a hit list of the media best suited to your target audience. Determine what publications your audience reads and what television programs they watch. Your publicist is an expert at this and should be able to prioritize a list.

Brainstorm with your publicist. Find the promotion angles that would grab the attention of newspapers, magazines and television. Different media have different needs. Your publicist should be well versed in the unique aspects and needs of various newspaper columns and talk shows.

Your publicist may not be aware of subtleties of your program that could be promoted to very specific audiences. Recall the most promotable elements in your program and couple them with your target audience's interests. Figure out how to deliver the message to them in the most effective manner. Sometimes it's through publicity. Sometimes it's through advertising. Usually, its through a combination of both.

Too frequently, producers do not conceive promotional angles for their programs. This is unfortunate because distributors, publicists and press need strong hooks and unusual angles to hang their stories on—that's what will grab the attention of your audience in a marketplace filled with programs. Many video programs have no stories to tell from a media writer's point of view. It becomes very difficult to interest the press and in turn sell the video to the public. The publicist is then forced to create an angle, and if that angle doesn't really pay off (when watching the program), interest in writing about the program may wane.

Some programs are loaded with promotable angles. The more angles you have the better. Different facets of the program may be promoted to different audiences in different media, giving you far more exposure. And the press will have more creative choices as they approach the subject matter of the program.

An example: Two friends, Lawrence and Loren Blair, produced RING OF FIRE, a travel adventure of the South Seas made up of four one-hour programs. Not only are they fascinating explorers and anthropologists in their own right, but their program is one incredible episode after another, including many things never before captured on camera. A reporter can pick up on one or more of dozens of stories—sailing with pirates, escaping active volcanos and giant man-eating lizards, surviving dangerous ritual ceremonies with headhunters, etc. Their program was shown on PBS and got outstanding press coverage. They had so much to offer both the print and broadcast media that reporters clamored to meet these two eccentric globetrotters and write about their adventures. They had themselves and their stories with which to promote their television series. The package (the explorers and the television shows) was loaded with promotable angles. The only downside to the story is that they waited too long before negotiating their home video deal and missed the great publicity push when their book and television program came out. They weren't positioned with their video in time to take advantage of the tremendous exposure they received. (RING OF FIRE is now distributed by Mystic Fire Video, New York.)

When you do publicity—as opposed to advertising—you have no control over what will be written. It could be good, bad or indifferent. The articles, if and when they do appear, may come too early or too late and even fail to mention necessary information like how the video may be ordered.

For producers working on limited budgets it is often wise to create a publicity driven campaign, if possible, rather than rely on advertising which is enormously expensive. Publicity, if carefully and effectively orchestrated, can produce big results.

Publicity and advertising go together. Prepare a marketing plan that incorporates both. They should be carefully coordinated and interlocking, with one building on the other. Do some publicity. Let people know—through well-placed ads—where they can buy the video (mail order and/or retail outlets); then repeat the cycle. The objective is to create multiple impressions of your program in the audience's mind at a time when they can rent or buy it.

Don't publicize your program too early. Many producers are so anxious for attention from the press that they give interviews too early. These interviews appear before the videos are in the stores. There is no payoff (other than ego gratification) and little likelihood that the same publication will do another article at a time that would help sales.

Although it is rarely discussed—because of inherent conflict-of-interest issues—you may get more editorial attention from a magazine when you place ads between their covers. This can never be addressed directly. Just make sure that the editorial people know that you are running advertising in their publication. Let the advertising people introduce you to the editorial staff. Then see what happens.

Hire a clipping service to compile your reviews. Send the best reviews to the video wholesalers and retailers. Use the best quotes in newspaper and magazine ads and on the cassette jacket.

Publicity Tours

A star (or host or author) may go on a multiple-city tour. Cities are selected where the star has a following and/or where the tape has the greatest likelihood of success. A publicist can set up television, radio and print interviews in these cities. A certain amount of lead time is required so that the tour may be coordinated. The hotter the star and the program are, the easier it is to arrange interviews.

The star/host may go on national and local TV talk or entertainment shows, do radio interviews, and meet with the press individually or at press conferences or press parties. Sometimes stunts or events are planned as well. The star/host may do selected in-store appearances to sign autographs and talk with fans.

The star's status has a lot to do with the quantity of publicity that can be generated. In large cities like Los Angeles and New York the press can choose among as many as thirty press conferences a day. Something exciting is always going on—lots of food, drink and other attractions that pull in the press. In smaller towns it is much easier to capture their attention.

Press Kits

Well-designed materials are needed to carry out a successful publicity campaign. The press kit is usually sent in a slip-sleeve which contains all or some of the following:

• The press release is the centerpiece of a press kit. It tells the basics of who, what, where, when and why. It contains a synopsis of the program and emphasizes its promotable elements. The price, length, distributor and retail outlets (where and how it can be bought) may also be mentioned.

• Biographies and photos (black-and-white and color) of the celebrities involved.

• A position paper or statement or letter about the cause or value of the program is sometimes included.

• Information on the company and principals who made the tape along with production and music credits.

• A product shot clearly showing the video package. Sometimes the video package is shot in an appropriate setting (e.g., the Beach Boys tape shot in a beach scene) and other times it is presented in limbo.

The product shot is used in both trade and consumer advertisements and for publicity purposes.

• A cover letter pitching the merits of the program.

• Screening copies of the tape. (Sometimes an electronic press kit is also included promoting and highlighting different aspects of the tape.)

The publicist will compile the hit list of newspaper, magazine, TV and radio reviewers and feature writers. The press kit will be sent to them. The publicist will then follow up with telephone calls.

OTHER ISSUES

"You must decide whether or not you want to be in the sales and distribution end of the business. "

Implementation

If you decide to distribute the program yourself, the first step is to hire experienced people to implement your marketing plan. A <u>marketing consultant</u> will evaluate your program (or program idea) and design all aspects of a sales and marketing campaign. An <u>art director</u> will design your packaging, flyers, one-sheets, point-of-purchase materials, etc. When you are ready to release your program a <u>publicist</u> will handle all the publicity for it. A <u>sales rep(s)</u> will sell to the various markets (video stores, bookstores, mass merchants, etc.). A <u>direct mail specialist</u> may design flyers and a direct mail test. A <u>tape duplication house</u> will manufacture and package the videos and send them to the <u>fulfillment house</u>, which will warehouse them and fulfill direct mail orders. (Some duplication houses will also fulfill for you.) A <u>mail order service</u> will send out direct mailers to your mailing list, which you buy from a <u>mail list broker</u>. An <u>accountant</u> will design an accounting and tracking system to track orders, make out payroll checks and do year-end tax statements. Sounds like a lot of work, yes? It is. Maybe that small royalty a manufacturer/supplier would give isn't so bad after all.

If you have only produced one program, your marketing costs may be so exorbitant that distribution is not feasible. You must decide whether or not you want to be in distribution business. If you do, you need to create or acquire a series of programs you can sell to the same markets, thus amortizing release costs. If your programming spans many genres, it will be more difficult to market because you will have to reach many different classes of buyer. If, on the other hand, you simplify your marketing strategy by designing a series of programs that have the same target audience, you may be able to very successfully sell your product line. Once you begin making sales, you can return to them with similar product. This strategy reduces costs enormously and may be profitable. You must be sure that this really is a business. You have to ask yourself the questions again, this time as a program supplier and marketer: What do you want to be?

Splintering Rights

You may find a manufacturer who will only handle some of the potential markets, although this is unlikely since most want as many markets as possible to increase their revenue streams. But let's say your manufacturer deals primarily with retail outlets—video stores, bookstores, toy stores and sports shops. In this case the manufacturer may agree to a distribution contract that allows you to splinter off (separate and keep) some of the other rights—premiums, mail order, catalog sales, museum shops, and other markets—which you can then license to third-party specialists such as direct mail marketing organizations or sales rep organizations that sell to the premium market. You could also ask the manufacturer to provide cassettes for you for these other markets (at cost plus 10 percent) and to fulfill your orders if they have a fulfillment service. The worst that can happen is that they just say no.

These kinds of arrangements are common in book publishing. Sometimes two publishers—one in the United States and one in Europe—join forces to publish a book. This is called co-publishing. It allows both parties to reduce manufacturing, packaging and promotion costs by sharing them. From time to time you may find this kind of arrangement in home video as well.

RELEASE MODELS

"A single idea or concept may be expressed through a variety of media."

Release Models

Not every idea is worthy of becoming a film or video. It's sad but true. Before blindly rushing down a path of no return, producers need to really examine their idea, the best form for its expression and their reasons for wanting to make that idea into a film or video—it might not be the most appropriate medium to use. Other possibilities might be better suited to that idea.

Each of the many media forms and formats has a unique way to communicate and make an impression on its audience. Think of this way: Producers make "communication pieces." A communication piece could be a feature film—but it could also be a video, a TV show, a radio show, an audio cassette, a painting, a poem or a poster. These forms of media are all different, all relevant, all useful in expressing ideas. Some ideas or concepts may be communicated best through only one form, while others may be expressed through a variety of media.

If yours is an idea that can really be communicated through a variety of formats <u>it is very important to sequence its release</u> in the different media. For example, rarely would you show something on television and then hope to show it in a movie theater. Why would theater owners book a film after it had been seen for free on television? Films are released first to theaters and then to television—that's a sequence.

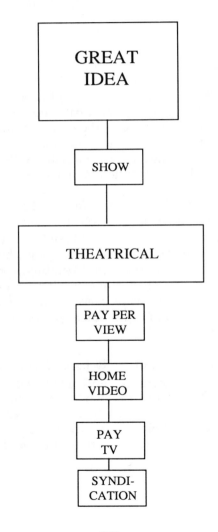

Great Idea

The first chart shows a "great idea." This idea is then made into a "show"—in this case a movie—which is released in theaters and then goes to pay-per-view (where cable television customers order and pay for it on an individual basis). Next it is released on videocassette; then it is shown on pay television and later in syndication. This is one example of a release sequence. Release models take many forms depending entirely on the content, substance, and timeliness of the show, as well as its intended market. There is a basic logic inherent in all forms of release: Whatever sequence generates the most dollars is usually the one selected.

In this section several different release models and strategies will be examined. As you begin to understand the hows and whys of release sequences, you can start to apply similar logic to your own ideas. You may find new opportunities for your ideas.

As an idea is being conceived, it is important for the producer to take a long, hard look at what medium he or she is producing the communication piece for. *Is it a theatrical film or is it really an after-school television special? Is it a home video or would it make a better book? Is it an hour-long film or is it really a segment for television?* Your concept must be appropriate for the medium in which you wish to release it. You need to also determine what the market needs are for the various formats to see if your idea is really feasible. Once you do so you can work out the release strategy for all other potential exploitable formats.

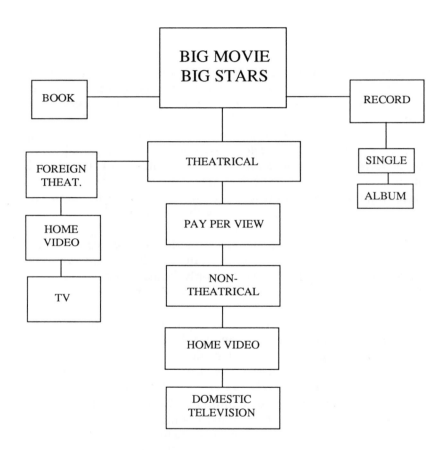

Big Movie, Big Stars

Let's look at a big picture first—a big movie, with big stars. In order for this high-budget production to recoup its cost, it must be released in a manner that will make the most money possible. The first exposure for the movie is in theaters. It then goes to pay-per-view, to home video (about six months or less after the theatrical window), to pay-TV (and at about the same time to the nontheatrical school and library market), and finally to television (either network or syndication). Concurrent with the theatrical release, a soundtrack record is produced. A single is released first, followed by the album. Paralleling the theatrical and album releases is a book release, which also appears serialized in a magazine. Shortly after the domestic theatrical exhibition comes foreign distribution, which follows the domestic pattern: theatrical exhibition followed by home video, pay-TV (in those countries that have it), and then television. There may be merchandising as well—dolls, pajamas, toys, games, etc. This model is of a film that has characteristics which make it "playable" in all markets. It could be a film like E.T., AN AMERICAN TAIL or DIRTY DANCING. When the film is created, the financiers are already looking to the potential of these markets.

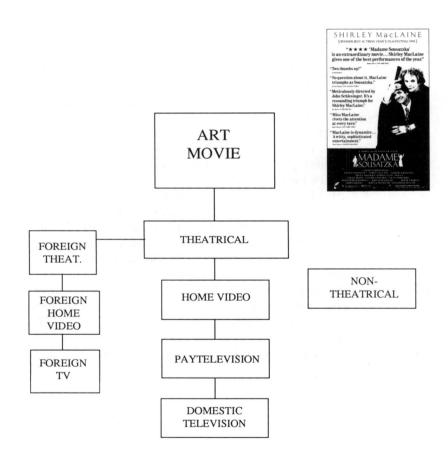

ART
MOVIE

THEATRICAL

FOREIGN
THEAT.

FOREIGN
HOME
VIDEO

FOREIGN
TV

HOME VIDEO

PAYTELEVISION

DOMESTIC
TELEVISION

NON-
THEATRICAL

Art Film

On a smaller scale is the art film, which may only be released in a few dozen theaters before going to home video (with unit sales of 5,000 to 40,000). Next comes pay television or, more likely, a basic or pay cable network like A&E (Arts & Entertainment) or Bravo. Rarely, an art film gets to domestic syndication. It depends entirely on the film and the current market conditions. There may be a nontheatrical market. Or, just possibly, a foreign market. Again, this will depend on the genre and whether these markets are appropriate for the product. Producers should not overestimate the desirability of their films in these markets. Although, if a producer is serious about capturing attention here, these markets can be held in mind when designing and writing a film.

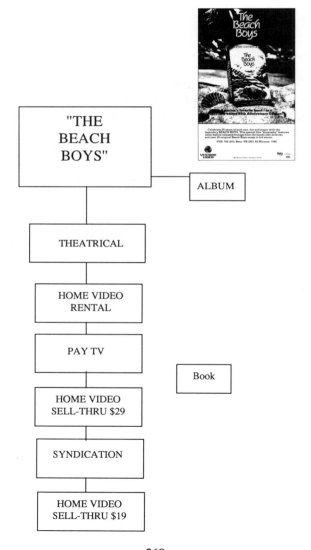

"THE
BEACH
BOYS"

ALBUM

THEATRICAL

HOME VIDEO
RENTAL

PAY TV

Book

HOME VIDEO
SELL-THRU $29

SYNDICATION

HOME VIDEO
SELL-THRU $19

"Rockumentary"

THE BEACH BOYS: AN AMERICAN BAND was a "rockumen-
tary." Though not really a movie-movie, it was sold like one.
Occasionally other music documentaries follow a similar strategy.
First it had a very limited theatrical release (ten theaters, two weeks
maximum). Then it was sold for $69 retail as a video movie before
going to pay-TV. Next it was resold to the home video market at the
"music video" price of $29. Finally it went to television syndication
and had a third release to home video, this time as a mass-merchan-
dised sell-through product at $19. This is called having your cake
and eating it twice. This strategy was implemented in non–English-
speaking territories as well.

No one expected the film to perform well theatrically. After all, who
but over-35 California Beach Boys fans would really come out for a
movie about their career? The theatrical release was to position the
program as a movie video and not a music video, so that video
retailers would pay the home video movie price. Without a theatrical release and its accompanying hoopla, the $69 movie price could
not be charged. It's a matter of perception—video retailers who see
a video as a music video will not pay over $29 for it. In this case, even
though the movie did not make money theatrically, it was well
worth the effort in terms of subsequent video and television sales.

A Beach Boys album and a book were released during the film/
video release. This was carried out by other companies and not
cross-promoted or marketed with the film to any significant degree.

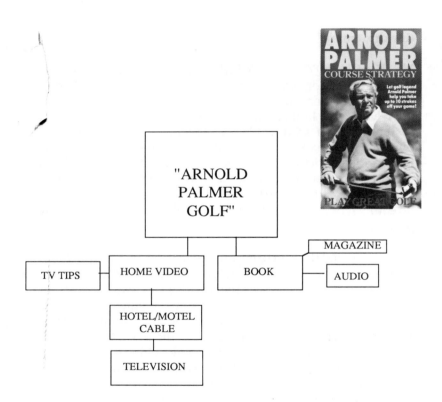

"ARNOLD PALMER GOLF"

TV TIPS

HOME VIDEO

BOOK

MAGAZINE

AUDIO

HOTEL/MOTEL CABLE

TELEVISION

Arnold Palmer Video

A video company (Vestron) and a publisher (Doubleday) approached Arnold Palmer at the same time. He agreed to do a video and a book at the same time. A still photographer would shoot on location during the videotaping. An editor would craft Arnold's teaching tips into a how-to book. The book and video would share similar cover graphics and be cross-promoted. This was decided at the outset of the production. This was one of the first times in my experience that a strategy between media companies was designed before video production began.

The video was shot so that one-minute golf tips could be extracted and sold to a sponsor. Imagine, for example, a series of spots like, *"Hertz presents the following one-minute golf tip from Arnold Palmer."*

While it didn't happen, an audio cassette could have been designed to release at the same time as the video and book. *Sports Illustrated* magazine published articles that drew on golf tips from the book.

Once the concept was fully exploited in book and video form, it was licensed to hotel/motel cable. A business traveler staying overnight in a hotel could punch up Arnold Palmer's program on a pay-per-view television monitor.

And finally, the program can go to television syndication once the revenues fall off from the aforementioned markets.

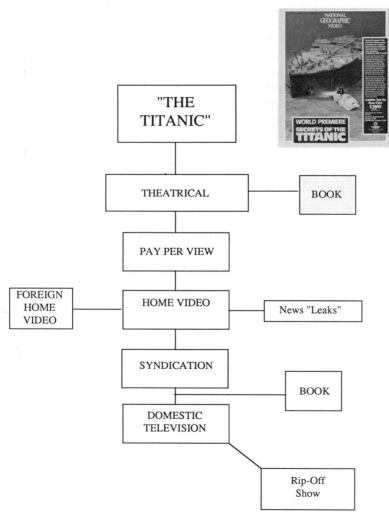

Secrets of the Titanic

There was so little time to get SECRETS OF THE TITANIC to the marketplace for Christmas that National Geographic had to forgo playing the program theatrically or on pay-per-view. Instead, it would premiere on home video.

Before the home video release, National Geographic ran selected photographs of the Titanic's discovery in their magazine and news clips were leaked to television newscasters announcing the discovery. This whetted the public's appetite: "What does the Titanic look like now? Is there any treasure?" Retailers and consumers alike waited anxiously for the video to be completed and released, because this would be the only way they could see the Titanic. The tape shipped the second week in December—right before Christmas. Vestron sold 150,000 copies.

Four months later the program appeared on WTBS where it set cable television ratings records. A photo book came out many months later. It was not cross-marketed in any significant way with either the television show or the video. Months later a French producer broadcast a program hosted by Telly Savalas in which the Titanic's safe was opened. The program, which was incredibly weak, still had enough appeal to garner very high ratings. Rumor has it that a home video of this program will soon be released. When will it end? The mystery and drama of the Titanic is clearly unusual; however, from time to time similar opportunities will arise.

In this example five different media producers (magazine, video, television, book and television again) exploited various communication pieces related to the Titanic.

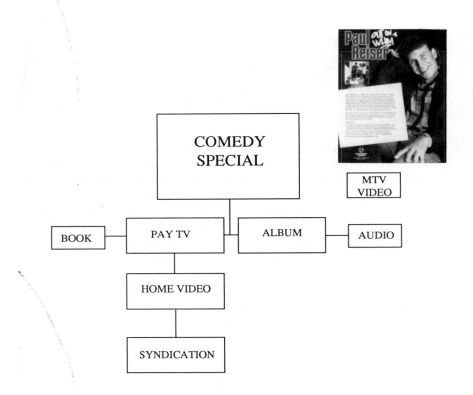

COMEDY
SPECIAL

MTV
VIDEO

BOOK — PAY TV — ALBUM — AUDIO

HOME VIDEO

SYNDICATION

Comedy Special

Comedy does not travel well. The difficulty inherent in translating colloquial speech and idiom limit a comedy's ability to deliver international laughs. Comedy specials are frequently produced for HBO or Showtime and then go directly to home video. Sometimes an album or book is generated from the same material (e.g., Joe Piscopo, Father Guido Sarducci, Steven Wright, etc.) Some comedians, like Piscopo or Weird Al Yankovich, do music video parodies which are shown on MTV, thereby promoting the album or video. Some specials appear in television syndication. End of story.

Rock Concert

These too are first released on pay television. Depending on the artist, they may play internationally since music—unlike comedy—is an international language. An accompanying album may cover the same material that is in the video concert, or it may contain studio versions of the same or similar material. In either case, the album and pay television pieces frequently serve to promote each other and are released with this in mind. MTV can be used as a promotional window through which the video or television special can be promoted by showing short music video or news clips. My feeling is that the sooner the home video release (after pay television and MTV exposure), the better. Most music and performance material plays off quickly, so you want to sell the home video while songs from the album are still on the charts. Some record companies want to fully exploit the record, tape and CD opportunities first. The concert may also appear in television syndication if the artist is sufficiently well known.

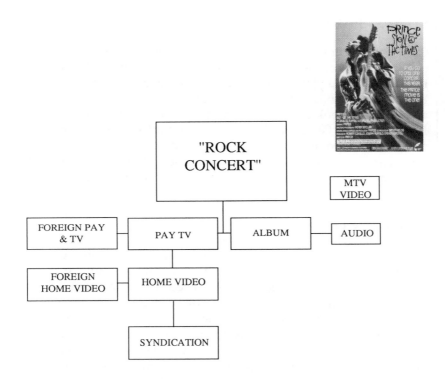

"ROCK CONCERT"

MTV VIDEO

FOREIGN PAY & TV

PAY TV

ALBUM

AUDIO

FOREIGN HOME VIDEO

HOME VIDEO

SYNDICATION

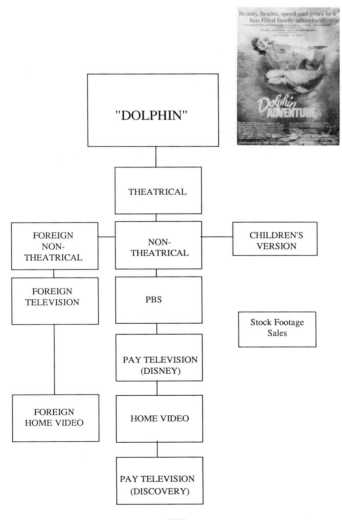

"DOLPHIN"

THEATRICAL

FOREIGN NON-THEATRICAL

NON-THEATRICAL

CHILDREN'S VERSION

FOREIGN TELEVISION

PBS

Stock Footage Sales

PAY TELEVISION (DISNEY)

FOREIGN HOME VIDEO

HOME VIDEO

PAY TELEVISION (DISCOVERY)

Dolphin

When I produced this independent documentary feature in 1978, I had not even marginally thought about how to release it. Like most filmmakers, I was so wrapped up in thinking about how to make the film, I didn't think about a release strategy. I simply assumed that I could always sell it to PBS.

Once we were deep in postproduction I felt we had something special, something theatrical. (Don't all producers!) DOLPHIN was released in a dozen theaters—mostly in California. It was booked for as long as a week and as short as a few days in repertory theaters. At the end of the run the ticket sales just paid for the advertising— it was a wash. (At the time I was disappointed; but now I realize, given the nature of the film, that was really quite good. It's just that our expectations were higher.)

Like the BEACH BOYS film scenario a decade later, the reviews stimulated future sales. DOLPHIN was released in the nontheatrical school and library markets, but because a 16-mm film print cost $770, there were not many sales. I later cut a children's version for the nontheatrical market which performed very well—and ten years later is still selling. Stock footage sales throughout the years also contributed income.

PBS took the first broadcast window and then, as pay television grew, DOLPHIN appeared on the Disney Channel. Then Vestron retitled the film DOLPHIN ADVENTURES and released it on home video. And a year later it played on the Discovery Channel.

There was some activity in England and Canada in the nontheatrical markets. The biggest market, however, was foreign television, where DOLPHIN played on thirty networks with many relicensing it for additional showings. While Vestron presently has the international home video rights, it is unlikely that it will be released on worldwide video. Enough new markets developed to give the film some legs beyond what we initially expected given the lack of foresight in regard to a release strategy.

Exercise

An exercise program is usually produced first as an original home video program. There are exceptions like the 20-MINUTE WORKOUT, which first appeared on syndicated television.

The release pattern is usually home video first, then (maybe) a limited pay cable run, and then television. Many exercise programs are also produced as audiotapes and appear in magazines and in book form. Some exercise programs can also be edited into one-minute tips for interstitial television programming.

EXERCISE

MAGAZINE

BOOK

HOME VIDEO

AUDIO

TV SPOTS

HOTEL/MOTEL CABLE

SYNDICATION

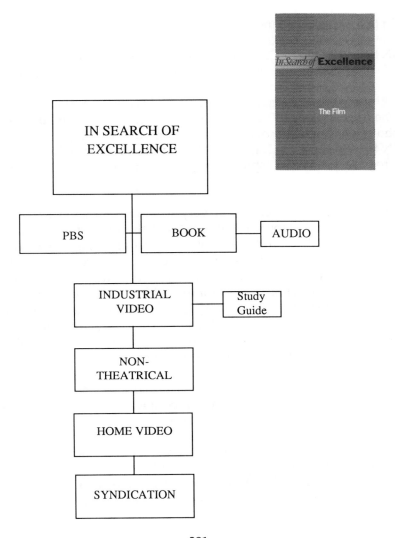

IN SEARCH OF
EXCELLENCE

In Search of **Excellence**

The Film

PBS

BOOK

AUDIO

INDUSTRIAL
VIDEO

Study
Guide

NON-
THEATRICAL

HOME VIDEO

SYNDICATION

In Search of Excellence

IN SEARCH OF EXCELLENCE was based on the best-selling book of the same title and profiled several successful entrepreneurs.

This television special demonstrates a release pattern that allowed one idea to expand successfully into nearly every medium. Although not initially conceived as a program for multiple markets, IN SEARCH OF EXCELLENCE has become a model which many program producers aspire to duplicate. The sequencing worked brilliantly.

The PBS program performed very well and garnered excellent ratings. An audiotape was produced with the author for the audiotape market. The producers (John Nathan and Sam Tyler) then taped new hosted sections with experts who commented on the material in the special. By combining these two elements they created an instructional video for the industrial market which was different from what had already been exposed on television. This video was accompanied by a study guide and other printed materials. In excess of 20,000 copies sold at approximately $400–$500 each. That's $8–10 million in gross receipts!

The video is still selling in the industrial market. Consequently the nontheatrical, traditional home video and syndication markets remain unexploited. That makes sense.

The producers obviously do not want to cannibalize on their success by releasing this program in markets with low retail prices until they sufficiently harvest high-price markets. Releasing IN SEARCH OF EXCELLENCE on home video (for $29 or even $59) would have a detrimental effect on their industrial sales. At the low end of $29 they would have to sell thirteen home videotapes for every one industrial tape to achieve the same revenues. Also, they distribute the industrial themselves (keeping all receipts), so their profits would be further diluted by going to home video where they would only receive a 20 percent royalty of the wholesale price. Why go into home video in this case until the very last industrial tape is sold?

Many other producers have followed this sequence with varying degrees of success. (The show itself, timing, public awareness and a variety of other factors come into play.) A simultaneous book release and PBS special cross-promote each other. The program then goes into home video and syndication. Very few programs are specialized enough to have an industrial or training video window.

Hardware Wars

I produced this popular 16-mm short together with Ernie Fosselius in 1977. We got lucky. It was seen everywhere. At the time, I didn't have the vaguest notion about how to sequence a film's release. We just fell into it and were fortunate enough to come out as well as we did. It helps to have a film that everyone wants.

The first window was nontheatrical. It was sold as a 16-mm film print for $325 to schools, libraries and corporations. (The defense department bought dozens of prints. I guess the title intrigued them. Go figure!) The film was then blown up to 35-mm and distributed in the United States and Australia. Since 1978 every pay-television broadcaster has played the film repeatedly. It was licensed to PBS and some independent stations at about the same time as to pay-TV. A year later Warner Home Video released the video version in a compilation with other short films. Shortened (six-minute) versions were then licensed to various network television shows such as DICK CLARK'S BLOOPERS AND BLUNDERS and SATURDAY NIGHT LIVE (although they chose not to broadcast it). After more than a decade it continues to spin off small revenues in all markets.

We also wanted to parody the merchandising of STAR WARS by selling posters and T-shirts. A halfhearted attempt was made, but we were filmmakers not concessionaires. The release model for this short film was extremely unusual. Parodying the top-grossing film of that time didn't hurt. Every time a new STAR WARS picture was released our sales jumped. The millions that 20th Century-Fox spent marketing STAR WARS didn't hurt either.

I always wanted Warner Home Video to promote HARDWARE WARS whenever CBS did a STAR WARS promotion. Why not ride in the jet stream of their promotion? I thought lots of units could be sold. Of course, a small film like ours falls below the threshold of major film corporations. Guerilla marketers might have employed this strategy. As of this writing CBS is doing a large STAR WARS promotion and offering all three titles at a discount. If Warner was opportunistic they would parody CBS's multimillion-dollar marketing campaign and rerelease HARDWARE WARS. I've always felt that if you do a film parody, you should go all the way with it and parody the marketing campaigns for it as well. But, unfortunately, such tactics are not what large manufacturers are about. After all, they have much bigger features to promote which they have paid a lot of money to either produce or acquire.

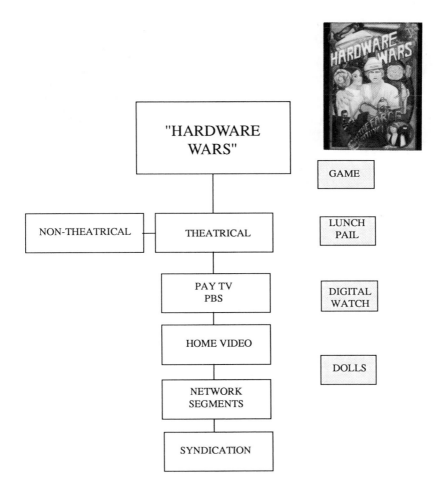

"HARDWARE
WARS"

GAME

NON-THEATRICAL

THEATRICAL

LUNCH
PAIL

PAY TV
PBS

DIGITAL
WATCH

HOME VIDEO

DOLLS

NETWORK
SEGMENTS

SYNDICATION

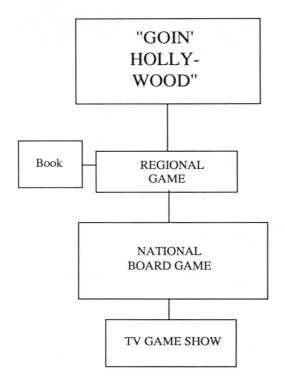

"GOIN'
HOLLY-
WOOD"

Book

REGIONAL
GAME

NATIONAL
BOARD GAME

TV GAME SHOW

Goin' Hollywood: The Movie-Making Game

Although GOIN' HOLLYWOOD is not a video or film, the marketing strategy for this board game exemplifies one which videos, films or books may employ on their way to wider exposure. In GOIN' HOLLYWOOD the players are producers willing to do anything to get their films made. It's a parody of the film business and the way films are made. Because that subject makes it an obvious home run in Los Angeles, the strategy is to make it a hit in the Los Angeles area first. This regional focus (on Los Angeles and, to a much lesser degree, New York) also maximizes limited marketing dollars. While there has been some national publicity (*Premiere, Spy, Newsweek*, wire services, etc.) which has helped drive direct mail sales, it hasn't affected the retail level because the game is only available in Los Angeles and New York. The national release will come after regional awareness is established.

Both Trivial Pursuit and Pictionary were regional hits before they rose to national attention. These best-selling games took two and three Christmas seasons to become well known. My partner Greg Johnson and I selected a similar release pattern after examining the recent phenomenon of hit games. These games probably didn't employ this strategy purposely; their success simply happened.

Once the game is a hit in Los Angeles, it will have built name value and recognition among the public. It's regional success will demonstrate its promotability, playability and excitement. And this can be extrapolated for the rest of the country (the game performed very well in tests with non-movie people). Once this value is built, GOIN' HOLLYWOOD can be licensed to a major game manufacturer/distributor like Parker Bros., Milton/Bradley, Western Publishing or Pressman Toys.

If the game can be made into a national hit, we could consider creating a television comedy or game show based on it. A humor book with the same title could also be released. The name itself will have value, and we might exploit that value by licensing the name for other merchandising.

Few people think of it, but at one time the Cokes, National Geographics and Ford Motor Companies were all one year old. A good product, commitment to marketing, long-term vision and patience can lead to success you may not see in the short run.

Summary

These conceptual models and real-life examples show the thought (and sometimes lack of thought) that can go into the release of a communication piece through the various media. Study them. Think about your own projects and ideas. What is possible? Dream a little. Then map out your strategy and see how each release serves to promote and stimulate the next market.

The release model is very important. All potential markets for your idea should be considered. Not all ideas are appropriate for features. That's OK. Find those media forms—books, television, records, games, or videos—that are appropriate for what you want to express. As you design your communication piece, use the proper format for the medium you've chosen and an already established distribution channel. It will make your life easier. Do not create a 36-minute television program, for example. It will fit into neither a half-hour nor an hour slot. Work in conventional forms and it will be much easier to license your property to a distributor. Once your product begins selling you can start exploring other more difficult-to-reach markets.

I began making films in the sixties. I wanted to buck the system. I'd make films of any length—not thinking about what I would do with the films when they were finished. It took me a while to learn that no matter how good they were, if they didn't fit distributable formats they would never be seen. Length and lack of foresight sabotaged many projects. Producers need to learn the limitations and formats of each medium and design their projects accordingly. After all, isn't the idea to get your work seen?

Map out the various potential markets that may be appropriate. Let the preceding release models stimulate your imagination.

I did not assign specific times or windows to each step. This is highly dependent on the product. A feature film, for example, may bomb. In that case, why wait six months for the video release? You want to get it to home video as quickly as possible—while the public still remembers the theatrical promotion and advertising. If a film plays successfully for many months, why hurry the home video release? You may wish to wait. Think about the kind of product you have and model its release after similar products that were successful.

ADVERTISING

"Advertising calls to action three classes of buyer."

Advertising

Advertising is paid communication to an audience through magazines, newspapers, mailers and electronic media such as radio and television. Advertising asks consumers to take action and buy a product. All ads demonstrate a benefit of and create a desire for a product or service. In the case of films, advertising creates a desire in the viewer to see the particular film advertised.

Consumers buy videotapes for entertainment or information or some other perceived value. Usually they also have an emotional reason, and this motivation must not be ignored when designing advertising for your video. What emotional benefits come with owning a tape? A National Geographic video is educational and consumers may purchase them for their kids or as gifts—they feel proud to be sharing knowledge with the recipients. Jane Fonda's exercise tapes bring the emotional promise of not only a new body, but the new life that is perceived to go with it. Besides the spiritual connotations of Shirley MacLaine's meditation video, there is also the implicit promise of self-knowledge. Find the single theme or note of your program and amplify it through advertising and packaging.

Advertising calls to action three classes of buyer: the wholesaler, the retailer and the consumer. The video wholesaler and retailer are reached through trade magazines and mailers. The video consumer is reached through all the media you can muster—newspapers, magazines, television and direct mail.

Ad Expenditures

Advertising is expensive. On average manufacturers spend 23–25 percent of their anticipated gross revenues for hard costs and marketing. Book publishers spend about 15 percent on marketing only. Another 3–4 percent goes to co-op advertising plans—the manufacturer shares some of the cost of advertising with the wholesaler or retailer, depending on the size of their orders.

Magazines

Magazines are an excellent advertising medium for video because they reach special interest groups with easily defined demographics. If you have an exercise tape, advertise in health and fitness or lifestyle magazines. Place ads for a childcare video in parenting magazines. Sell an aviation tape through aviation magazines, and so forth. Many magazines are a clear match for special-interest tapes in such areas as opera, sports, golf, nature documentary, and so on. You must be sure that subscribers to the magazine also have and use VCRs. The teenage subscribers to *Teen Beat*, for example, will not have VCRs.

Classes of Magazines

Through consumer magazines you can communicate directly to the potential buyer with ads that address women or men or business professionals or health advocates or whoever the class of reader is. The ad calls the reader to action—to buy your tape through a mail order or a toll-free telephone call. Sometimes the effectiveness of a magazine ad is hard to measure. In addition to any direct results, it may influence retail sales by bringing readers into the video store to rent or buy the tape.

Trade magazines are read by manufacturers, wholesalers, retailers, hardware manufacturers and producers, who use these magazines to communicate with one another. Some of these magazines and newsletters are *Home Video Publisher, Video Insider, Video Business, TWICE, Variety,* and the *Hollywood Reporter.*

Retail magazines communicate to retailers and store owners. These magazines help them with merchandising, title selection, sales tips and other subjects related to the operation of their business. Some magazines that address retailers are *Video Software Dealer, Video Store,* and *Video Week.*

The libraries are an important component of the book publishing industry. In recent years libraries have begun and are expanding their video collections. Video marketers are now seriously courting the library business (especially Baker and Taylor and Ingram Video, who service libraries with books). There are magazines which review books and videos for librarians. Positive reviews in these magazines are extremely important. Examples of the most influential library magazines are *Library Journal, Media and Methods,* and *Video Librarian.*

You may find many more magazines that will be valuable for publicizing and advertising specific videos. See *Bacon's Publicity Checker* in the reference section of your local library.

Newspapers

Newspapers reach consumers directly. The good thing about newspapers is that they reach a very specific geographic area during specific periods of time. Since many videos are given as gifts, most video advertising appears during the Christmas season; although this is changing as retailers learn that people buy and collect videos all year long.

Attention Span

Think of your own experience in looking at ads in newspapers and magazines. If you are like me, you flip through publications very quickly. An ad has only a few seconds to grab my attention. If it does, I'll stop and look at it for another ten or twenty seconds. If I read the headline or sense that the product or service could benefit me, I may read the copy. If the copy convinces me this is a "must have," I may order it. More likely, I'll tear out the ad and file it. Weeks later when I look at it again, more often than not I change my mind and do not order it.

I extrapolate from my own experience of looking at ads when I design them. The graphics must be very strong and the copy line simple and to the point. If you get too clever, you get a smile instead of a sale. I am of the school that you want to get your message across as quickly as possible and have someone respond. Therefore the ad must hit the most powerful single note inherent in your program. It must be that one note which will resonate with the reader of that publication. When placing magazine ads, remember that you are not trying to hit everyone who reads that magazine. You are only trying to appeal to the segment of readers who are potential buyers of your product. As much as you'd like to think so, that's not everybody. Only address those readers who are really potential buyers. This focused approach on a more specific demographic will, in the long run, make your ad more powerful.

Plenty of books on advertising and copy theory are available to help you in your thinking about advertising. An ad agency should be able to help match your product with the appropriate advertising vehicles as well as craft the message you want to send.

Trailers

Trailers are generally three- to five-minute coming attractions that are screened in theaters to promote upcoming movies. Video trailers have the same goal—to communicate what a program is about. They may run for 60 to 90 to 120 seconds and are used to sell wholesalers on a program. They will watch a short video trailer in a sales meeting, but they may or may not ever watch a whole tape.

Video trailers are also shown in booths at video conventions or at other marketing meetings. Rarely are they shown in video stores.

There are new cable services, like Movietime, that show hundreds of movie trailers. It is only a matter of time before a cable service broadcasts home video trailers—a home video version of MTV.

More and more, specialized video programs are using in-store videos to sell video and other products. Cosmetic counters and department store boutiques use videos to sell their product. The video trailer is like a live point-of-purchase display. It can repeat endlessly within the retail environment.

Trailer Testing

It's done for movies, why not video? Cut a trailer, make several dubs with different titles, and test them to see which is most effective.

Some producers make a trailer for their unproduced program to use in pitch meetings to financiers and suppliers. A trailer (and poster mock-up) is really doing the marketers job for them. If well done, it can help demonstrate to the supplier that you have a hot program—one which is promotable.

TV Advertising

Television is used to advertise movies primarily to young audiences. Why? Because young people get much of their information from television. (Older audiences read newspapers.)

The marketing objective is to get your video program in front of its target audience. Since audiences gather their information in different ways, pick the media form that best communicates to the audience you are trying to reach. If you really understand your target audience, you will also understand which form of media they respond to. You will know what television shows they watch and what magazines and newspapers they read. You will know where they shop, what they spend, and what they buy. You will know the best way to get your program in front of them. Manufacturer's and wholesaler's marketing people act on these considerations. As stated frequently in this book, forethought about marketing can only benefit you when you select, create and produce your videos.

Retailers demand advertising because they know it has many indirect benefits. Video retailers are calling out to wholesalers for more video advertising. They say, "If you want us to buy your videos, then advertise so that people will come into our stores." Advertising builds awareness among consumers. A consumer may not take action the first time he or she sees your ad, but after multiple impressions it starts to have an effect. This may result in an in-store sale if the consumer sees your tape there. Every time a consumer sees an ad on television or in a newspaper or comes in contact with publicity about a program, it builds awareness.

The trade commonly refers to "push-and-pull" marketing. You "push" product through the distribution chain from wholesaler to retailer with a variety of marketing spiff and promotions. At the same time, you advertise to the consumer to get him or her to "pull" product through at the retail level. Most successful marketing approaches address both audiences. You sell the stores. You sell the consumers. You sell to both sides of the cash register.

VIDEO PROMOTION MATERIALS

"Arnie's personal message to the sales staff made them work even harder. After all, he 'talked' to them directly."

Preproduction

If you know prior to production the kind of marketing materials you may need, you can schedule and budget special photography. During production you can produce footage to be used for sales and marketing reels. For example, when we shot the ARNOLD PALMER: PLAY GREAT GOLF video we had Arnie do some special testimonials and messages to both our in-house sales staff and to the wholesalers. Arnie's personal message to the sales staff made them work even harder. After all, he "talked" to them directly. This kind of thing can go a long way.

These are some of the things you may wish to consider doing during production for later use:

1. The VSDA (Video Software Dealers Association) convention is where manufacturer/suppliers announce new product. Shoot special footage with your star and edit it for a luncheon presentation or for looped screenings in the booth on the convention floor. This might include a special message: Hello to VSDA Retailers...

2. Shoot special footage to introduce the star and the program to video wholesalers. We once had Mick Jagger do personalized hellos to field reps using their names. Mick found ways of weaving little bits of personal information (that were collected for him) into these hellos. This, of course, really knocked the salespeople off their feet. Hopefully, they went to some extra effort to help sell Mick's tape.

3. It would be impractical to attempt customized versions of a hello trailer for all 30,000 video retailers, but a generic tape for store monitors could be useful.

4. You may also wish to shoot footage that could be incorporated into direct response television commercials or to shoot stills for print ads.

To really do a good job, you have to know in advance what these materials will be so that the various marketing clips, segments and spots can be designed and written prior to production.

Depending on the complexity the spots require, additional time may be necessary. We never designed anything that took more than a few hours to produce because, obviously, the production of the program itself is the most important thing. Still, do not think that you can always do additional taping or filming later. Getting your star to return for another day of shooting could be very difficult and expensive.

The additional sales benefit of these marketing tools is well worth the effort and minor expense involved because they offer a unique way to get your product more attention. And when you go that extra mile for the people who must sell the program, they may do something special for you—like buy your product and really push it.

This doubling up—doing additional shooting during production for other uses—can really pay off. When I worked at The Movie Channel we produced hundreds of Star Profiles segments. We'd go out to a star's home or on location and do a ten-minute interview which was shown between the movies on the network, often to soft-sell an actor's upcoming movie. At the end of each interview we'd ask the star if they'd do a little bump for us and say, "Hi, I'm Sean Connery [or whoever] and you're watching The Movie Channel." We'd composite this footage with paint-box effects and build a promo spot. Shooting this additional material took about five minutes and cost nothing. Most of the time the stars were very cooperative. After about six months of this we had hundreds of spots sprinkled throughout the breaks; it seemed as if every major star was supporting the network. The benefit to the on-air look was enormous. We couldn't have afforded to pay for it! This strategy was developed long before we went out to shoot the interviews. You must understand the needs of the sales and marketing group. Think these things through prior to production and be prepared to take advantage of additional opportunities as they happen.

Electronic Press Kit (EPK)

Electronic press kits are discussed in greater detail in the film section of the book. Their components are really the same for video. A videotape is prepared that contains various B-roll clips (these are various unedited segments with or without sound) that local television stations can revamp by adding their own hosts and voice-overs to them (this visual material is accompanied by a script). The EPK could contain (1) a trailer, (2) other promotable elements from the video which can stand on their own, (3) a special message from the star, (4) behind-the-scenes clips and (5) interviews with stars or experts. Electronic press kits are not appropriate for all original video programs. This depends entirely on the nature of the video and how the marketing and publicity folks want to promote it. Because of the considerable expense involved in preparing and distributing them, electronic press kits are usually reserved for movie promotion.

P. O. P.

Numerous P.O.P. (point-of-purchase) materials can be designed and printed to promote videos at the retail level—posters, banners, mobiles, counter cards, tents, "take-ones" (flyers containing an order coupon), stand-ups, special racks and spinner stands, header and shelf cards, etc. Walk into a supermarket and just look at all the promotional material that is used to attract a buyer's attention to a product. It's so much a part of the environment that we forget the

399

overall effect this merchandising can have on the decision to buy. Similar techniques may also be used to sell video. Until rather recently, the video retailer was not terribly sophisticated and did not take advantage of these sales tools provided by the wholesaler to promote product. Today, sales seminars, retailer magazines and the assistance provided by wholesalers are making retailers much more adept at using P.O.P. materials. An example:

Inside Shirley MacLaine's P.O.P.

What follows are some of P.O.P. materials that Vestron used to promote and market Shirley MacLaine's INNER WORKOUT. Look carefully at the material to understand the thinking that went into these sales materials.

Cassette Package

First, the video package. The key selling element is Shirley herself. Her name is the first thing you read. Her picture is the very first thing you see. She is immediately recognizable. This is very important. Any other treatment of this video would be a real mistake. When you have a star as big as Shirley, you use her.

Note that the title treatment and photos (all from the same series) are consistent throughout the materials. It is important to imprint in the buyer's mind the title and the look of the series so that the impressions build and the "personality" of the tape begins to emerge.

The word *workout* in the title and the pose in the key photo imply that this is an exercise tape. People understand what exercise tapes are; you don't have to explain them to the video trade or the consumer anymore. The marketers used this as a place to start in explaining the tape. But it is not an exercise tape, it is a meditation tape. The word *inner* implies this major difference. The distinction is further reinforced by the subheading: *Meditations for Relaxation and Stress Reduction.*

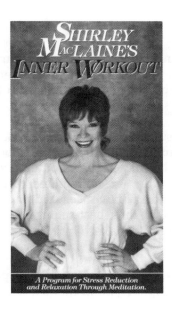

We still don't really know what the tape is about. But we are intrigued. Anyone who knows about Shirley—either through her books, appearances, TV movie, or publicity—knows that in addition to being an actress, she is an explorer of metaphysical and spiritual possibilities. To find out more, we turn the package over.

On the back the purpose of the tape is restated: *a complete program for stress-reduction and relaxation*. A softer picture of Shirley appears with her explanation that the tape is a comprehensive workout using meditation and relaxation techniques that have been used for centuries in Asia and India.

The standard display of credits, copyright, close-caption information, and so on also appear on the back of the cassette package.

Sell Sheet

The sell sheet is an expensive four-color, four-page fold-out. The first page is a tease suggesting that a bestseller is on the way. This is exactly what the retailer—who is looking for the next bestseller—wants to hear.

The inside pages support this promise. Shirley's achievements—her Oscar and Emmy awards, best-selling books, etc.—are reiterated for anyone who may have forgotten. The importance of the subject—stress-reduction—is highlighted. A headline tell us that 7 million copies of her books have been sold, and a photograph shows the tape in context with these best-selling books. What assumption is the retailer expected to make? This tape is going to be big! Better order a lot.

Throughout there is an association with Jane Fonda's videos. Both in the title, which implies a more subtle inner workout, and in the message—here comes another bestseller; get your copies now. The subject of the tape—stress-reduction—is expanded on and reinforced: Stress is linked to disease; therefore, the reduction of stress can lead to overall health.

Shirley's audience of millions is emphasized again. This is her first home video. Expectations are built. The main sales points are bulleted: Video debut; sold-out seminars; biggest name in New Age; comprehensive stress-reduction program; major promotional campaign, tour, advertising; state-of-the-art special effects and music; sell-through pricing; cross-promotion with her new book. In less than a minute, the retailer can see the manufacturer/supplier's commitment to the program.

Basic information—the order number, release date and order date—is included. If you order the six-pack, the tapes come in a counter display for P.O.P. sales.

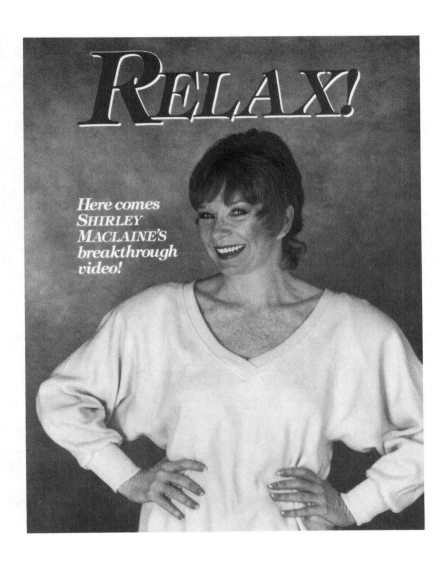

rs a New Age!

A program for stress-reduction and relaxation through meditation

Stress-related illnesses are a leading cause of discomfort and disease in today's society. Heart disease, nervous disorders, ulcers, among others, can all be linked to stress. Doctors and other health specialists have stated repeatedly that reducing stress is key to overall health — meaning a daily stress-reduction program is just as important as daily physical exercise.

Now you can improve the health of your business *and* your customers with Shirley MacLaine's breakthrough stress-reduction video aimed at people with stress — that's *everyone!*

SHIRLEY MACLAINE'S *INNER WORKOUT* is one of the most highly anticipated non-theatrical programs to reach the home video market ever! Shirley MacLaine's high profile as star and author have brought her millions of followers. Now with her breakthrough debut on home video she is sure to add many more! Stock up on SHIRLEY MACLAINE'S *INNER WORKOUT* because home video is about to enter a New Age!

Sales Points:

• The home video debut of the techniques that make Shirley MacLaine's seminars sell-out nationwide.

• The only comprehensive stress-reduction and relaxation home video program available.

• Backed by a major promotional and marketing push including: a national Shirley MacLaine publicity campaign beginning in April; extensive national consumer advertising; powerful P.O.P.; and much more.

• Personalized meditation designed by Shirley MacLaine specifically for high repeatability.

• Features state-of-the-art special effects and some of the top New Age musical composers.

• Priced to sell-through and sell-out at only $29.98 ($39.98 in Canada).

• Cross-promotion and simultaneous release of the Bantam book *Going Within* by Shirley MacLaine.

VHS: VA5270; Beta: VB5270; 70 Minutes;
ISBN: 0-6051-0627-8; UPC: 2848515270
6-Pack: VHS VA5315; ISBN: 0-6051-0707-X; UPC: 2848515315

**NATIONAL RELEASE DATE: MARCH 15, 1989
ORDERS DUE: FEBRUARY 15, 1989**

ly $29.98!
39.98 in Canada)

VESTRON VIDEO®

© 1989 Vestron Video
P.O. Box 10382
Stamford, CT 06901
Prices shown are suggested retail price

The back of the sell sheet is an ad mat. Wholesalers will use it in the catalogs they send to retailers. Retailers may use it for newspaper ads or promotional mailings to their customers.

P.O.P. Display

Just to make sure that the consumer doesn't miss it, a header card is provided for the six-pack. This mini-poster sits on the counter directly in back of the six-pack.

Consumer Poster

A poster emphasizing the benefits of the tape is also provided to help retailers sell INNER WORKOUT to their customers. The poster creates another impression in consumers' minds; they cannot fail to notice that this tape has been released. Whether or not they are interested in it, by the time they leave the video store they probably have seen at least three different shots of Shirley (tape, poster, P.O.P.).

CONVENTIONS

VSDA (Video Software Dealers Association) holds a convention every August where video dealers from all over the country convene. At the convention the major suppliers/manufacturers hold luncheons, dinners and parties to announce their new product, reaffirm relationships and make new friends. Every supplier, large or small, has a booth, hands out flyers, shows video clips, and tries, in a vast circuslike environment, to do something memorable to sell videocassettes. It is the one event every year when manufacturers, wholesalers, and retailers have a chance to get together and find ways to help each other. Everyone has the same goal: to sell more cassettes.

In August 1988, Vestron was at VSDA to promote Shirley MacLaine's INNER WORKOUT video and other product. Even though Shirley was in the middle of filming a new movie, STEEL MAGNOLIA, she came to VSDA for less than a day. During that time she held a standing-room-only press conference to discuss the video and answer questions. She met privately with the owners or principals of nearly every major wholesaler. On the convention floor more than more than a thousand people lined up to meet Shirley, receive an autographed photo and have a Polaroid of themselves taken with her. Vestron very cleverly gave out a frame for the Polaroid— you can be sure that the happy retailer won't lose a moment proudly displaying the Vestron-framed photo near the cash register for all to see. When order day rolls around and it's time to sign up for copies of Shirley's new video, that retailer will be there! The photo is a constant reminder to customers and staff of the availability of her tape.

VIDEO BUSINESS

"The economics that works for the manufacturer is very different than that of the producer—the manufacturer makes a profit long before the producer."

Video Business

The sales potential of every video program needs to be analyzed very carefully. Both producer and manufacturer must be convinced that the tape merits production. The manufacturer must be convinced that enough tapes will be sold to reap a profit. The economics that works for the manufacturer is very different than that of the producer. Simply stated, the manufacturer makes a profit long before the producer. How does that happen?

Contribution Analysis

Manufacturers do a *contribution analysis* to help them decide whether or not to finance or acquire a video program. It's also called "running the numbers." The assumptions are computed and if the program can be successfully sold, a positive contribution to the bottom line will be made. In this model, not only the traditional video store is analyzed but the mass merchant (K-Mart, etc.) as well.

The program costs $75,000 (line 2). The distributor advances this money to the producer to make the video. The producer/director's fee, which probably doesn't exceed 10 percent, is included in the $75,000 budget. In the analysis the budget is split fifty-fifty between each market (line 20), with $37,500 each shown.

The retail price in both markets is $29.95. Each market has a different discounting standard—38 percent among video retailers and 50

411

percent among mass merchants. The wholesale price received by the manufacturer is less from the mass merchant ($14.98) than it is from the video store ($18.57). The manufacturer's costs are the same: tape and duplication costs are $4 per unit (line 12), overhead (staff, building, etc.) are figured in at 15 percent (line 13), and returns are anticipated at 10 percent (line 14).

The manufacturer estimates spending $50,000 (line 16 divided by the two markets) on marketing for the release of the tape. This is calculated at about $2.01 per tape. (The marketing cost per tape goes down when sales volume increases. Large initial marketing costs are hard to avoid because it takes a minimum expenditure of $50,000 to get a respectable level of awareness in the video marketplace.) Marketing dollars go for posters, one-sheets, paid advertising, publicity, etc. (More will be spent after the tape takes off.) This is divided equally between the two markets in this demonstration; some marketing, such as consumer ads, would benefit both markets and drive customers into both video and mass merchant stores.

The net per unit to the manufacturer is $7.92 from the video retailer and $5.22 (line 22) from the mass merchant account.

To demonstrate, let's assume that our fictitious tape sells 12,450 units in each market. The net subtotals collected by the manufacturer are $61,104 and $27,489 respectively. From this balance the production costs ($37,500 x 2 = $75,000) are deducted. The total net balance remaining from both markets is **$88,593**. Remember this number.

This analysis so far has been from the manufacturer's point of view. Given the number of cassettes sold (nearly 25,000), $88,593 is in the bank at the end of the day.

Now let's look at this analysis from the producer's point of view. The producer received a fee to produce the videotape. He or she is also entitled—in this particular deal—to a producer's royalty calcu-

	CONTRIBUTION ANALYSIS			
1				
2				
3	Based on Retail Price Point:		$29.95	
4	Production Budget/Advance:		$75,000	
5				
6	**Video Retail Store**		**Mass Merchant**	
7				
8	**INCOME**			
9	Wholesale Price	$18.57		$14.98
10	(% Retail)	.62		.50
11				
12	**EXPENSES**			
13	Tape/Dup Costs	-4.00		-4.00
14	Overhead %	.15	-2.79	.15	-2.25
15	Returns %	.10	-1.86	.10	-1.50
16	Marketing	25,000	-2.01	25,000	-2.01
17				
18	**NET/UNIT**	**$7.92**		**$5.22**
19				
20				
21	Projected Sales	12,450		12,450
22	at Net/Unit	$7.92		$5.22
23			$98,604		$64,989
24	Budget/Advance		-37,500		-37,500
25				
26		NET	$61,104	NET	$27,489
27				
28	Total Units Sold			24,900
29	**TOTAL NET BOTH MARKETS**			**$88,593**
30				
31				
32	**PRODUCER'S SHARE**			
33		**Video Store**	**Mass Outlet**	
34	Wholesale	$18.57	$14.98	
35	Royalty 20% of Wholesale	3.71	3.00	
36	10% Returns	-.37	-.30	
37	**Producer's Net Per Unit**	3.34	2.70	
38				
39	Units Sold each Market	12,450	12,450	
40				
41	**Royalty Each Market**	**$41,583**	**$33,615**	
42				
43				
44	**Less Combined Royalties**			**$75,198**
45	Budget/Advance			($75,000)
46	*Overages*			*$198*
47				
48	Producer's Overages Begin at 24,900 units.			

lated as a percentage, 20 percent in this case (line 35), of the wholesale dollars (called gross wholesale receipts). The total received from each of the two markets differs (line 37); the producer sees about 24 percent more from the video market than from the mass market. Deducted from the royalty is an amount for returns—we assume 10 percent (line 36). Even though the returns have already been calculated by the manufacturer (line 15), this further reduction is made as a buffer to ensure that money is not paid out to the producer that must be returned to the wholesaler later. The royalty in our model is multiplied by the number of units sold and yields $41,583 and $33,615 or a total for both markets of $75,198 and change. Hey! That's almost the same amount as the budget. Right. The budget advances (line 45) are deducted from the royalty earned (line 44) with a negligible result ($198). This is called a break-even scenario for the producer.

Remember the number? The manufacturer has banked $88,593 at this point and recouped the entire production advance. From this point on the producer will receive royalty checks ranging from $2.70 to $3.34 for every additional tape sold. So, even though the manufacturer has made a profit, the producer has not (other than the producer's fee that was part of the production budget). In other words, the manufacturer has made a profit on the video even though the program did not "recoup" it's production cost. If this sounds strange it's probably a matter of semantics. Yes, more money came in than was expended on the budget. But the way the accounting figures it, the program has still not recouped and the producer is not yet entitled to royalty payments.

Let's summarize. A video was produced on a budget of $75,000, advanced by the manufacturer and recouped from gross receipts. At a retail price of $29.95 and selling an equal number of tapes to both video and mass merchant stores, the manufacturer comes out with a net profit of $88,593 after all costs, including production, have been recouped. The producer is now in a position to receive a royalty per tape for every tape sold hereafter.

This explanation should make it clear that a manufacturer can make a profit on a video program that has not "recouped" it's production cost. You'd think that if the production cost hadn't been recouped, no one would have made any money, but that's not true. The distributor will always make money before the producer.

On the other hand, it's easy to overlook the fact that the manufacturer's money allowed the program to be made in the first place. If the program doesn't sell, the manufacturer may see a loss. When you use someone else's money, they are usually entitled to make a profit on their money first. That's business.

The example we've just examined is a simple model. Many other deductions may come into play which will reduce the producer's profit share even more. A contract can protect the basic royalty from deductions—or allow them. What follows is a detailed look at the video distribution contract—the result of "the deal."

THE DEAL

"The final contract is a reflection of how good your negotiation skills are and how valuable the buyer perceives your program to be."

The Deal

The deal's the thing. Although this discussion comes at the end of the book, the deal will come long before the marketing plans are executed. It's very important to consider the details of a contract carefully, because they can significantly affect the marketing of your program and your profits.

When you sit in the distributor's (manufacturer/supplier's) office and they offer you their "standard contract," let a little smile break out on your face. Don't say anything. Look into their eyes and remember: *There is no such thing as a standard distribution contract.*

The standard contract is the contract that they would like you to sign; it is not the contract that you would like to sign. After all, it's all negotiable. The final contract will be a reflection of how good your negotiation skills are and how valuable the buyer perceives your program to be. If you push too far, you'll get a "no." If they push too far, you should retort with a "no" unless you are absolutely sure you won't get a better deal elsewhere. Another factor that may affect your deal will be the climate and health of the marketplace in general while you are making your deal.

Basic Contract Terms

Now that we have gone through all the steps involved with marketing and assuming the program has had some success, the producer's net income will depend on not only how well the marketing plan was carried out, but also how good a deal was negotiated prior to distribution.

The manufacturer will always have an advantage over the producer, because he or she is the one supplying the contract and creating the context from which all negotiation will spring. If you can turn this around and set your own agenda, you can control the direction in which the conversation will go. If you start with the standard contract, chip away at it until it is acceptable. Whereas if you set the stage and provide the contract (which is unlikely but possible), you can set the context for future negotiations; and you may, therefore, be able to include issues that normally wouldn't come up but are important to you.

The following are basic terms (found in most contracts) with comments on how to improve what may be offered:

Exclusive right to distribute. The manufacturer/supplier will want to have the exclusive right to distribute your program. Even if they don't distribute to all the markets that this includes, they may want to throw a net over everything in case their distribution expands in the future. Or, they will acquire all the home video rights they can and then go to smaller subdistributors. It is good that the manufacturer will try every available venue; but when they subdistribute, rather than doing it themselves, a piece must be paid to the subdistributor. This will dilute the producer's share. If the distributor does not market to special markets, book clubs, or do direct mail, these may be rights the producer should hold on to and either do personally or find distributors to handle. Besides home video, the producer will have television (pay, basic cable, network, syndication and foreign) as well as book rights, audio rights (which the home video supplier may sometimes try to capture even when they do not distribute to these markets) and merchandising. The reason a supplier wants as much as possible is to cover the production/ acquisition cost in the likelihood that things do not pan out in home video. Or simply because enough isn't enough. It's sometimes the nature of business to be greedy and put more on your plate than you can handle.

Advance. An advance put forth either as a straight acquisition or as payment for the production will be recouped from royalties. We've already discussed how a manufacturer is making profits before the program has recouped. A manufacturer may try to charge interest on the money paid out as an advance until it is recouped. In this case, the financing of the production is no different than going to a bank. You, not the manufacturer, have to pay the interest. Advances should always be refundable. If a manufacturer pays for the production, a clause may be included in the contract that asks for any under-budget monies to be returned.

Most producers believe that the advance is all the money they will ever see from a production. For a great many this is correct. They try to get as big a fee in the production budget as possible. They may also budget items (office, overhead, equipment rental and the like) which flow back to the producer.

Formats. This refers to all the formats, in any and all media, that exist now or may exist in the future. They could be various formats of videocassette (Beta, VHS, 8-mm) and videodisc, as well as digital, audio and other formats. When the Beatles signed their record deal with Capitol there were no CDs. Later, that "any and all media" line was interpreted by Capitol to mean that they had the CD rights; but there was no definition of royalties in the agreements because the CD hadn't been developed yet. The Beatles and Capitol have been haggling over a contract for some time. It's important to specify only those rights which we now understand. Manufacturers want

all format rights in order to protect themselves from unseen techno-
logical changes. Remember that various CD videos are coming into
the marketplace, along with digital tape, which may influence the
markets for other formats.

Royalty. Royalties are the monies that the producer receives from
the sale and distribution of his video. The definition of royalties is
extremely critical. Some manufacturers give and then take away.
They agree in one part of the contract on a royalty rate and then the
boilerplate toward the back of the contract starts to chip away at it
with things like packaging deductions, return allowances and the
like. It is very important to use a lawyer familiar with the contract
form that the manufacturer is offering. If your lawyer has been
through this field of land mines before, you may stand a better
chance of getting through unscathed.

Gross Receipts. This term should be interpreted as all monies received by the manufacturer from the wholesalers and other accounts. The manufacturer's lawyers will work long and hard to find
as many legitimate deductions as possible to reduce this pool of
money and thus make the royalty significantly smaller. Once you
start with deductions, you open the door to more and more dilution.
Once committed to an agreement, these deductions become legal.
Your lawyer will only get as much as he or she can, which in the end
will be based on how much they want your program. Your lawyer's
job is to push long and hard until he or she comes up to deal-
breaking points and must back off.

Returns. They can destroy your royalty. Cassettes are frequently
sold on a "guaranteed" or "return" basis. This means that at some
future date the wholesaler or rack-jobber may return the cassettes
for credit or different product. The manufacturer will not pay a royalty on tapes returned. They didn't make any money on what they
thought was a sale, so neither will you. That's fair enough. Two
concepts regarding returns should be discussed so that the proper
wording appears in the contract and so that everyone understands
one another.

Returns Reserve. This means that a reserve—a bank account—is being maintained. This reserve holds money that would normally go to the producer, except that the manufacturer anticipates that there will be returns which will reduce the money owed the producer. The returns reserve is usually 5–20 percent, which is held until such time as all the returns have come back. The time will be negotiable. Some returns will come in within six months and others will take longer. The manufacturer will want to extend the time before the returns reserve will go to the producer, because during this time the manufacturer has use of this money and may be able to make some interest on it. Any "reserve" or money held back from the producer will cut into the royalty until the returns reserve is liquidated.

Returns Allowance. It sounds the same as, and is often talked about as being the same as, a returns reserve, but it has an entirely different meaning. Here is where one word in the contract can make a significant dent in the producer's bottom line. A returns allowance means that the manufacturer is allowed to <u>deduct and keep</u> the returns allowance. It is an allowance, not a reserve.

<u>A producer may think he or she is getting one deal and actually end up with something quite different, since the accounting is based on interpretation of the words and phrases in a contract.</u>

Pricing. The contract may have language that will allow for the reduction of video royalties prorated against the wholesale price. It is very difficult to audit and find out what the real selling price may have been. Remember, too, that different classes of trade get different discounts. The royalty should be stated very specifically in case the initial selling price is changed. The producer may try to get a fixed dollar amount per cassette rather than a percentage of the gross receipts. While it is tough to negotiate such a deal, you don't have to worry about what price the distributor will sell the tape at;

you only have to know how many cassettes are sold. It makes the math very easy. And it makes it tough for accountants to do disappearing acts with your money.

For example, a producer may get a royalty of 20 percent for a tape with a retail price of $59.95 or higher, 15 percent for $39.95 and up, 10 percent for $29.95 and up and 5 percent for anything lower. The 20 percent may look very good on paper, but the distributor may be planning to release the tape at $19.95. Therefore, forget about a 20 percent royalty—you are really getting 5 percent.

Most distributors will try to avoid a pricing clauses in the contract because they will not want to fix a price until they are ready to release the tape. The market has stabilized somewhat in the last few years, so anticipating pricing is a bit easier than it had been. The royalties will vary from 10–20 percent (of gross wholesale receipts) based on the retail price. Therefore, if you can get a commitment from a distributor on the pricing, you can tie your royalty (or a dollar amount per tape sold) to the retail price. To cover all contingencies, have the royalties for various retail prices fixed in the contract. That way you always know where you stand.

Release. Specify the release date. Sometimes manufacturers will offer to pay you an acquisition price for your program upon release. This sounds fair enough but unless it is in writing, release dates change all the time. The manufacturer may come across a hotter property and bump yours in order to get the hotter one out first. Any acquisition payment should come upon signing the contract. Then you get your money regardless of the release date. It is tough to do, but you might try to negotiate a specific period by which they must release the tape or the rights revert back to you. If the tape isn't released, it isn't making any money for you beyond your advance.

Term. The term is the period of time the licensing of your program to the distributor will be in effect. That could range from a low of a few years to forever. Five, or seven or ten years is about average.

Territories. This refers to the geographic locations where the distributor may sell the program. It could be the United States or North America (the U.S. and Canada) or Japan. It could be worldwide. (If so, the distributor will probably use subdistributors in each territory. You could license your program worldwide yourself by going to distributors on a territory-by-territory basis. While this is more lucrative, it is very time consuming to understand and make the deals and then administer them. Plus, it is very difficult to supply marketing materials to a variety of distributors and coordinate any sort of release. If it is not coordinated, the opportunity for pirating to take place increases. The pirate can beat the distributor to market.)

Delivery Date. This is the date specified in the contract by which the producer will deliver all the master tapes and "delivery materials" to the distributor. The distributor needs to fix this date in order to schedule the release date. The producer must understand what these "delivery materials" consist of, because he or she may or may not have them.

Delivery Materials. They include the master videotape, which conforms to specific technical requirements; key artwork; a trailer; errors and omissions insurance (E&O), which protects the distributor from rights lawsuits; music and effects (M&E) tracks; color slides; black-and-white prints; a music cue sheet; and backing rights, agreements and clearances.

If you control the master marketing elements (key artwork and photographs), you have considerable control over the look of the marketing materials. Big stars will frequently have control over the photos and art used, the title selected, and the press releases and other supplementary marketing materials.

Holdbacks. A holdback is the period of time during which the program is held back from other media. For example, SECRETS OF THE TITANIC was held back from television broadcast until four months after the video release. Holdbacks of releases in each medium should be specified. (Study the chapter on release schedules and the various models to see how to best plan the holdbacks of different media.) If you don't make the holdbacks contractual, you could have a television release before home video, which (in some cases) could be harmful.

Marketing Commitment. Although it may be extremely difficult, try to get a marketing commitment in dollars from your distributor. Prior to acquiring or financing a production, they will have assessed the number of cassettes they can sell. (See contribution analysis.) They will know how much to spend to generate that level of sales, even though they may be unwilling to commit this amount to paper. Without an expenditure of marketing dollars the many promotional, publicity, and marketing ideas discussed in this book will be very difficult to arrange. The greater expenditure by the distributor, the greater their commitment to your program. If they decide to take it on, spend very little and it performs poorly, that's the end of the story. If they spend a lot, they'll work much, much harder trying to get their money back. The greater expenditure will help (although not ensure) wider exposure and will make the program more competitive in the marketplace.

Warranty. Any distribution agreement will contain a section where the rights holder (the producer) will represent to the distributor that he or she, the rights holder, has the right to grant the video rights, including all literary, artistic, musical and other property rights, to the distributor. The producer will warrant to the distributor that the program is copyrighted.

Indemnity. The producer also indemnifies, or holds harmless, the distributor and the distributor's licensees, affiliates, employees and agents against any claims that may occur from other parties.

Accounting Period. The accounting period is the time period after which the producer will receive a royalty statement. Distributors report quarterly, semi-annually and annually. Normally the distributor will send a royalty report forty-five to sixty days after the end of the accounting period (which could be quarterly, semi-annually or annually).

Audit Rights. Audit rights will allow the producer to audit the distributor's books during reasonable business hours in case of any dispute over royalties. If a producer thinks that his or her tape is more successful than royalties show, an audit might be in order. Because of the expense of hiring auditors, the producer must feel that the royalties reported to date are significantly underreported. Producers whose tapes are hits may want to consider auditing. When there is a lot of money moving through the system, it is prudent to make sure that you are receiving your just desserts. (In this case, find an auditor who has audited your distribution company before. This will save time because he or she will be familiar with the distributor's accounting system.)

Use the same strategy when looking for a lawyer to negotiate your distribution contract. Find one who has negotiated contracts with your distributor in the past and therefore may be able to start with a prenegotiated contract. The lawyer might say, "Listen, let's just cut through all the bull and start with the same terms that you gave me on [a star's] video." Most likely your lawyer will get something much better than the "standard contract."

Legal fees can run from $50 to $275 per hour. And this is not the time to look for bargain-basement lawyers. Your distribution contract is the basis of your business.

THE ESSENCE OF MARKETING

"At one time, these were mere intangible ideas that became real after months or years of step-by-step hard work."

The Essence of Marketing

Marketing is a very exciting part of the creative process. Usually film- and videomakers talk about the shooting, the creation of images, as the most exciting part. Or they talk about the thrill of postproduction when it all comes together. Creative thinkers will also be inspired as they come up with innovative ways to get their films and videos out into the world. It is very satisfying to see your film in a theater, your video in a video store, your book in a bookstore, or your game in a toy store. Especially since, at one time, these were mere intangible ideas that became real after months or years of step-by-step hard work. And although the results of marketing aren't really seen until the product is finished and distributed, its seeds come at the very beginning—when a project is being designed.

Marketing is a combination of elements. It is both a strategy and an action plan that enables your film or video to reach its market with energy, enthusiasm and imagination behind it. And if so designed, it will capture the energy, enthusiasm and imagination of others— the press, the promoters, the marketers, the retailers and the many buyers.

As we've explored in this book, marketing is not one thing. It is a combination of advertising and promotional strategies which affect all levels of buyers and sellers. The more ways you discover to promote and cross-promote your film or video, the more successful your marketing will be.

Marketing is not something that happens all at once. You must be committed to seeing it all the way through, otherwise you'll never get the real fruits of your labor. Like your time, marketing is an investment which pays off down the road. You must be patient and persistent in seeing your plan to its completion. Too many movies and videos are dropped by their distributors when instant results aren't accomplished. That's bad for the creators of those films and videos but good for marketers willing to go the long haul.

Whether you've created a film or a video or some other product, you need to make it visible to your target audience. They have to begin to gain confidence in that product. They have to hear that it's entertaining, or informative, or good. This takes time. They have to feel a certain familiarity or comfort level with your product to begin to want to see it, or rent it, or buy it.

And finally, after this long process of marketing yourself and your product, you should be prepared to go back to the well and come up with another product. After you've learned how to get to an audience you can do it again and again, each time refining and modifying your techniques. If they've responded favorably to your film or video they will be willing to see your next film or rent your next video. It is absolutely critical that you don't turn your back on the audience you've spent so long developing. Instead, nurture your market and it will draw others to your future products, it will expand exponentially. The satisfaction in getting your film seen or your video bought is tremendous. I hope that this book has given you some ideas about how to do just that.

THE FUTURE

"The electronic revolution has brought capital equipment into people's hands, enabling them to produce highly sophisticated work."

The Future

Home video had it's origins in forms of programming that predate video. Originally, tons of X-rated tapes were sold and rented. Here was a way to view this material privately instead of going to seedy neighborhood theaters. Later video became a showcase for all kind of movies. You could rent them whenever you wanted and see movies you missed or weren't inclined to see during their theatrical release.

Then suppliers culled the vaults of television producers and put tons of television shows on home video. Innovative producers developed forms of programs that had not existed before. Some of these original programs—like Jane Fonda's Workout—did spectacular business. Other ideas flopped.

Home video will probably be dominated by movie videos for a long time; it is unlikely that any other form of programming will capture the lion's share of the home video market. However, the sheer volume of programs being bought and sold indicates that people do want to own new forms of original programs.

Economics is one factor that has held back the proliferation of many original program ideas. It has simply been too expensive to produce high-quality videos that could find great enough acceptance to create profits for producers and recoup production costs. Fifty thousand dollars is a lot of money for most original programs, whose sole outlet is home video. The tape better be entertaining, educational or broad enough in its appeal to sell sufficient copies. Otherwise distributors, retailers and wholesalers alike will not even take the program on.

Because of high production costs for video, many special-interest videos will not be successfully produced; however, this is likely to change significantly in the next few years.

In music and book publishing the arrival of synthesizers and desktop-publishing computers has enabled people with musical and literary ideas to produce high-quality music albums, audio-tapes and books on minimal investments. The electronic revolution has brought capital equipment into people's hands, enabling them to produce highly sophisticated work. No longer do you have to assemble dozens of musicians to produce an orchestral-sounding score. No longer do you need to employ typesetters and graphic designers to lay out your books. Because it is cheaper to produce desktop products, a whole niche has arisen for suppliers, distributors and retailers who sell this product to specialized audiences. In attending the ABA (American Booksellers Association) Convention, you see not only the major book publishers—the Random Houses—but also the thousands of new mom-and-pop publishers who actually make a living publishing very specialized kinds of books. Any trip to your local record store will turn up a plethora of New Age music tapes which, for the most part, were produced in home recording studios.

This same phenomenon is now coming to home video. Electronics and the home computer will give producers the means to produce with very limited investments. Equipment and software are now available that combine the technologies of video recording, music production, sound and picture editing and computer graphics. This hardware and software give producers the opportunity to create entirely new forms of acoustical and visual expression. The new software that will emerge from these "desktop video" or "desktop movie" producers will be very different in style and form from much of today's original video programming. Some of it will find it's way into mass market distribution. Other, more specialized programs will be sold through direct mail distribution. The reduced cost of production will mean that fewer tapes will need to be sold before everyone in the video food chain realizes a profit. This fact alone will allow entry for more producers to create product. A lot of it will be sheer junk—as exemplified in the music industry, where synthesizers made almost anyone a "musician." But there will also be some landmark pieces that will create new forms of programming that will be entertaining, educational and surpass what can be done with today's equipment. The video revolution is far from over.

APPENDIX

GOIN' HOLLYWOOD:
THE MOVIE-MAKING GAME

"Do Lunch. Take a Meeting. Cheat Your Friends."

GOIN' HOLLYWOOD: THE MOVIE-MAKING GAME

It's not a video. It's not a movie. It's a board game. Then what's it doing in this book? Normally a case study like this would have no place here; however, the marketing strategy for the game utilizes all the principles of film and video promotion, so I've included it. In addition to its business potential, the board game provided an excellent and unusual entrée for my move to Los Angeles in October 1988—everyone's got a script, but who's got a game?! Plus, it's a lot of fun.

The Idea

The game was conceived by my partner Greg Johnson in August 1987. I've been pitched lots and lots of ideas, but rarely do I see the whole program and marketing strategy in a single sweep. As soon as Greg told me the idea—to devise a game where players are producers trying to get their movies made—I saw that the game could be irreverent and comedic, have hip graphics and be promoted first to the Los Angeles entertainment community and then broaden out from there. And that's what we did.

The Copy Line

Wheel and Deal.
Schmooze and Steal.
Do Lunch. Take a Meeting.
Cheat Your Friends.

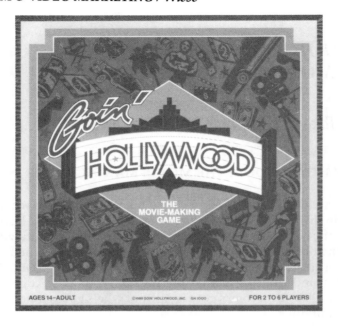

The Goal

Our objective is to create a regional hit in the Los Angeles area. *Pictionary* and *Trivial Pursuit* also started out as regional successes. It took a few Christmases before they became national hits. We knew that we didn't want to become a national game company. Board games are a tough business—the ratio between the total number created and those that hit is even worse than it is for movies. Only one or two games break out each year!

The goal was to make it the hottest game in Hollywood—the hippest Christmas gift you could give.

If we could create a fun, exciting game, get good press coverage and make a healthy number of sales we were confident that we could then license the game to a major toy company like Milton-Bradley, Western Publishing, or Pressman Toys for national distribution.

Development

Greg and I spent a year developing the game. We started on our hands and knees with a large piece of cardboard, two pencils and some erasers. We just kept working with these basic materials until we'd sketched out something we liked. We made up the rules as we went along and kept refining it. Art director Scott Mednick developed several prototypes. We're very happy with the final artwork. It is very upscale, hip and trendy—just right for our target audience.

Simultaneously we wrote all the cards for each of the three categories: scripts, actors and lifestyle. Over the course of many months four writers (Ernie Fosselius, HARDWARE WARS; Bob James and Andy Goodman, American Comedy Network Radio; and Bruce Handy, staff writer for *Spy* magazine) enhanced, rewrote and generated new material.

From a few visits to our local game stores we learned that all successful games have three things in common: they are easy to learn, challenging and fun. We also felt that the game should be very interactive and engaging. Yes, the game should be funny, but we also wanted the people who play the game to be funny with each other. The game was therefore designed to force people to make deals with each other, cheat each other, co-produce films and the like. This creates alliances and tensions between the players—just like real life!

The Financing

During the development phase we raised $125,000 from one investor in exchange for about a 30 percent share of the corporation we formed. We would raise more money when we needed it. This money would cover design, printing and manufacturing, shipping and the part-time salaries of three people for about six months.

Many business plans and spreadsheets were drawn up and revised. The cost of everything down to the penny was figured in, from how much each game piece would cost to manufacturing, advertising, hiring a public relations firm, air travel, etc.

Focus Groups

Once we had a playable prototype I asked friend and marketing consultant Malcolm Baker (Baker, Restaino and Schulman of Sausalito, California) to design focus groups and questionnaires that would tell us how well the game played—its *playability*.

Couples were recruited because we figured that you would usually play the game with at least one person you knew. We tried to re-create the environment of a living room. Those recruited were *not* in the entertainment industry. We assumed that industry people would like the game but that group in itself is not a big enough market. We hoped the game would appeal to everyone who simply liked movies. Therefore those recruited (1) were between the ages of twenty-five and forty-five, (2) had played a board game at least once in the last year, and (3) liked movies.

We hosted two focus groups where four to six people played the game. We sat behind one-way mirrors and watched them stumble through the game. It was painful. Every time they made a mistake we cringed. Then we took voluminous notes on what changes we'd have to make. By the time it was over we saw that we'd have to simplify the game tremendously. But we also were relieved to find that people really liked the game.

The sample group were asked to take the game home and play it with friends. Then they were to complete an extensive questionnaire about it and return it along with the game. The results confirmed our feeling that the game was too complicated. We also learned that some of the cards were a bit too raunchy for our audience so we toned them down—a little. We wanted the game to have an irreverent edge to it, sort of "Saturday Night Live" meets *National Lampoon/Spy* magazine.

Sponsorship

In the game, producers move around a "wheeling-and-dealing track" as they try to package their scripts with actors and directors. As in real life, we created squares on the board for hotels and restaurants ("power spots"). If a producer lands on a power spot, good things happen in his or her career. We decided to use the names of famous places to further increase the fantasy aspect of the board. Betsy Zeidman, who also worked on marketing the game, solicited sponsors for the first printing and got L'Ermitage, Mondrian, Chateau Marmont, Nicky Blair's, Hugo's and the Sports Connection to sponsor squares. We were paid in cash and/or barter to put their corporate logos on the board. We also signed up various trade media—the *Hollywood Reporter, Variety, Spy* magazine and *Premiere* magazine—to sponsor squares. When you land on the *Premiere* square, for example, it means that the magazine has written about you. You draw a lifestyle card to see what they say.

Creatively, the addition of these sponsors worked well within the context of the game because these are real places in Hollywood. It adds to the fantasy of the game and also the bottom line. We did not want to junk up the board with unnecessary advertisements.

Two Businesses

As it turns out, we had two distinct businesses. The first business was selling board games, the second was selling advertising space. This created two sources of potential income. It was difficult to get sponsors at first. We'd never published a board game before. Hollywood is loaded with get-rich-quick schemes so we weren't taken very seriously—until we had the finished artwork.

Publicity

We hired Parker Public Relations to help with various stunts and press events. The first thing we did was to host "game salons" at our sponsors' hotels: L'Ermitage, Mondrian, and Chateau Marmont. (Part of our deal with these sponsors was for hotel suites.) We set up a prototype—the actual games were still being manufactured—and invited the press to play. We did this about half a dozen times. The press are normally observers and rarely participate, but this time they really got into it. This was great because it gave each of them their own experience of the game (which never plays the same way twice), and they could write about it from their own point of view. We started the press salons before we had the games because our big push was to establish GOIN' HOLLYWOOD for Christmas and the games were not finished until mid-October.

Advertising

With the help of our sponsor deals we ran ads in *Spy, Premiere, Variety* and the *Hollywood Reporter*. We also took out ads in the back of *New Video*, a membership magazine for video retailers in New York City. While we were trying to keep the focus mostly on L.A., this was something we wanted to try. We also did some "per

441

inquiry" (P.I.) ads in *Hollywood* magazine and others. We didn't pay for inclusion of the ad in the magazine, except for the costs of the design and mechanicals; however, every game sold through the magazine generates a royalty for them. We hired a fulfillment center in Los Angeles to fill all orders via mail and an "800" number.

For *Premiere* magazine we took a more traditional approach:

For *Variety* and the *Hollywood Reporter* we we copped an attitude again:

NEED $25 MILLION FOR YOUR MOVIE? NO PROBLEM. STUDIO APPROVAL GUARANTEED*... Then in small type ...*when you play GOIN' HOLLYWOOD: THE MOVIE-MAKING GAME.

For Valentine's Day the *Hollywood Reporter* ad had this headline:

Happy Valentine's Day
Cheat On Your Lover
When you play GOIN' HOLLYWOOD...

Direct Mail

We did a direct mail test to 9,000 people who had bought my books or attended AFI seminars. The results were minimal and hard to track. We suspect they added to the retail store purchases. The most important thing for a new product's launch is to get visibility and awareness—so the direct mail piece helped on this level.
game one-sheet graphic

Volume Discounts

We also started a push to sell volumes of the game as premiums to studios, agents and producers. We encouraged them to give it to their clients and employees. *Premiere* bought 500 games to give to their key advertisers. Movietime, Chateau Marmont, and some of the restaurant owners bought copies to give to celebrities and special clients. Movietime, a basic cable service, also gave away games to their clients. This was terrific for us because it got the games into the hands of every studio head and every senior vice president and vice president at the studios, advertising agencies and production houses. The community was well seeded through corporate gift giving.

The response was terrific. Since the gift-giving sponsors were also on the board it looked like a custom gift. They got a lot of points for such an original Christmas gift.

Retail Stores

We sold to various retail outlets including game stores, gift stores, hotel stores, and video store chains. Waldenbooks put the game into sixty stores throughout Southern California. It got so busy at Christmastime that we had a guy in a pizza truck delivering games to the stores a few hours after they placed an order! The retail stores loved this special attention. Of course, we had to do this to make sure the games were on the shelves as quickly as possible. It is highly unusual for any store to keep reordering because they are so busy selling, but in this case the product was hot and they reordered frequently.

To further promote the game we did numerous in-store appearances where we demonstrated the game, signed copies, etc. Usually not too many games sold that day, but a few days later the stores would experience a pickup in sales. Plus, thousands of people walked by the stores and saw that something was going on. (Another impression!)

Press Coverage

As of this writing articles have appeared in the *Hollywood Reporter*, *Los Angeles* magazine, the *Daily News*, *USA Today* ,*Premiere*, *Variety*, the *Los Angeles Times*, *TWICE*, *Hollywood* magazine, *Associated Press* syndication, *Billboard* and many smaller local papers. We are expecting another dozen articles to appear in March and April from work started in late November.

TV Coverage

Movietime, our basic cable television network, did a five-week GOIN' HOLLYWOOD promotion where the winner got a night on the town, tickets to the premiere of TWINS, etc. The second prizes were copies of the game. This exposed the game to nearly 10 million people. They used our logo and did some funny segments with a "producer-type and some babes" in the back seat of a limo playing the game.

I also did interviews and game demonstrations on Movietime, the "Hollywood Magazine Executive Report" and KHJ's "Nightly News." "Entertainment Tonight," the KGO "Morning Show" and MTV did their own pieces about the game. The BBC included the game in a documentary they were doing about Hollywood. More television coverage is expected.

Stunts

We took a very guerrilla approach to marketing Goin' Hollywood, in keeping with the irreverent tone of the game. We were originally going to go out with a big, fancy launch party, but Morgan Smith wisely pointed out to me that we were becoming the very thing the game was parodying. Besides, a Hollywood-style event would nearly wipe out our entire promotion budget. We aren't a studio, so we shouldn't act like one. We needed to be more innovative and get a bigger bang for our buck. As an underdog, we decided to take the "Spike Lee" approach to the board game business.

We decided to launch the game on several Southern California campuses (USC, UCLA, CalState) with either game parties for the students or demonstrations tied in with the campus bookstores. This helped to sell games. We also got several student reps from the film departments to play the game, tell their friends and sell copies. They got a commission on sales. This also enabled the game to travel back home with the students at Thanksgiving and Christmas— traditionally a great time for playing board games.

Another idea we had was to run a teaser in the trade papers that would read: "Eisner and Diller Bout. See tomorrow's issue for details." A full-page ad the next day would say something like: "Congratulations Michael Eisner. You are the heavyweight deal-making champion of GOIN' HOLLYWOOD: THE MOVIE-MAK-ING GAME." The ad would include a picture of the game and a picture of Michael Eisner—not the head of Disney, but the house painter from Encino with the same name. While we thought this was ever so clever, we chickened out.

Game Parties

For months our friends set up game parties in the their homes with any movers and shakers they knew. Producers, agents, actors, lawyers, directors, crew people and ordinary folks played the game—then bought multiple copies for their friends. We had to get a large number of people to play the game and like it. Because without real folks having real game-playing experience, it would never be talked about. This is tough because the only way to get that word of mouth is to get people to actually play GOIN' HOLLY-WOOD. (This is very different than a book, which you can flip through, or a movie, where you can see a trailer—and decide on that basis alone whether or not to buy it.)

The Next Step

We manufactured 5,000 games and sold nearly every one by December thirty-first. We are now planning our strategy for the rest of the year. In February we will go to Toy Fair in New York, where we will be meeting with many major toy and game companies. We've put together our sales and reorder history with the retail stores (which included bookstores, gift stores, toy stores, department stores, video stores and college, hotel and studio stores), and we've compiled a portfolio of our local and national magazine and newspaper press. We also have edited together all the television interviews and segments on the game. The publicity and impressions we've generated are cumulatively worth millions.

We are now looking to make a licensing deal with a major game company that can take the game national for next Christmas. If we do not make a satisfactory deal we will continue to do what we've been doing. We will expand our retail store base in Los Angeles and prepare to market regionally to half a dozen selected cities next year. Fortunately for a game, you've got several seasons of Christmases to build a reputation for your product. We were careful last Christmas not to push so many games out that there would still be games on the shelves after Christmas and we'd get returns. If that had been the case, retailers would have remembered the game as not doing so well—"We had to return games."—and they might not have been inclined to reorder for next year. If, on the other hand, they remember that they kept running out of games—"That game was really hot!"—they will have this positive impression in their minds when reorder time comes.

Mistakes

In the video, movie or book business the acquisitions people are always looking for ideas for products. They read newspapers and magazines and watch television with this foremost in their mind. They scour the media for new product. We were certainly in enough publications that any video, movie or book person would have come into contact with our product. Unfortunately, this has not proven to be the case with the toy and game industry. They did not find us. We now have to go to them and sell our success story—they missed it. Strategically, we made the assumption that they would find us. Perhaps this is too much to expect. As of this writing we've only been in the marketplace for nine weeks. Perhaps in another six months we'd have been "discovered," but we don't have that long to wait. We need to have a national distribution deal in place fairly soon for next Christmas. (The toy and game business works a year or more in advance.)

Summary

We did not set out to be in the national game business. Rather, we endeavored to create a presence that would look significant (profitable) to major game companies. We did not want to be among the thousands of people who go with their games under their arms to the game companies saying, "Please help me." We wanted to prove that we could develop an audience, a promotional and advertising campaign, and—through guerrilla marketing—look like a much bigger company than we really were. What we did was create a company with multimillion-dollar potential with the efforts of just three people, a well-organized strategy, a good product and the use of lots of mirrors! Hopefully we will have built value in the name and be able to do films, books, computer games or a television game show from the franchise in the name. It's a long shot but why not? Others have done it before. That's the vision of "what we want to be". Now let's see if we can bring it into reality.

FILM DISTRIBUTORS

ABC CIRCLE FILMS, 2040 Avenue of the Stars, 5th Floor, Los Angeles, CA 90067, (213) 557-6860

ALIVE, 8271 Melrose Avenue, Los Angeles, CA 90046, (213) 852-1100

ATLANTIC ENTERTAINMENT GROUP, 8255 Sunset Boulevard, Los Angeles, CA 90046-2400, (213) 650-2500

BUENA VISTA/TOUCHSTONE, 500 S. Buena Vista Street, Burbank, CA 91521, (818) 840-1000

CANNON GROUP, INC., 640 San Vicente Boulevard, Los Angeles, CA 90048, (213) 658-2100

CINECOM INTERNATIONAL FILMS, 1250 Broadway, 33rd Floor, New York, NY 10019, (212) 239-8360

CINEPLEX ODEON CORPORATION, 1925 Century Park East, Suite 300, Los Angeles, CA 90067, (213) 553-5307

CINETEL FILMS, INC., 9200 Sunset Boulevard, Suite 1215, Los Angeles, CA 90069, (213) 550-1067

COLUMBIA PICTURES INC., Columbia Plaza, Burbank, CA 91505, (818) 954-6000

CROWN INTERNATIONAL PICTURES, INC., 8701 Wilshire Boulevard, Beverly Hills, CA 90211, (213) 657-6700

DE LAURENTIIS ENTERTAINMENT GROUP, 8670 Wilshire Boulevard, Beverly Hills, CA 90211, (213) 854-7000. Also: 720 Fifth Avenue, Suite 100, New York, NY 10019, (212) 399-7700

EXPANDED ENTERTAINMENT, 2222 S. Barrington, Los Angeles, CA 90064, (213) 473-6701

FOX INC., 10201 W. Pico Boulevard, Los Angeles, CA 90035, (213) 277-2211. Also: P.O. Box 900, Beverly Hills, CA 90213

HEMDALE FILM CORPORATION, 1118 N. Wetherly Drive, Los Angeles, CA 90069, (213) 550-6894 and 550-6856

HI-TOPS, 5730 Buckingham Parkway, Culver City, CA 90230, (213) 216-7900

HBO PICTURES, 1100 Avenue of the Americas, 10th Floor, New York, NY 10036, (212) 512-1000

INTERNATIONAL FILM MARKETING, 9440 Santa Monica Boulevard, Suite 707, Beverly Hills, CA 90210, (213) 859-3971

ISLAND PICTURES, 9000 Sunset Boulevard, Suite 700, Los Angeles, CA 90069, (213) 276-4500

LORIMAR TELEPICTURES CORPORATION, 10202 W. Washington Boulevard, Culver City, CA 90232-3783, (213) 280-8000

MGM/UA, 10000 W. Washington Boulevard, Culver City, CA 90232, (213) 280-6000

MIRAMAX, 18 E. 48th Street, Suite 1601, New York, NY 10017, (212) 888-2662.

NEW CENTURY/VISTA FILM CO., 1875 Century Park East, Suite 200, Los Angeles, CA 90067, (213) 201-0506

NEW LINE CINEMA, 575 Eighth Avenue, 16th Floor, New York, NY 10018, (212) 239-8880. Also: 1116 N. Robertson Boulevard, Suite 808, Los Angeles, CA 90048, (213) 854-5811

NEW WORLD, 1440 S. Sepulveda Boulevard, Los Angeles, CA 90025, (213) 444-8100

ORION PICTURES INTERNATIONAL, and ORION CLASSICS, 711 Fifth Avenue, New York, NY 10022, (212) 758-5100. Also: 9 W. 57th Street, New York, NY 10019, (212) 980-1117. Also: 1888 Century Park East, Los Angeles, CA 90067, (213) 282-0550

PARAMOUNT PICTURES CORPORATION, 5555 Melrose Avenue, Los Angeles, CA 90038-3197, (213) 468-5000. Also: 1 Gulf & Western Plaza, New York, NY 10023, (212) 333-4600

ROSEBUD RELEASING CORP., 8670 Wilshire Boulevard, Beverly Hills, CA 90211, (213) 652-8459

SAMUEL GOLDWYN COMPANY, 10203 Santa Monica Boulevard, Suite 500, Los Angeles, CA 90067-6403, (213) 552-2255

SKOURAS INTERNATIONAL, 1040 N. Las Palmas, Hollywood, CA 90038, (213) 467-3000

TRANS WORLD ENTERTAINMENT, 6464 Sunset Boulevard, Suite 1100, Hollywood, CA 90028, (213) 461-0467

TMS PICTURES, INC., 11111 Santa Monica Boulevard, Suite 1850, Los Angeles, CA 90025, (213) 478-4230

TRI STAR PICTURES, 1875 Century Park East, 7th Floor, Los Angeles, CA 90067, (213) 201-2300. Also: 711 Fifth Avenue, 12th Floor, New York, NY 10022, (212) 758-3900

UNITED ARTISTS PICTURES, INC., 450 N. Roxbury Drive, Beverly Hills, CA 90210, (213) 281-4000

UNIVERSAL PICTURES, 100 Universal City Plaza, Universal City, CA 91608, (818) 777-1000. Also: 445 Park Avenue, New York, NY 10022, (212) 759-7500

VESTRON INC., 1010 Washington Boulevard, Stamford, CT 06901, (203) 978-5636. Also: 9255 Sunset Boulevard, Suite 420, Los Angeles, CA 90069, (213) 551-1723

WARNER BROS., 4000 Warner Boulevard, Burbank, CA 91522, (818) 954-6000

VIDEO MANUFACTURER/SUPPLIERS

ABC VIDEO ENTERPRISES, 2040 Avenue of the Stars, Los Angeles, CA 90067, (213) 557-6600

ACTIVE HOME VIDEO, 9300 W. Pico Boulevard, Los Angeles, CA 90035, (800) 824-6109

ADLER VIDEO MARKETING INC., Old Dominion Drive, #360, McLean, VA 22101, (703) 556-8880

AIMS MEDIA, 6901 Woodley Avenue, Van Nuys, CA 91406, (818) 785-4111 or (800) 367-2467

ARTHUR CANTOR FILMS, 2112 Broadway, Suite 400, New York, NY 10023, (212) 496-5710

AMERICAN HOME VIDEO LIBRARY, 1500 Broadway, Suite 1807, New York, NY 10136, (212) 869-2616

BARR FILMS, 12801 Schabarum Avenue/P.O. Box 7878, Irwindale, CA

BEACON FILMS INC., 21601 Devonshire Street, Evanston, IL 60202, (800) 322-330

BEST FILM AND VIDEO CORP., 98 Cutter Mills Road, Great Neck, NY 11021, (516) 487-4515

BFA EDUCATIONAL MEDIA, 468 Park Avenue South, New York, NY 10016, (212) 684-5910

BLACKHAWK FILMS, 595 Triumph Street, Commerce, CA 90040, (319) 323-8637

BOOK OF THE MONTH CLUB, INC., 485 Lexington Avenue, New York, NY 10017, (212) 867-4300

BOOKSHELF VIDEO, 301-B W. Dyer Road, Santa Ana, CA 92702, (714) 957-0206

BULLDOG FILMS, Oley, PA 19547, (212) 779-8226

BUDGET VIDEO, 1540 N. Highland Avenue, Los Angeles, CA 90028, (213) 466-2431

CAPITAL CITY/ABC VIDEO ENTERPRISES, 1825 7th Avenue, New York, NY 10019, (212) 887-6655

CBS VIDEO CLUBS/CBS VIDEO LIBRARY, 1400 N. Fruitridge Avenue, Terre Haute, IN 47811. Also: 1211 Avenue of the Americas, New York, NY 100036, (212) 975-4875

CBS/FOX VIDEO, 1211 Sixth Avenue, New York, NY 10036, (212) 819-3200

CHILDREN'S VIDEO LIBRARY (CVL), 1010 Washington Boulevard, Stamford, CT 06901, (203) 987-5400

CHRONICLE VIDEO CASSETTES, 4628 Fawn Hill Way, Antioch, CA 94509, (213) 858-0141

CHURCHILL FILMS, 622 N. Robertson Boulevard, Los Angeles, CA 90069, (213) 657-5110

CINEMA GUILD, 1697 Broadway, Suite 802, New York, NY 10019, (212) 246-5522

CINERGY ENTERTAINMENT, 858 12th Street, Suite 8, Santa Monica, CA 90403, (213) 451-2513.

COLISEUM VIDEO, 430 W. 54th Street, New York, NY 10019, (212) 489-8130

CORINTH VIDEO, 34 Gansevourt Street, New York, NY 10014, (212) 463-0305

CORONET/MTI, a division of Simon and Schuster, 108 Wilmot Road, Deerfield, IL 60015, (312) 940-1260 or (800) 621-2131

COVENANT VIDEO, 3200 W. Foster Avenue, Chicago, IL 60625, (800) 621-1290

CRITIC'S CHOICE VIDEO INC., 1020 31st Street, Suite 130, Downer's Grove, IL 60515-5503, (312) 969-8895

CROWN VIDEO, 225 Park Street, New York, NY 10003, (212) 254-1600

DIRECT CINEMA LIMITED, Box 69589, Los Angeles, CA 90069, (213) 656-4700

DISCOUNT VIDEO TAPES, 3711 Clark Avenue, Suite B, Burbank, CA 91521 (818) 843-3366

DISNEY HOME VIDEO, 500 S. Buena Vista Street, Burbank, CA 91521, (818) 840-1000

DO-IT-YOURSELF, 712 Euclid Avenue, Charlotte, NC 28203, (704) 342-9608

EMBASSY HOME ENTERTAINMENT, 1901 Avenue of the Stars, Los Angeles, CA 90067, (213) 553-3600

FAITH FOR TODAY, 1100 Rancho Conejo Boulevard, Newbury Park, CA 91320, (805) 499-4363

FAMILY HOME ENTERTAINMENT, 21800 Burbank Boulevard, Woodland Hills, CA 91365, (800) 423-7455

FANLIGHT PRODUCTIONS, 47 Halifax Street, Boston, MA 02130, (617) 524-0980

FILMS FOR THE HUMANITIES, INC., P. O. Box 2053, Princeton, NJ 08543, (609) 452-1128

GREENLEAF VIDEO INC., 3230 Nebraska Avenue, Santa Monica, CA 90404 (213) 829-7675

HARMONY VISION, 116 N. Robertson Boulevard, Suite 701, Los Angeles, CA 90046, (213) 652-8844

HBO VIDEO INC., 1370 Avenue of the Americas, New York, NY 10019, (212) 977-8990

HOLLYWOOD VIDEO INC., 15951 Arminta Street, Van Nuys, CA 91406, (818) 908-1274

INCREASE VIDEO, 8265 Sunset Boulevard, Suite 105, Hollywood, CA 90046, (213) 654-8808

INDEPENDENT UNITED DISTRIBUTORS (IUD), 430 W. 54th Street, New York, NY 10019, (800) 223-0313

INDEPENDENT VIDEO SERVICES, 401 East Tenth Avenue, Suite 160, Eugene, OR 97401

INTERNATIONAL FILM EXCHANGE, 201 West 52nd Street, New York, NY 10019, (212) 582-4318

INTERNATIONAL VIDEO ENTERTAINMENT (IVE), 7920 Alabama Avenue, Canoga Park, CA 91304, (800) 423-7455

IRS VIDEO, 633 N. La Brea, Los Angeles, CA 90036

JOURNAL FILMS INC., 21601 Devonshire Street, Evanston, IL 60202, (800) 323-5448

J2 COMMUNICATIONS, 10850 Wilshire Boulevard, Suite 1000, Los Angeles, CA 90024, (213) 474-5252

KARL/LORIMAR HOME VIDEO, 3970 Overland Avenue, Suite 205, Culver City, CA 90230, (213) 280-0190

KAROL MEDIA, 22 Riverview Drive, Wayne, NJ 07470, (201) 628-9111

KARTES VIDEO, 10 E. 106th Street, Indianapolis, IN 46280, (317) 844-7403

KID TIME VIDEO, 2340 Sawtelle Boulevard, Los Angeles, CA 90064, (213) 452-9006

KULTUR, 121 Highway 36, West Long Beach, NJ 07764, (201) 842-6693

LAWREN PRODUCTION INC., 21601 Devonshire Street, Evanston, IL 60202, (800) 323-9084

LIBERTY PUBLISHING CO., INC., Suite B-3, 440 South Federal Highway, Deerfield, FL 33441, (305) 360-9000

LIGHTNING VIDEO, 1010 Washington Boulevard, Stamford, CT 06901, (203) 978-5400

MALJACK PRODUCTIONS, 15825 Rob Roy Drive, Oak Forest, IL 60452, (800) 323-0442

MCA HOME VIDEO, 100 Universal City Plaza, Universal City, CA 91608, (818) 777-1000

MEDIA HOME ENTERTAINMENT, 5730 Buckingham Parkway, Culver City, CA 90230, (800) 421-4509

MEDICAL ELECTRON EDUCATION SERVICE INC., 21601 Devonshire Street, Evanston, IL 60202, (800) 323-9084

MEGEL & ASSOCIATES, 3575 Cahuenga Boulevard West, Suite 249, Los Angeles, CA 90068, (213) 850-3306

MGM/UA HOME VIDEO, 1350 Avenue of the Americas, New York, NY 10019, (212) 708-0300 or (800) 468-7600

MONTEREY HOME VIDEO, 7920 Alabama Avenue, Canoga Park, CA 91304, (818) 888-3040

MTI TELEPROGRAMS, 3710 Commercial Avenue, Northbrook, IL 60062, (800) 323-5343

NATIONAL AUDIOVISUAL CENTER (GSA), Washington, DC 20409, (301) 763-1881

NATIONAL HEALTH VIDEO INC., 12021 Wilshire Boulevard, Suite 550, Los Angeles, CA 90025, (213) 472-2275

NELSON ENTERTAINMENT, 1901 Avenue of the Stars, Los Angeles, CA 90067, (213) 553-3600

NEW AGE VIDEO INC., P.O. Box 669, Old Chelsea Station, New York, NY 10113, (212) 254-1482

NEW DAY FILMS, 7 Harvard Square, Brookline, MA 02146, (617) 566-5914

NEW WORLD VIDEO, 1888 Century Park East, 5th Floor, Los Angeles, CA 90067, (213) 201-0741

NFL FILMS, 330 Fellowship Road, Mt. Laurel, NJ 08054, (609) 778-1600

NIGHTENGALE-CONANT CORP., 7300 N. Lehigh Avenue, Chicago, IL 60648, (800) 572-2770

NORSTAR VIDEO CORP., 1580 Old Bayshore Highway, San Jose, CA 95112, (408) 280-0522

NOSTALGIA MERCHANT, 6255 Sunset Boulevard, Hollywood, CA 90028, (213) 216-7900

PACIFIC ARTS VIDEO, 50 La Cienega Boulevard, Suite 210, Beverly Hills, CA 90211, (213) 657-2233

PARAMOUNT HOME VIDEO, 5555 Melrose Avenue, Hollywood, CA 90038, (213) 468-5000

PBS VIDEO, 1320 Braddock Place, Alexandria VA 22314, (800) 424-7963

PENNSYLVANIA STATE UNIVERSITY, Audio Visual Services, Specialty Services Bldg., University Park, PA 16801, (814) 865-6314

PERENNIAL EDUCATION INC., 21601 Devonshire Street, Evanston, IL 60202, (800) 323-9089

PHOENIX FILMS/BFA EDUCATIONAL MEDIA, 468 Park Avenue South, New York, NY 10016, (212) 648-5910

PIONEER VIDEO, 200 West Grand Avenue, Montvale, NJ 07645, (201) 573-1122

POLARIS, 2 Park Avenue, 24th Floor, New York, NY 10016, (212) 684-3232

PRISM, 1875 Century Park East, Suite 100, Los Angeles, CA 90067, (213) 277-3270

PROFESSIONAL RESEARCH INC., 21601 Devonshire Street, Evanston, IL 60202, (800) 421-2363

PYRAMID FILM AND VIDEO, Box 1048, Santa Monica, CA 90406, (213) 828-7577

RANDOM HOUSE VIDEO, 201 E. 50th Street, New York, NY 10022, (212) 751-2600

RCA/COLUMBIA HOME VIDEO, 3500 W. Olive Ave., Burbank, CA 91505, (818) 953-7900

RHINO VIDEO, 1201 Olympic Boulevard, Santa Monica, CA 90404, (213) 450-6323

SBI VIDEO, 4901 Forbes Road, Lanham, MD 20706, (301) 459-8000

SONY VIDEO SOFTWARE, 1700 Broadway, New York, NY 10019, (212) 757-4990

SPINNAKER SOFTWARE, One Kendall Square, Cambridge, MA 02139, (617) 494-1200

TEACHING FILMS INC., 21601 Devonshire Street, Evanston, IL 60202, (800) 323-9084

TERRA-NOVA FILMS, 9848 S. Winchester Avenue, Chicago, IL 60643, (312) 881-8491

THE KITCHEN, 512 W. 19th Street, New York, NY 10011, (312) 443-3793

THORN EMI/HBO VIDEO INC., 1370 Avenue of the Americas, New York, NY 10019, (212) 977-8990

TIME-LIFE VIDEO, 1271 Avenue of the Americas, New York, NY 10020, (212) 552-5940

TODAY HOME ENTERTAINMENT INC., 9200 Sunset Boulevard, Los Angeles, CA 90069, (213) 278-6490

TRAVELNETWORK, P.O. Box 11345, Chicago, IL 60611, (312) 266-9400

NATHAN TYLER PRODUCTIONS, 451 D Street, Boston, MA 02210, (617) 439-9797

UMBRELLA FILMS, 60 Blake Road, Brookline, MA 02146, (617) 277-6639

UNIVERSITY OF CALIFORNIA, Extension Media Center, 2176 Shattuck Avenue, Berkeley, CA 94704, (415) 642-0460 and 642-5578

USA HOME VIDEO, 7920 Alabama Avenue, Canoga Park, CA 91304, (818) 888-3040

VESTRON VIDEO, 1010 Washington Boulevard, Stamford, CT 06901, (203) 978-5400

VIDAMERICA, 235 E. 55th Street, New York, NY 10022, (212) 355-1600

VIDEO CASSETTE MARKETING, 137 Eucalyptus Drive, El Segundo, CA 90245

VIDEO DATA BANK, 280 South Columbus Avenue, Chicago, IL 60603, (312) 443-3793

VIDEODISC PUBLISHING INC., 381 Park Avenue South, Suite 1601, New York, NY 10016, (212) 685-5522

VIDEO GEMS, 731 N. La Brea Avenue, Los Angeles, CA 90038, (213) 938-2385 or (800) 421-3252

VIDEO NATURALS, 2590 Glen Green, Suite 6, Los Angeles, CA 90068

VIDEO PUBLISHING HOUSE INC., 10011 E. Touhy Avenue, Suite 580, Des Plaines, IL 60018, (312) 827-1191

THE VIDEO SCHOOLHOUSE, 167 Central Avenue, Pacific Grove, CA 93950, (408) 375-4474

VIDEOTAKES, 220 Shrewsbury Avenue, Red Bank, NJ 07701, (201) 747-2444

VIDEOTAPE CATALOG, SMW Video Inc., 803 Russell Boulevard, #2, Davis, CA 95616, (800) 547-0653

VIDEO TREASURE INC., 87 Essex Street, Hackensack, NJ 07601, (201) 489-7998

VIDEO YESTERYEAR, P.O. Box C, Sandy Hook, CT 06482, (203) 426-2574

WARNER HOME VIDEO, 4000 Warner Boulevard, Burbank, CA 91522, (818) 954-6000

WIZARD VIDEO/FORCE VIDEO, 1551 N. La Brea Avenue, Los Angeles, CA 90028, (213) 850-6563

WOOD KNAPP, 140 E. 45th Street, 39th Floor, New York, NY 10017, (212) 983-8192

XEROX INFORMATION RESOURCES GROUP/PUBLISHING, One Pickwick Plaza/P.O. Box 6710, Greenwich, CT 06836, (203) 625-5675

VIDEO WHOLESALER/DISTRIBUTORS

AMERICAN VIDEO NETWORK, 830 S. Myrtle Road, Monrovia, CA 91016, (818) 358-7761 or (800) 523-5193

ARTEC INC., 1 Pine Haven Shore Road, Shelbourne, VT 05482, (802) 985-8401

B.A. PARGH COMP. INC., 1283 Murfreesboro Road, Nashville, TN 37217, (800) 227-1000

BAKER & TAYLOR VIDEO, 8140 N. Lehigh Avenue, Morton Grove, IL 60053, (312) 647-0800

BEST VIDEO, INC., 50 N.W. 44th Street, Oklahoma City, OK 73118, (405) 557-0066

BIG STATE DISTRIBUTING CORP., 4830 Lackawana, #121, Dallas, TX 75247, (214) 631-1100

BLACK SWAN ENTERPRISES, 1100 Centennial Boulevard, Suite 248, Richardson, TX 75081, (214) 644-7926

CAPITAL RECORDS VIDEO DISTRIBUTION, 1750 N. Vine Street, Hollywood, CA 90028, (213) 462-6252

CHANNEL 3 Inc., 2901 White Plains Road, New York, NY 10467, (212) 881-7480

COAST VIDEO DISTRIBUTION INC., 500 N. Ventu Park Road, Newbury Park, CA 91320, (818) 884-3800

COMMERCIAL DISTRIBUTORS, 8 Sommerset Street, Portland, ME 04101, (207) 879-5400

COMMTRON, 2450 Bell Avenue, Des Moines, IA 50321, (515) 224-1784

DISCOUNT VIDEO INTERNATIONAL, 1765 Woodhaven Drive, Bensalem, PA 19006, (800) VIDEO-44

EAST TEXAS DISTRIBUTING, 7171 Grand Boulevard, Houston, TX 77054, (800) 231-6648

FIRST VIDEO EXCHANGE, 17503 S. Figueroa, Gardena, CA 90248, (213) 516-6422 or (800) 247-2351

G.G. COMMUNICATIONS INC., 111 French Avenue, Braintree, MA 02184, (617) 843-4860

GLOBAL VIDEO DISTRIBUTORS INC., 7213 N.W. 79th Terrace, Medley, FL 33166, (305) 887-1986 or (305) 887-2000

HANDLEMAN COMPANY, 500 Kirts Boulevard, Troy, MI 48084, (313) 362-4400

HOME ENTERTAINMENT DISTRIBUTORS (a subsidiary of Ingram), 9549 Penn Avenue South, Minneapolis, MN 55431, (612) 887-9500

INDEPENDENT VIDEO INC., 10364 Rockingham Drive, Sacramento, CA 95827, (916) 361-7181

INGRAM VIDEO, 347 Readwood Drive, Nashville, TN 37217, (615) 361-5000

INTERNATIONAL MOVIE MERCHANTS, 25115 S.W. Parkway Avenue, Suite C, Wilsonville, OR 97070, (503) 682-3545

LIBRARY VIDEO COMPANY, Box 40351, Philadelphia, PA 19106, (215) 627-6667

LIEBERMAN ENTERPRISES, INC. (a subsidiary of IVE), 9549 Penn Avenue South, Minneapolis, MN 55431, (612) 887-5300

LISTENING LIBRARY INC., One Park Avenue, Old Greenwich, CT 06870, (203) 637-3616

M.S. DISTRIBUTING COMPANY, 1050 Arthur Avenue, Elk Grove Village, IL 60007, (312) 364-2888

METRO VIDEO, 92 Railroad Avenue, Hasbrouck Heights, NJ 07604, (201) 288-0400

MOVIE TAPE EXCHANGE INC., 9380 Route 130 North, Pennsauken, NJ 08109, (609) 665-5775

MSV DISTRIBUTORS, 40 S. Caroline Street, Baltimore, MD 21231, (301) 675-1400

PRIVATE EYE VIDEO, P.O. Box 2796, Capistrano Beach, CA 92624-0796, (714) 240-5144

SCHWARTZ BROTHERS, INC., 4901 Forbes Boulevard, Lanham, MD 20706, (301) 459-8000

SIGHT AND SOUND DISTRIBUTORS, 2055 Walton Road, St. Louis, MO 63114, (314) 426-2388

SOUND/VIDEO UNLIMITED, 8140 N. Lehigh Avenue, Morton Grove, IL 60053, (312) 647-0800

SOURCE VIDEO, 1100 Hillsboro Road, Franklin, TN 37064, (615) 790-5300

SOUTHERN ELECTRONICS DISTRIBUTORS INC., 4916 N. Royal Atlanta Drive, Tucker, GA 30054, (404) 491-8962

SPRING ARBOR DISTRIBUTORS, 10885 Textile Road, Belleville, MI 48111, (313) 481-0900

STAR VIDEO ENTERTAINMENT, 550 Grand Street, Jersey City, NJ 07302, (201) 333-4600

THE MOVIE WAREHOUSE CO., 605 Harrison Avenue, Leadville, CO 80461, (303) 486-3883 or (800) 535-3400

VIDCOM, 175 W. 2700 S., Salt Lake City, UT 84115, (801) 487-8888

VIDEO BROKERS INTERNATIONAL, 6902 Grand Ave, Maspeth, NY 11378, (718) 457-1617

VIDEO CLOSEOUTS OF AMERICA INC., 261 Central Avenue, Suite 42, Jersey City, NJ 07307, (201) 333-3802 or (800) 221-4391

VIDEO MARKETING AND DISTRIBUTING, 14001 Ridgedale Drive, Suite 290, Minneapolis, MN 55343, (612) 544-8588 or (800) 328-4815

VIDEO MOVIE BROKERS, 7640 Gloria Avenue, Suite C, Van Nuys, CA 91406, (818) 908-8966 or (800) 235-6644

VIDEO ONE VIDEO, 1600 124th Avenue NE, Bellevue, WA 98005, (206) 454-5992

VIDEO PRODUCTS DISTRIBUTORS, 2428 Glendale Lane, Sacramento, CA 95825, (916) 971-1809

VIDEO SHUTTLE NETWORK, 445 Eighth Avenue NW, St. Paul, MN 55112, (612) 639-0622

VIDEO TREND, 12900 Richfield Court, Livonia, MI 48150, (313) 591-0200

VSI DISTRIBUTORS INC., 3333 Commercial Avenue, Northbrook, IL 60062, (312) 498-4130

VTR INC., 173 Industry Drive, Pittsburgh, PA 15275, (412) 787-8890 or (800) 245-1172

VVI DISTRIBUTORS, 2940 Interstate Street/P.O. Box 667309, Charlotte, NC 28208, (704) 399-4660 or (800) 532-0150 and 438-8273

WAX WORKS VIDEOWORKS, 325 E. Third Street, Owensboro, KY 42301, (502) 926-0008

WIN RECORDS AND VIDEO, 76-05 51st Avenue, Elmhurst, NY 11373, (718) 786-7667

ZBS INDUSTRIES, 701 Beta Drive, Mayfield Village, OH 44143, (216) 461-6275

SELECTED DUPLICATORS

Allied Film and Video, Chicago, IL (312) 348-0373

Allied Film and Video, Detroit, MI (313) 871-2222

All Mobile Video, New York, NY (212) 757-8919

C & C Visual, New York, NY (212) 684-3830

Capitol Video Communications, Washington, DC (202) 965-7800

Century III Teleproduction, Boston, MA (617) 267-6400

Communications Concepts, Cape Canaveral, FL (305) 783-5232

Creative Video Services, Street Cloud, MN (612) 255-0033

Dallas Post-Production Center, Irving, TX (214) 556-1043

Devlin Productions, New York, NY (212) 582-5572

Editel/Chicago, Chicago, IL (312) 440-2360

Editel/Los Angeles, Los Angeles, CA (213) 931-1821

Editel/New York, New York, NY (212) 867-4600

First Communications, Atlanta, GA (404) 980-9773

Image Transform, North Hollywood, CA (818) 985-7566

Innovision Teleproduction, Lawrence, KS (913) 843-9148

Interface Video Systems, Washington, DC (202) 861-0500

International Production Center, New York, NY (212) 582-6530

Koplar Communications Center, St. Louis, MO (313) 454-6324

Media Associates, Mt. View, CA (415) 968-2444

Midtown Video, Denver, CO (303) 778-1681

MTI, New York, NY (212) 355-0510

Northwest Teleproductions, Kansas City, MO (816) 531-3838

Northwest Teleproductions, Minneapolis, MN (612) 835-4455

PCA Teleproductions, Matthews, NC (704) 847-8011

Polycom Teleproductions, Chicago, IL (312) 337-6000

Skaggs Telecommunications, Salt Lake City, UT (801) 539-1427

Southwest Teleproductions, Dallas, TX (214) 243-5719

Telemation Productions, Seattle, WA (206) 623-5934

Third Coast Video, Austin, TX (512) 473-2020

VCA/Technicolor, Des Plaines, IL (312) 298-7700

Versatile Video, Sunnyvale, CA (408) 734-5550

BIBLIOGRAPHY

PRODUCTION

Video Editing and Post-Production: A Professional Guide, available from Knowledge Industry Publications, 701 Westchester Avenue, White Plains, NY 10604

Professional Video Production by Ingrid Weigand, available from Knowledge Industry Publications, 701 Westchester Avenue, White Plains, NY 10604 (1985)

Reel Power by Mark Litwak, New American Library, New York, NY (1986)

Television Production by Alan Wurtzel, McGraw-Hill, New York, NY (1983)

Television Production Handbook by Herbert Zettl, Wadsworth Publishing Company, Belmont, CA (1984)

The Independent Producer: Film & Television by Hourcourt, Howlett, Davies, Moskovic, Faber & Faber, London (1986)

The Video Production Guide by Lon McQuillin, Howard Sams Publishing, Indianapolis, IN (1983)

Producers on Producing: The Making of Film & Television by Irv Broughton, MacFarland Publishing (1986)

DISTRIBUTION

The Independent Film and Videomakers Guide by Michael Wiese, Revised and Expanded 1986, available from Michael Wiese,

3960 Laurel Canyon Boulevard, #331, Studio City, CA 91604—$18.95 postpaid

Doing It Yourself: A Handbook on Independent Film Distribution by AIVF, Inc. by Julia Reichert, 99 Prince Street, New York, NY 10012 (1977)

Entertainment Industry Economics by Harold L. Vogel, Cambridge University Press, New York, NY (1986)

Making Films Your Business by Mollie Gregory, available from Schocken Books, New York, NY (1979)—$6.95

The Film Industries: Practical Business and Legal Problems in Production, Distribution and Exhibition by Michael F. Mayer, available from Hastings House, New York, NY (1978)—$11.50

Motion Picture Distribution—Business or Racket? by Walter E. Hurst and Wm. Storm Hale, Seven Arts, Hollywood, CA (1975)

16mm Distribution by Judith Trojan & Nadien Convert, available from Educational Film Library Association, 43 W. 61st Street, New York, NY 10023—$6

Distribution Guide by the Independent Film Journal, 1251 Avenue of the Americas, New York, NY

Producing, Financing and Distributing Film by Farber and Baumgarten, Drama Book Specialists, New York, NY (1973)

The Movie Business: American Film Industry Practice by William Bluem and Jason Squire, Hastings House, New York (1972)

BUDGETS

Film Scheduling Or, How Long Will It Take To Shoot Your Movie? by Ralph S. Singleton, Lone Eagle Publishing, 9903 Santa Monica Blvd., Beverly Hills, CA 90212 (213) 471-8066 (Features)

Film Scheduling/Film Budgeting Workbook and Movie Production by Ralph S. Singleton, Lone Eagle Publishing, 9903 Santa Monica Blvd., Beverly Hills, CA 90212 (213) 471-8066 (Features)

Budget Forms Instantly! by Ralph S. Singleton, Lone Eagle Publishing, 9903 Santa Monica Blvd., Beverly Hills, CA 90212 (213) 471-8066 (Features)

Film and Video Budgets by Michael Wiese, available from Michael Wiese, 3690 Laurel Canyon Boulevard, #331, Studio City, CA 91604 (818 905-6367). (Revised 1988)—$18.95 postpaid. (18 budget formats—features, docs, comedy, original programs, etc.)

The Hollywood Guide to Film Budgeting and Script Breakdown by Danford Chamness, available from Stanley J. Brooks Company, 1416 Westwood Boulevard, Suite 201, Los Angeles, CA 90024 (1977). Telephone: (213) 470-2849—$20 (Features)

1987-1988 Brooks Standard Rate Book, available from Stanley J. Brooks Company, 1416 Westwood Boulevard, Suite 201, Los Angeles, CA 90024. Telephone: (213) 470-2849—$28

Production Boards and Strips: For Features and Television available from Stanley J. Brooks Company, 1416 Westwood Boulevard, Suite 201, Los Angeles, CA 90024. Telephone: (213) 470-2849

1989 Motion Picture Almanac & Television Almanac (2 books), available from Quigley Publishing Company, 159 W. 53rd Street, New York, NY 10019

VIDEO

Home Video: Producing for the Home Market by Michael Wiese, available from Michael Wiese, 3690 Laurel Canyon Boulevard, #331, Studio City, CA 91604—$18.95 postpaid

Guide to the Sponsored Video by Doug Duda, et al, available from Knowledge Industry Publications, 701 Westchester Avenue, White Plains, NY 10604 (1987)

Guide to Videotape Publishing, ed. by Ellen Lazer, available from Knowledge Industry Publications, 701 Westchester Avenue, White Plains, NY 10604 (1986)

Video Product Marketplace by Martin Porter, Martin Porter & Associates Publications, Port Washington, NY (1987)

Home Video Publishing: The Distribution of Videocassettes 1986-90 by Presentation Consultants Inc. White Plains, NY: Knowledge Industry Publications, Inc., 1986.

Variety's Complete Home Video Directory, R.R. Bowker, New York, NY (1988)

The Video Tape & Disc Guide to Home Entertainment, National Video Clearinghouse, Inc., Syosset, NY (annual)

Video Shopper, P.O. Box 309, Fraser, MI 48026, (313) 774-4311

DIRECTORIES

1988 Film Directors, 1988 Film Producers, Studios and Agents Guide, 1988 Cinematographers, Production Designers, Costume Designers & Film Editors Guide by Kate Bales, available from Lone Eagle Publishing, 9903 Santa Monica Blvd., Beverly Hills, CA 90212 (213) 471-8066

Motion Picture, TV and Theater Directory, Motion Picture Enterprises, Tarrytown, NY 10591—$4.25

New York Feature Film and Video Guide, 90 Riverside Drive, New York, NY 10024—$5

The Producer's Master Guide, New York Production Manual Inc., 611 Broadway, Suite 807, New York, NY 10012—$69.95 per year

TRADE PUBLICATIONS

AD AGE, 200 E. 42nd Street, New York, NY 10017

ADVERTISING AGE, Crain Communications, Inc., 740 N. Rush Street, Chicago, Il 60611

ADWEEK, 49 E. 21st Street, New York, NY 10010

AMERICAN CINEMATOGRAPHER, 220 E. 42nd Street, Suite 930, New York, NY 10017—$15.95 per year

AMERICAN FILM, The American Film Institute, Washington DC

BACKSTAGE, 5151 Wilshire Boulevard, Suite 302, Los Angeles, CA 90036—$35 per year

BILLBOARD, 9107 Wilshire Boulevard, #2265, Los Angeles, CA 90036. Also: 1515 Broadway, New York, NY 10036—$148 per year.

BROADCASTING, 630 Third Street, 12th Floor, New York, NY 10017. Also: Broadcasting Publications Inc., Washington, DC

CHAIN STORE AGE, Lebhar-Friedman, Inc., New York, NY

CHANNELS, 19 West 44th Street, #812, New York, NY 10036

CHANNELS OF COMMUNICATION, Media Commentary Council, Inc., New York, NY

CHILDREN'S VIDEO, John L. Weber for Children's Video Magazine, Inc., Brooklyn, NY

COMING ATTRACTIONS, Convenience Video Corp., Jersey City, NJ

CONVENIENCE STORE NEWS, BMT Publications, Inc., New York, NY

DAILY VARIETY, 1400 N. Cahuenga Boulevard, Los Angeles, CA 90028

DEALERSCOPE, North American Publishing Co., Philadelphia, PA

DIRECT MARKETING, Hoke Communications, Inc., Garden City, NY

DM [Direct Marketing] NEWS, c/o DMN Corp., 19 W. 21st Street, New York, NY 10010, (212) 741-2095

ELECTRONIC MEDIA, 220 East 42nd Street, #1306, New York, NY 10017

ELECTRONIC RETAILING, Fairchild Publications, New York, NY

FILM COMMENT, 140 W. 65th Street, New York, NY 10023

FILM JOURNAL, 244 W. 49th Street, #305, New York, NY 10019

FOLIO, Folio Magazine Publishing Corp., New Canaan, CT

HOLLYWOOD REPORTER, 1501 Broadway, New York, NY 10036. Also: 6715 Sunset Boulevard, Hollywood, CA 90028—$89 per year.

HOME VIDEO PUBLISHER, Knowledge Industry Publications, 701 Westchester Avenue, White Plains, NY 10604

HOME VIEWER, 11 N. Second Street, Philadelphia, PA 19160, (215) 629-1588

INTV JOURNAL, 80 Fifth Avenue, New York, NY 10011

LIBRARY JOURNAL, R.R. Bowker Co., New York, NY

MART, Morgan-Grampian Publishing Co., New York, NY

MILLIMETER, 826 Broadway, New York, NY 10003—$40 per year

MOVIELINE, 1141 S. Beverly Drive, Los Angeles, CA 90035-1139

MULTI-CHANNEL NEWS, 7 E. 12th Street, New York, NY 10003

NEWS & VIEWS, 1560 Broadway, #714, New York, NY 10036

PAUL KAGAN ASSOCIATES, 126 Clock Tower Place, Carmel, CA 93923

PHOTOMETHODS, Ziff-Davis Publishing Co., New York, NY

PHOTO WEEKLY, Billboard Publications Inc., New York, NY

PREMIERE, 755 Second Avenue, New York, NY 10017

PUBLISHERS WEEKLY, R.R. Bowker Co., New York, NY

ROCKAMERICA MAGAZINE, 27 E. 21st Street, New York, NY 10010—$3.50 per issue

SCREEN INTERNATIONAL, 8500 Wilshire Boulevard, Beverly Hills, CA 90211

SIGHT & SOUND MARKETING, Dorbaugh Publications, New York, NY

SPLICE, 10 Columbus Circle, #1300, New York, NY 10019

TAPE BUSINESS, Knowledge Industry Publications, 701 Westchester Avenue, White Plains, NY 10604

TELEVISION DIGEST, Television Digest Inc., 475 Fifth Avenue, Suite 1021, New York, NY 10017

TOYS, HOBBIES & CRAFTS, Harcourt Brace Jovanovich Inc., New York, NY

TV/RADIO AGE, 1270 Avenue of the Americas, #502, New York, NY 10020

TWICE, 5900 Wilshire Blvd, #700, Los Angeles, CA 90036

V, THE MAIL ORDER MAGAZINE OF VIDEOCASSETTES, Fairfield Publishing Co., Inc., New York, NY

VARIETY (weekly edition, also available as a daily), Variety, Inc., 154 W. 46th Street, New York, NY 10036—$75 per year.

VIDEO BUSINESS WEEKLY, 345 Park South, New York, NY 10010

VIDEO INSIDER, 223 Conestoga Road, Wayne, PA 19087

VIDEO MAGAZINE, 460 W. 34th Street, New York, NY 10001, (212) 947-6500

VIDEO MARKETING NEWSLETTER, 12052 Montecito Road, Los Alamitos, CA 90720

VIDEO MARKETPLACE, World Publishing Corp., Evanston, IL

VIDEO PREVIEW, P.O. Box 561467, Dallas, TX 75356-1476, (214) 438-4111

VIDEO REVIEW, 902 Broadway, New York, NY 10010, (212) 477-2200

VIDEO SOFTWARE DEALER, 5519 Centinela Avenue, Los Angeles, CA 90066

VIDEO STORE, 545 Fifth Avenue, New York, NY 10017. Also: 1700 E. Dyer Road, Santa Ana, CA 92705

VIDEO STORE (and ENTERTAINMENT MERCHANDISING), Magacycle Inc., Irvine, CA

VIDEO WEEK, 475 Fifth Avenue, New York, NY 10017

VIEW MAGAZINE, 80 Fifth Avenue, #501, New York, NY

VIEW: THE MAGAZINE OF CABLE TV PROGRAMMING, Subscription Services Department, P.O. Box 5011, FDR Station, New York, NY 10022—$36 per year

MARKETING & ADVERTISING

Adweek's Marketers Guide to Media, c/o A/S/M Communications Inc., 49 East 21st Street, New York, NY 10010

Advertising Manager's Handbook, Dartnell Corporation, Chicago, IL

American Demographics, Dow Jones and Company Inc., Syracuse, NY

Ayer Directory of Publications, Ayer Press, One Bala Avenue, Bala-Cynwyd, PA 19004

Bacon's Publicity Checker: Magazine and Newspapers, Bacon's Publishing Company, Inc., 332 S. Michigan Avenue, Chicago, Il 60604, (312) 922-2400

Business Publications Rates & Data, Standard Rate and Data Service, Inc., 3004 Glenview Road, Wilmette, IL 60091

Direct Mail List Rates and Data, Standard Rate and Data Service, Inc., 3004 Glenview Road, Wilmette, IL 60091

The Direct Marketing Association, Inc., 6 E. 43rd Street, New York, NY 10017, (212) 689-4977

The Direct Marketing Market Place: The Directory of the Direct Marketing Industry, c/o Hilary House Publishers, Inc., 1033 Channel Drive, Hewlett Harbor, NY 11557

How to Make Your Advertising Make Money by John Caples, Prentice-Hall, Englewood Cliffs, NJ (1983)

Inside the Leading Mail Order Companies, c/o NTC Business Books, 4255 West Touhy Avenue, Lincolnwood, IL 60646.

Maximarketing, The New Direction in Promotion, Advertising and Marketing Strategy, McGraw-Hill, New York, NY

Marketing & Media Decisions, 342 Madison Avenue, New York, NY 10017

Media: The Second God by Tony Schwartz, Random House, New York, NY (1981)

NATPE International Pocket Station Listing Guide, NATPE International, 342 Madison Avenue, Suite 933, New York, NY 10173

Ogilvy on Advertising by David Ogilvy, Crown Publishers, New York, NY (1983)

Response Television by John Witek, Crain Books, Chicago, IL (1981)

Television and Cable Contacts, Larimi Communications Associates, Ltd., 5 W. 37th Street, New York, NY 10018, (212) 819-9310

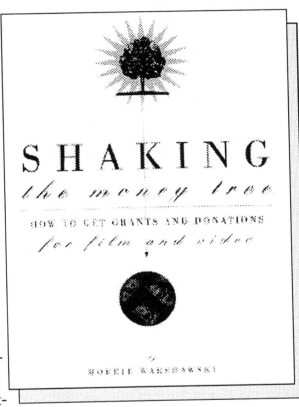

SUCCESSFUL FINANCING & DISTRIBUTION

THE INDEPENDENT FILM & VIDEOMAKERS GUIDE

By Michael Wiese
Revised Edition 1990, 392 pages, 45 illustrations.
ISBN 0-941188-03-5, $18.95

A classic best-seller and independent producer's best
friend. Advice on limited partnerships, writing a
prospectus, market research, negotiating, film markets, lists of pay TV and home video buyers.

- Financing
- Partnership Agreements
- Income Projections
- Investor Presentations
- Finding Distributors
- Promotion

*"The book is full of practical tips on how to get a film or video project financed, produced, and
distributed without sacrificing artistic integrity."* **CO-EVOLUTION QUARTERLY**

FILM AND VIDEO BUDGETS

By Michael Wiese
Revised 1990, 348 pages, 18 budgets
ISBN 0-941188-02-7, $18.95

This is a basic "how-to" budget guide for many types of films. Clearly written, informal in style, and generously illustrated with detailed budgets. Readers can look up sample budgets similar to their own and find a wealth of information on costs and savings. Includes:

- Money-Saving Tips
- Computer Budgets
- Line Items
- Accounting Procedures
- Negotiations
- Union and Guild Contacts

"...must reading. This is a common-sense book written with a touch of ironic humor. If you want to make your life easier in the financial arena of film/video making—buy the book. Enjoyable reading for those who like profits." **INFORMATIONAL FILM PRODUCERS ASSOCIATION**

FADE IN:
THE SCREENWRITING PROCESS

By Robert A. Berman, 240 pages, 1988
ISBN: 0-941188-07-8, $18.95

A concise method for developing a "story concept" into a finished motion picture screenplay. Includes: The Basics of Dramatic Writing; Creating Three-Dimensional Characters; Screenwriting Form, Techniques, and Terminology; Writing Techniques; Collaboration; Adaptations; Plus Index. Includes the original screenplay: THE CRIMSON MOON.

- Screenplay Structure
- Dramatic Structure
- Plot Points
- Story Pacing

"Writers should find his concise screenwriting methods inspiring and valuable in enhancing their own creative skills." **MICHAEL WIESE**

485

FILM DIRECTING
CINEMATIC MOTION
A Workshop for Staging Scenes
by Steven D. Katz

1992, approx. 225 pages, approx. 220 illus.
ISBN: 0-941188-14-0, 7 x 10, $24.95 paper
Available November 1992

A practical guide with 24 basic staging and
blocking examples covering many dialogue and
dramatic situations. Unique to this approach is the
evaluation of each creative staging strategy from
the production point of view through interviews
with well-known production professionals—John Sayles (writer/director), Van
Ling (special effects and visualizations "Terminator 2"), Dusty Smith (key grip),
Ralph Singleton (producer/director)....and other top professionals!

Chapters include: *Staging: The Director, Scheduling: The Production Manager,
Staging Without Dialogue, Staging in Confined Spaces, Choreography in Confined
Spaces, Choreography in Larger Spaces, Zone Vs. One on One Staging,* and *Sequence
Shots.*

By providing the practical information that directors usually discover the hard
way—like running out of time on the set—the book becomes an indispensable
resource for producers, directors, cameramen, production designers, screenwriters
and actors.

Learn how to prepare your ideas for the realities of production.   Directors
cannot do without this book!!

Steven D. Katz is the author of the best-selling book FILM DIRECTING
SHOT BY SHOT. Katz, an award-winner filmmaker with 20 years
experience has worked as an editor, director and writer. Katz is also an
accomplished artist and drew the 200 illustrations for the book. He has
recently created techniques for realizing and animating storyboards on
Macintosh computers.

FILM DIRECTING–SHOT BY SHOT:
Visualizing From Concept to Screen

by Steven D. Katz

About 380 pages, 7" x 10" paper
Approx. 400 illus. and photos
ISBN 0-941188-10-8, $24.95

Available January 1991

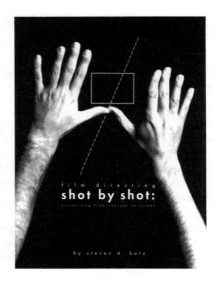

FILM DIRECTING SHOT BY
SHOT is a complete catalogue of
visual techniques and their stylistic implications for both film and
video directors — "a text book"
which enables working
filmmakers (as well as screenwriters and producers) to expand their
stylistic knowledge.

Extensively illustrated and well-written, it should find an enthusiastic audience
among both seasoned and novice filmmakers.

Includes illustrations, photos and storyboards from:

- Alfred Hitchcock's *THE BIRDS* and *TORN CURTAIN*
- Steven Spielberg's *EMPIRE OF THE SUN*
- Orson Welles' *CITIZEN CANE*
- N.C. Wyeth and Howard Pyle artwork
- David Byrne's illustrations from *TRUE STORIES*

Contents include: Camera Techniques, Storyboard Style, Screen Ballistics,
Framing and Compositional Techniques, Graphic Properties, Lenses, Moving
Cameras, Style, How Directors Interpret Script Scenes, Blocking, Editing and
Transitions, Image Organization, Symbolic Meaning, and Modern Tech-
niques.

FILM & VIDEO FINANCING

By Michael Wiese
1991, Approx. 300 pages, 6 x 8 paper
ISBN 0-941188-11-6, $22.95

The most important—and most elusive—element in any producer's life is the ability to raise production monies.

Financing Film & Video offers the independent producer a plethora of approaches to the complex and arduous task of financing the low-budget features and home video programs.

Contents include information on current attitudes and approaches to finding investment through limited partnerships, equity investments, banking issues, split-rights deals, debt equity deals, blocked funds, foreign pre-sales, and much more.

Rounding out the volume are insider's tips from independent producers and money raisers for such films as *sex, lies and videotape, Dirty Dancing, Blue Steel, Trip to Bountiful,* and *Kiss of the Spider Woman*.

This is a book that should be on the desk of practicing film and video producers as well as anyone contemplating a venture into this field.

THE WRITER'S JOURNEY
Mythic Structure for Storytellers & Screenwriters
by Christopher Vogler
1992, approx. 200 pages
ISBN 0-941188-13-2, 6 x 8, $22.95
Available November 1992

Learn how the top Hollywood studios and screenwriters mine mythological treasures for story ideas. This practical writer's guide reveals the secret patterns of mythology including a powerful set of myth-inspired tools for structure and character that divulge the universal mythic structure behind all narrative writing.

Step-by-step guidelines show you how to structure your plot and create realistic characters. Innovative exercises help you troubleshoot and improve your own work. These ideas have been tested and refined by professional screenwriters, playwrights and novelists and will empower your command of storytelling through the ancient wisdom of myth. One of Hollywood's most powerful studio heads made the rough draft of this book *"required reading"* for the entire executive staff.

As a story analyst, **Chris Vogler** has evaluated over 6000 screenplays for major motion picture studios including Walt Disney, Warner Bros., 20th Century Fox, United Artists, Orion Pictures, The Ladd Company, Touchstone Pictures and Hollywood Pictures. He has also specialized in fairy tale and folklore consulting for Walt Disney Feature Animation.

Mr. Vogler is deeply indebted to the work of scholar Joseph Campbell and has enjoyed applying Campbell's ideas on mythology to screenwriting solutions. Mr. Vogler teaches classes in story analysis, motion picture development, and mythic structure in film at UCLA Extension Writers Program.

MICHAEL WIESE PRODUCTIONS offers a CONSULTING SERVICE to producers, directors, writers, media creators, distributors, suppliers, publishers and others to provide expert advice and strategies for film and home video. Clients include NATIONAL GEOGRAPHIC, THE SMITHSONIAN INSTITUTION, THE AMERICAN FILM INSTITUTE, MYSTIC FIRE VIDEO, PBS HOME VIDEO, WNE, KCET, THE APOLLO THEATER and many others. For more information call (818) 379-8799.

BUY **ANY 4** ITEMS — GET A **FREE** BOOK OF YOUR CHOICE!

MICHAEL WIESE PRODUCTIONS
4354 LAUREL CANYON BLVD., SUITE 234
STUDIO CITY, CA 91604
800-379-8808 • FAX: 818-986-3408

**$** **=**

SEND THIS FREE BOOK:

_____

_____

_____

I HAVE ORDERED 4 ITEMS OR MORE.

SUBTOTAL		
SHIPPING (SEE CHART)		
8.25% SALES TAX (CA ONLY)		
TOTAL ENCLOSED		

CREDIT CARD ORDERS
CALL
1-800-379-8808
OR FAX YOUR ORDER
818-986-3408

PLEASE MAKE CHECK OR MONEY ORDER PAYABLE TO
MICHAEL WIESE PRODUCTIONS.

SHIPPING

1 ITEM	$4.00
2 ITEMS	$6.00
3 ITEMS	$7.00

FOR EACH ADDTL. ITEM ADD $1.00
(FOR EXAMPLE, SIX ITEMS = $10.00)

FOREIGN ORDERS
MUST BE PREPAID

EACH BOOK SURFACE MAIL $ 5.00
EACH BOOK AIR MAIL $ 8.00

PLEASE ALLOW 2-3 WEEKS FOR DELIVERY.
ALL PRICES SUBJECT TO CHANGE WITHOUT NOTICE.

(CHECK ONE) ❑ MASTER CARD ❑ VISA ❑ COMPANY P.O. #

CREDIT CARD NUMBER _____

EXPIRATION DATE _____

CARDHOLDER'S NAME _____

CARDHOLDER'S SIGNATURE _____

UPS 2ND DAY
DELIVERY.
ADD $10.00 U.S. ONLY.

WHEN MAILING ORDERS,
PLEASE INCLUDE THE
ADDRESS LABEL BELOW TO
HELP US PROCESS YOUR
ORDER. THANK YOU.

NAME _____

ADDRESS _____

CITY _____ STATE _____ ZIP _____

COUNTRY _____ TELEPHONE _____